Northwest Vista College
Learning Resource Center
3535 North Ellison Drive
San Antonio, Texas 78251

POVERTY, NATURAL RESOURCES, AND PUBLIC POLICY IN CENTRAL AMERICA

D1708536

POVERTY, NATURAL RESOURCES, AND PUBLIC POLICY IN CENTRAL AMERICA

■

Sheldon Annis and contributors:

Oscar Arias
James D. Nations
Stephen B. Cox
Alvaro Umaña
Katrina Brandon
Stuart K. Tucker
John D. Strasma
Rafael Celis

Transaction Publishers
New Brunswick (USA) and Oxford (UK)

ISBN: 1-56000-015-5 (cloth)
ISBN: 1-56000-577-7 (paper)
Printed in the United States of America

Library of Congress Cataloging-in-Publication Data

Annis, Sheldon.
    Poverty, Natural Resources, and Public Policy in Central America/Sheldon Annis and contributors.

(U.S.-Third World Policy Perspectives: No. 17)
Includes bibliographic references.
    1. Central America—Economic policy. 2. Agriculture and state—Central America. 3. Rural poor—Government policy—Central America. 4. Rural development—Government policy—Central America. 5. Conservation of natural resources—Government policy—Central America. I. Annis, Sheldon. 1944- . II. Series: U.S.-Third World Policy Perspectives, No. 17.

HC141.P68   1992   333.7'09728—dc20   92-29662   CIP
ISBN: 1-56000-015-0 (cloth)
ISBN: 1-56000-577-7 (paper)

Director of Publications: Christine E. Contee
Publications Editor: Jacqueline Edlund-Braun
Edited by Anne M. Byers
Cover and book design by Tim Kenney Design, Inc.

Contents

Foreword vii

I. Overview: Poverty, Natural Resources, and Public Policy in
    Central America
    Sheldon Annis 3

II. Summary of Chapter Recommendations 31

    1. A Call for Central American Peace Parks
        Oscar Arias and James D. Nations 43

        Introduction..................................... 43
        A Regional Approach 44
        Learning from the Peace Process 45
        Seeking Solutions to Regional Environmental
            Problems 48
        Benefits of Parks for Peace...................... 49
        Peace Parks and People 54
        The Challenge Ahead 55
        Toward a Process of Creating Peace Parks 57

    2. Citizen Participation and the Reform of Development
        Assistance in Central America
        Stephen B. Cox 59

        Obstacles to Effective Development Assistance 59
        An Alternative: Rigor in Process 66
        Institutional Reforms in Delivering Development
            Assistance 76
        Conclusion 81

    3. Inventing Institutions for Conservation:
        Lessons from Costa Rica
        Alvaro Umaña and Katrina Brandon 85

        Introduction..................................... 85
        Costa Rica's System of Protected Areas 86
        Reorganization of Conservation Management 88
        Integrating Conservation into the
            Development Process 99
        Conclusion 106

4. **Equity and the Environment in the Promotion of Nontraditional Agricultural Exports**
Stuart K. Tucker 109

    Introduction...................................... 109
    The Promise of Nontraditional Crops 111
    Obstacles to Easing Poverty Through Nontraditional
        Agriculture 114
    Environmental Impacts 121
    Policy Failings in the Promotion of Nontraditional
        Agriculture 122
    Policy Recommendations 128
    Principles for Advocacy 134

5. **Land Taxation, the Poor, and Sustainable Development**
John D. Strasma and Rafael Celis 143

    Introduction...................................... 143
    Poverty, Population, and Fragile Lands 144
    Overview of Land and Tax Policies in
        Central America 145
    Nonrevenue Advantages of Land Taxes 149
    Problems and Accomplishments of Land Reforms in
        Central America 151
    Land Markets and Land Banks as a Proposed Solution
        for the Landless 155
    Squatters and Trees 156
    Agricultural Credit: A Market or a Welfare System? .. 157
    Trees, Tenure, and Taxes: A Suggested Strategy 159
    Creation of a Modern Land Tax 162
    Revenue Potential of a Modern Land Tax 164
    Uses of the New Revenue 165
    Conclusion 165

IV. **Appendix**
Compiled by Beatrice Bezmalinovic and Cynthia Knowles 171

About the Overseas Development Council 194
About the Authors 197

Foreword

Given Central America's tiny size, populations, and economic resources, it would have been impossible to predict the extent to which this impoverished region has consumed U.S. foreign policy interest over and over again during the twentieth century. In this final and truly remarkable decade launching the post-Cold War era, the United States has an obligation to be closely involved in this troubled region, but the nature of its ties no longer need be overwhelmed by strategic military interests.

Responding more to Washington's short-term political interests than to Central America's long-term development needs, the United States squandered millions of dollars in poorly conceived aid programs throughout the 1980s. And it should be of no surprise that there is shockingly little to show for these efforts.

An effective foreign policy for the 1990s requires that security concerns be balanced against increasingly prominent political, economic, humanitarian, and environmental issues which are also of vital interest to the United States. Moreover, its longstanding relationship with the governments, economies, and militaries of Central America gives the United States a responsibility to take action on a new set of cooperative policies which recognizes these fundamentally changed interests.

For nations that have been devastated by wars, this has not come a moment too soon. Not only must much of Central America rebuild itself, but it must do so in the context of fragile and vulnerable democratic governments, enormous and still growing poverty, and economies still largely dependent on the export earnings of a few primary commodities. Also, this agrarian region must greatly accelerate its pace of development with less help from a once rich and vast base of natural resources. Instead, Central American development planners now contend with poisoned waters, eroded soils, disappearing forests, depleted fish stocks, etc. In short, their old development models *failed,* leaving weak political systems, still undiversified economies, much more poverty, and a greatly deteriorated environment in their wake.

Thus, one of the most pressing challenges for Central America is advancing more sustainable development alternatives in both an economic and environmental sense. The contributors to this volume are among the most perceptive analysts of the dual economic-environmental challenge that the region faces. In the pages that follow, they help to fill the crucial gap in our understanding by setting forth a concrete agenda and giving specificity to the ambiguous but critical task of charting a course for the economy that meets economic and social objectives while also maintaining the health of the environment.

When getting down to business at the national and local scale, as this study does, it becomes increasingly obvious that the interventions needed are complex, costly, and time-consuming, and require skilled and committed institutions and individuals. There are no short cuts—especially to setting in motion those measures that can reduce poverty, stabilize rapidly expanding populations, *and* safeguard the environment and natural resources on which these countries so greatly depend.

Two earlier works by the Overseas Development Council set the stage for the more focused discussion here: John P. Lewis's *Strengthening the Poor: What Have We Learned?* and *Environment and the Poor: Development Strategies for a Common Agenda* by H. Jeffrey Leonard. As Lewis shows, there is much that is known and can be done about improving the well-being of poor people in poor countries. *Environment and the Poor* focuses specifically on the huge and still rapidly growing numbers of very poor people (perhaps as much as six out of ten of all of the developing world's poor) who are being forced onto ecologically vulnerable lands—tropical forests, hilly areas, arid zones and the periphery of large urban centers.

This study builds on the analytical frameworks provided by Lewis and Leonard. In particular, *Poverty, Natural Resources, and Public Policy in Central America* devotes considerable attention to measures that alleviate poverty and empower the poor. This is no accident. Better environmental policies must deal head on with reconciling fiercely competing interests over how resources should be used—or not used. Fortunately, in most cases, policies that eradicate poverty will also ease pressures on natural resources.

Much of the local, national, and international dialogue on sustainable development, however, still focuses on the tensions rather than the fundamentally common agenda between strengthening the poor and protecting the environment. Indeed, preparations leading up to and during the 1992 Earth Summit were filled with tensions over how to balance environment and development priorities. The South wanted the conference to take concrete action on their unmet development needs, while the North pressed to keep the agenda more targeted on environmental concerns, especially global warming and massive species and forest loss. ODC's recent *Policy Essay* on "North-South Environmental Strategies, Costs, and Bargains" by Patti Petesch examines this unparalleled environmental diplomacy.

The contributors to this volume have provided valuable analyses and proposals for a Central American policy agenda that is at once pro-poor and pro-environment. Both rich and poor countries can only make progess on priorities of concern to them by taking up this challenge.

The Overseas Development Council gratefully acknowledges the support of the Rockefeller Brothers Fund and The Tinker Foundation, Inc. for their grants in support of this project. In addition, The Ford Foundation, The Rockefeller Foundation, and The William and Flora Hewlett Foundation contribute generously to the Council's overall program, including the U.S.-Third World Policy Perspectives series of which this study is a part.

October 1992
John W. Sewell, President
Overseas Development Council

Overview

Poverty, Natural Resources, and Public Policy in Central America

Sheldon Annis

It is now hardly necessary to tell anyone that Central America faces an environmental crisis—or that this environmental crisis mirrors an even deeper poverty crisis.

But it is wrong to say that nothing is being done. To the contrary, Central America's policymakers have responded with a plethora of new ministries, task forces, and high-level commissions. They have issued a stream of urgent priority statements, strategy documents, laws, and regulations. Bilateral and multilateral aid agencies have supported their efforts with tens of millions of new dollars for natural resource and rural development programs. International foundations have mobilized to support rainforest protection, biospheres, population programs, and research into sustainable agriculture. The airwaves of Central America now resound with exhortations not to litter, not to pollute, not to destroy. The region's school children are being taught to draw their own tapirs, guacamayas, and toucans (rather than elephants, giraffes, and zebras). And ever more loudly, their parents are voicing concerns about local resource problems—not just in universities and among the middle class, but in village committees, in urban *barrios*, and through well-organized popular organizations.

Central Americans understand perfectly well that poverty and environmental deterioration are mutually reinforcing. Yet despite anger and debate, new policies and programs, and a substantial investment of public and private money, three inescapable realities remain:

- Poverty has generally gotten worse, not better.

■ The region's physical resources are being depleted at an ever accelerating rate.

■ Current responses—though often positive—are neither reversing poverty nor stemming the drain of physical assets.

This book examines these troubling realities and sets forth several concrete proposals on what can be done. In presenting these ideas, we are all too aware of underlying obstacles that tend to undercut all such programs of good intention—a $28 billion debt overhang,[1] a weak international trade position, a legacy of violence, and enduring political conflict. Moreover, a region that had a population of about 12 million in 1960 will have a population of approximately 63 million in 2025 (Appendix, Figure 1).[2]

Yet, if the situation is not exactly bright, neither is it hopeless. Central America is changing, and many of the changes are for the better.

Perhaps the most significant change is relative peace. Since the peace process began in the mid-1980s, formerly contentious parties have been talking to each other, and a mood of reconciliation has prevailed. After 12 years of bitter warfare, a political settlement has finally been reached in El Salvador. After more than a century of dispute, Guatemala has formally acknowledged Belize as an independent nation with recognizable borders. With more than 45,000 dead in a country of less than 4 million people, Nicaragua continues to disarm.[3] And the parties to the region's longest and most intractable war—the guerrilla insurgency in Guatemala—are at least negotiating an end to the strife.

It is premature to say that economic recovery is taking place. It isn't, and certainly not for the poor. But some positive signs are visible. Costa Rica, Guatemala, and El Salvador registered positive real growth rates in 1990 (3.5, 3.8, and 2.5 percent, respectively)—far stronger than the negative or flat rates of the early and mid-1980s. Compared to the mid-1980s, inflation is coming under control.[4] Some economic sectors, such as tourism, are vigorous and promise to expand. In Costa Rica and Guatemala, nontraditional agricultural exports have increased. Investor confidence, relative to the 1980s, is up; capital flight is down. Although only Costa Rica has actually negotiated a significant reduction package for commercial debt, at least the precedent has been established, and the Enterprise for the Americas Initiative formalizes a procedure for reducing official debt.

In general, Central American governments are more stable and technocratic (in a good sense) than they used to be. The transition from military to civilian rule, though far from complete, is probably irreversible. The region's governments share a remarkable consensus on the need for market-driven economies, freer trade, continued restructuring of the public sector, and greater regional economic integration. With the cooling of external and internal warfare, they have an opportunity to redirect substantial military expenditures into economic and social investments. For almost the first time in history, these countries are in approximate agreement with their powerful northern neighbor on economic policy goals, especially in regard to foreign investment.

Finally, the extraordinary groundswell of popular revolution that has swept the world in the last three years also has reached Central America. Though less dramatically apparent than elsewhere, fundamental political changes are taking place. Throughout the region, a broadening spectrum of social actors—including the poor—are becoming engaged in debate and decisionmaking. Democracy is taking on practical meaning beyond nominal elections.

This book asks whether and how these positive trends can offset the continuing expansion of poverty and environmental depletion. In addressing this problem, we pose several future-oriented questions:

■ What kinds of regional arrangements can address cross-border environmental problems? How can national boundaries be respected, yet accommodate natural ecological boundaries and reduce political tension?

■ How can the new social energy and political activism of the poor be better incorporated into the political process? Specifically, can development assistance programs be reformed to reinforce and constructively build upon these new energies and capabilities?

■ What types of public-sector institutions need to be created to link the sometimes contrary objectives of poverty alleviation and resource conservation? In particular, how do Central American nations establish multiple-use protected areas that fairly reconcile human needs with the protection of forests and wildlife?

■ What agricultural strategies will the region need to embrace? In particular, how can modern, nontraditional agriculture include the poor?

■ What can be done about the inherent maldistribution of land in market-oriented economies? Are there practical measures that can redistribute assets in ways that are fair and conducive to rural development and environmental protection?

POVERTY IN CENTRAL AMERICA TODAY

No one knows, really, how many poor people there are in Central America. Indicators are imperfect, at best, and data are uneven.[5] However, estimates are that about 14.5 million Central Americans, or 56 percent of the population, are "poor." Of these, about 9.1 million people, or 35 percent of the population, are "extremely poor." In *rural* areas only, about

70 percent of the population is "poor," 47 percent of which is "extremely poor." (For a breakdown of poverty distribution by country, see Appendix, Figure 10.) Even with a wide margin for possible overstatement or error, this is a huge and unacceptable amount of poverty by any reasonable moral standard.

If poverty is clearly endemic in Central America, is it improving, stabilizing, or worsening?

For some countries there is no doubt. Nicaragua, for example, had a 1990 real growth rate in GDP of -5.5 percent; in Honduras it was -3.8 percent.[6] Even though hard statistical data are scarce, no one who has witnessed firsthand the economic devastation in Nicaragua, the visible malnourishment in Honduras, or the effects of a bloody war in rural El Salvador doubts that poverty has worsened.

The situation in Guatemala is mixed. On the one hand, the Guatemalan economy grew at a moderate 3.5 percent rate in 1990, following several years of positive growth; but, at the same time, substantial inflationary pressure hit the poor especially hard (see Appendix, Figure 8).[7] During the 1980s, both poverty and inequality increased in Guatemala. According to the World Bank and the Economic Commission for Latin America and the Caribbean (ECLAC), the proportion of Guatemalan households under the poverty line rose to nearly 70 percent by the mid-1980s, of which 43 percent were considered "extremely poor." The gini coefficient (the most commonly used statistical measure of relative inequality) for family income rose from 0.48 in the 1979-1981 period to 0.53 in the 1986-87 period—meaning that family income distribution worsened in a society that was already among the most inequitable in the hemisphere.[8]

Costa Rica is the only Central American nation in which it is plausible to argue that absolute and relative poverty may have declined overall in recent years. From the early 1960s through the end of the 1970s, Costa Rica enjoyed a period of sustained economic growth. Poverty and income inequality declined substantially. But at the outset of the 1980s, the economy collapsed. Real per capita income fell by nearly 25 percent and poverty shot up. Since the mid-1980s, the economy has expanded steadily. Yet the evidence on poverty and income inequality is mixed and contradictory. Economist Gary Fields, who has done the most systematic review on this subject, says that *if* indeed there have been improvements in inequality, they could not have been large ones.[9]

One simple way to translate abstract data about poverty into human terms is to think about what most rural Central Americans earn in light of what it actually costs them to live. Consider, for instance, the prevailing daily wage rates paid to agricultural laborers: about $2 per day in Guatemala, $4 a day in Costa Rica, $6 to $7 per day in Belize, $2.50 per day in El Salvador, and $3 per day in Honduras.[10] Whether working on their own land or on someone else's, most rural people earn cash or in-kind incomes relatively close to these rates.

Now, compare these incomes for a full day of backbreaking labor to the cost of common goods and services:

■ In Guatemala, most rural people eat tortillas and salt as a staple food, beans sometimes, eggs if they have their own poultry, and meat and milk rarely. That is because a gallon of milk costs about $1.60—more than 80 percent of a rural worker's daily salary; the price of a kilogram of ground beef is about $3.25, more than a day and a half of a full-time salary. A single gallon of gasoline to operate a truck is roughly equivalent to a co-op member's total daily income. If a landless farmer wants his own farm, a single hectare of high-quality land will cost about $1,600—roughly twice his income for a year.[11]

■ In the Nicaraguan countryside, the price of a minimal food basket for a family of four is about $110 a month, approximately *twice* the salary of a primary school teacher or rural nurse.[12] To build a home, a rural family will have to pay about 60 cents apiece for cinder blocks and about 30 cents a pound for 3-inch nails—just under the price for similar materials in a country hardware store in the United States. But the relative price in Nicaragua is much higher: 90 cents for the block and nails represent nearly *half a day's* wage for a rural Nicaraguan *albañil* (a skilled mason who builds homes), while they mean about 3 or 4 *minutes* of wages to a skilled American carpenter.[13]

■ In rural Belize, the average food expenditure for a family of six, living in a United Nations-funded refugee settlement project, is about $86 per month. That allows approximately 50 cents a day to feed each person. Yet the prices for goods, such as eggs ($1.20 per dozen), milk (90 cents a quart), a coke (50 cents), a bottle of local beer (about $1) are approximately the same or more than they are in the United States.[14] Meanwhile, if wages are a fraction of real food costs, the price for helping development is relatively much higher. A box of perforated computer printer paper used by a relief organization runs about $60 in Belize's capital, Belmopan (compared to about $25 in the United States); a ream of 500 sheets of photocopy paper costs approximately $10 in Belmopan (about $3 in the United States).

One need not search very far to see what these discrepancies between wages and the cost of living mean. Central America's "pockets" of endemic poverty have stretched so large as to now take in most of the region: virtually all of Nicaragua; most of Honduras; nearly all of Guatemala's northwest highlands and much of the east; war-ravaged departments in El Salvador, such as Chalatenango and Morazán; sizeable sections of Costa Rica, such as Nicoya and Puriscal; Colón and much of central Panama; and the large Toledo district that makes up southern Belize.

Even in relatively prosperous areas—the modern cotton farms along Guatemala's Pacific coast, the well-to-do small coffee and vegetable farms of Costa Rica's Central Valley, and the new melon-exporting regions of Honduras—poverty is displaced rather than truly absent. The poor live between prosperity's cracks as squatters on public land or camped out on vacant property, as seasonal laborers in temporary housing, and as tenant farmers, refugees, and urban slum dwellers who often commute to the countryside for low-paying harvest jobs.

It is no accident that environmental problems (deforestation, massive erosion, watershed destruction, agrochemical saturation, and degradation of marine estuaries) tend to be worst in the areas of most extreme poverty. Take, for example, Choluteca on the Pacific coast of Honduras. Once green, it is now deforested and sprouting cacti. Despite occasional satellite dishes and Mercedes diesels roaring between the capital city and the coast, the landscape is ragged; crops grow indifferently; houses are left unattended as workers seek jobs elsewhere.

The central highway that connects Choluteca with Tegucigalpa is pitted with potholes. To the south, traffic slows every few kilometers for what appears to be road construction. As a motorist approaches, the workers raise their hands to wave . . . well, not actually to wave, but to beg; for these workers are ragged gangs of roadside children—two here, three there, perhaps as many as 20 in small groups.

Some of these children are as young as four; few are older than 10. Their job is to fill in the potholes that they already "repaired" yesterday. With a busy flurry of activity to slow the speeding traffic, the youngest children pile sod or scoop roadside gravel onto scraps of plastic. They then dump this material into the potholes, sweeping in more roadside gravel and stomping on the fill. They beg for tips from the motorists who must slow and swerve to miss both the potholes and the waving children.

The homes in which these children live have dirt floors rather than concrete, cooking fires rather than stoves, and latrines rather than toilets. Much of their family diet consists of salted tortillas and store-bought sweets. Food is scarce, there are few possessions, and little or no cash is kept at home. Their parents typically came to this area a generation ago. When these children are older, they too will probably move on.

How Poverty in Central America is Different Today

In traveling and talking with rural Central Americans such as these, it is clear that the social character of poverty in the 1990s is very different from that of previous generations. These changes have important implications for the ways in which the population uses natural resources.

First, though as economically impoverished as ever, the rural poor of the 1990s are no longer necessarily isolated or "traditional."

Today's rural poor are not generally self-contained subsistence farmers or a backwater population waiting for development to happen. In Choluteca, for example, modern agriculture and the Green Revolution arrived years ago; mechanized farms, roads, power lines, and billboards stretch in every direction. The hardware of development projects peppers the landscape: Peace Corps rabbit hutches, CARE latrines, World Neighbors terraces, EEC farm implements, USAID schools, and IDB health posts, and government officials hurry in their acronym-initialled, four-wheel drive vehicles.

Rather, these rural poor are what is left over *after* development. They are not waiting for the modern economy; they *are* the modern economy. And for precisely this reason, the poverty they face is in many ways more deeply ingrained and more intractable than the "traditional" village poverty of their parents' generation.

On the other hand, these people are better educated and more media connected than their parents were. Between 1960 and 1980 alone, rural literacy rose from about 38 to 62 percent.[15] Few people still live in villages where no one can read a newspaper and where petitioners must sign documents with thumbprints. Virtually everyone is a radio listener, and most are television watchers. By now, their consciousness has been raised by Freirian educators, their souls contested by evangelical preachers, their children vaccinated by health post workers, and their communities organized by a half-dozen brands of community organizers. Of course none of this means that they are not still poor and powerless. But they are nonetheless better informed, better connected to ideas and to the outside world; and in some respects, they are better posed to challenge the conditions of their lives.

Second, today's rural poor are less rooted to place. To have asked a Honduran *campesino* 20 years ago, "Where are you from?" would have been pointless because the answer was largely self-evident: "From here." Now, however, the query seems as natural and conversational as it does in, say, transient Washington, DC. The rural population is mobile. As many as 3 million people—roughly a fifth of the rural inhabitants of Central America—have been displaced by war, fear of political violence, endemic poverty, and depletion of physical resources.[16] This displaced population also includes a very large number of rural offspring who did *not* inherit their parents' farms. To say that someone is "among the poorest of the rural poor" no longer suggests a poor but stable *campesino*, but rather a person who is transient, probably unwelcome among more permanent neighbors, and in many respects a "forager" on the landscape. Neither subsistence farming nor rural wage labor can fully absorb this widening fraction of the population.

In many cases, these uprooted people move from country to country—the human flotsam of the region's bitter warfare. For example,

Belize, with a 1991 population of about 200,000, has absorbed some 30,000 refugees from El Salvador and Guatemala, ranking it tenth in the world in the proportion of refugees to native-born citizens.[17] During the early 1980s, Mexico absorbed as many as 200,000 political refugees from the highlands of Guatemala (and an estimated 42,000 still remain).[18] In turn, Guatemala has endured cross-border incursions from landless Mexican farmers (as well as waves of archaeological looters and wildlife poachers).

In the late 1980s, tens of thousands of Nicaraguan contras operating in southern Honduras destroyed much of the forested border zone. As many as 20,000 ex-contras have laid down their arms and, with their dependents, are now seeking land.[19] While up to 350,000 Nicaraguans were internally displaced by the war, perhaps as many as half a million refugees fled the country.[20] Some 20,000 "official" refugees and an estimated 100,000 undocumented Nicaraguans are expected to remain in Costa Rica for the foreseeable future.[21]

Third, because much of the social fabric of rural Central America has been shredded by violence, dislocations, and loss of resources, today's poor are now less bound together within families and stable social institutions. "Village" once implied a web of multigenerational, extended family households. Today's rural poor are more likely to be "family fragments." The proportion of the poorest population that is made up of single, adult females has increased enormously. In countries such as El Salvador and Guatemala, where as many as a quarter of the households are now headed by women,[22] this perverse "feminization of poverty" can be partially attributed to men being killed or forced to flee. In less violent places, it has more to do with the splitting up of families because of poverty and work-related migration. One way or another, female-headed households have fewer working members, lower average wage earnings, and less access to productive resources.[23]

Indirectly, the dramatic increase in street children[24] in many of the region's cities is caused by the fragmentation of family life that is taking place in the countryside. In Guatemala, it is estimated that about 5,000 abandoned, homeless children sleep on the streets, while as many as 1.45 million children and youths (though they may have some kind of family or home base) earn their livelihood and roam the streets at least semi-independently.[25]

Men, women, and children of rural Central America who were previously bound within webs of linked nuclear families now find themselves in social situations that were once atypical of village life: serial, common-law unions that produce children who do not fit easily into the social space or inheritance structure; polygamy, especially by men who move between city, coast, and village; renting or homelessness among elderly villagers not incorporated into the households of their children; and semi-independence among rural teenagers who are the children of family fragments. Domestic servitude in middle-class urban households has long been an escape route for unattached village women. But while live-in maids once worked a lifetime as "members" of a family, now they tend to change employers frequently, usually without security or job benefits.

THE ENVIRONMENTAL COST OF CHANGED POVERTY

Most of these changes in the social character of modern Central American poverty have a direct and devastating impact on the environment. This is because resource use by the new "very, very poor" (i.e., squatters, landless laborers, refugees, sub-subsistence farmers, family fragments) is fundamentally different from resource use by the old "merely poor" (i.e., most *campesinos*). Moreover, the deepening structural entrenchment of poverty, the separation of the poor from place, and the tearing of the social fabric have all increased the number of people who are "very, very poor" relative to those who are "merely poor."

The problem is that the more modern "very, very poor" have neither the minimum assets nor the economic incentives to invest in conservation of physical resources. This is not because of a lack of education, environmental insensitivity, or agronomic ignorance. It is a matter of practical survival. Necessarily, the "very, very poor" have a short time horizon when it comes to investing in places in which they themselves are impermanent. They have fewer personal disincentives to cut forest cover, consume wildlife, and plant annual crops on slopes that will erode.

By contrast, "merely poor" farmers (i.e., *campesinos* with secure land tenure) are committed to place, and their livelihood depends on the continued integrity of the resource base. It makes sense for them to invest in windbreaks, fallowing, terracing, and protecting springs. Such poor, but not impoverished, farmers typically manage resources with great care, even elegance. They optimize the use of every microscopic scrap of resource—every ridge of soil, every tree, every channel of water, and every angle of sunlight.[26] They protect what they must depend on for their families' future. It is for this reason that the changed character of modern poverty—which has increased wealth for a few but caused landlessness and rootlessness for a great many more—has had such a deleterious effect on the environment.

The population boom, too, has accelerated environmental consumption. The more people there are in a small area, the harder it is to conserve what remains, despite the importance of conservation. When faced with this dilemma in the past, one solution for the "very, very poor" was to leave. And, indeed, there was usually somewhere else to go—to the agricultural frontier, to cities, to vacant tracts of land, to agrarian reform or colonization projects.

Today, the safety-valve places are mostly filled, and the welcoming frontiers are gone. In immense areas of Central America—virtually *all* of El Salvador for example—deforestation is now so complete that a potential slash-and-burn settler is hard pressed to find somewhere left to slash. The Pacific coast, Central America's great agricultural frontier of the past generation, is now cut by highways, urbanized, and given over to cotton, cattle, sugar, bananas, and African palm almost everywhere from southern Mexico through Panama City. A resident work force, primarily in new cities, now supplies most of the seasonal and permanent farm labor that used to be drawn from the highlands.

In highland Guatemala, which can no longer shed surplus population to the Pacific, departments such as Totonicapán have population densities approaching those of Sumatra or rural Belgium.[27] Cities provide a partial answer at best. In the recessionary 1980s, life for the urban poor in Central America became so bad that in many cases the flow of migration was *reversed*, back to the countryside.

In Guatemala, one historic option for the landless has been migration to the Petén, the country's last remaining large tract of sparsely populated forestland. But since the late 1960s, agriculture has penetrated and is now virtually irreversible as far north as Flores. And aside from the fact that the Petén's tropical soils are not particularly well suited for the subsistence crops of the highlands, today's land seekers are discovering that they must join a long, combative line of others who also want access to the remaining territory—commercial loggers, Mexican lumber poachers, wildlife poachers, marijuana growers, nature tourism operators, petroleum companies, Mayan archaeologists, chicle tappers, *xate* growers, 40,000 Guatemalan refugees living in Mexico, and conservationists who want to establish an international Mayan biosphere reserve.

The Environment and the Rich

The preceding discussion does not imply that Central America's worsening environmental crisis is the fault of the poor. To the contrary, there is another side to the story: the environmental crisis was created by the well-to-do, who, like the poor, are accustomed to viewing natural resources as the stuff from which personal wealth is manufactured.

Agrarian elites in Central America tend to be wealthy precisely *because* they have been able to convert public resources into personal wealth. Like the new "very, very poor," wealthy farmers typically inhabit an economic environment that is not based on incentives to conserve or even necessarily to produce. During the 1960s and 1970s, in particular, large farmers throughout Central America greatly benefited from the ease with which they could transfer resources to themselves by using political clout to manipulate states that were weak, corrupt, or controlled by the military. They were able to put in place policy choices and incentives that transferred resources to make the rich richer, the poor poorer, and helped to accumulate the region's dual "economic and environment debt."[28] These measures, which created grist for the economic reform agenda of the late 1980s, included:

- plentiful production loans for large farmers at negative real interest rates;
- overvalued exchange rates that effectively lowered the cost of expensive imported machinery and heavy equipment;
- reductions of and exonerations from tariffs on imported agricultural inputs;
- government-financed crop insurance programs that strongly favored large-farm crops;
- low tax rates on the traditional commodity exports;
- low rates or nonexistent taxes on land;
- generous fiscal incentives for export agriculture;
- privileged access to agricultural ministries;
- a banking system heavily biased toward large-farmer loans;
- research and agricultural extension services geared toward the needs and technology of large farms;
- willingness of banks to make seemingly endless bridge loans and to tolerate low repayment rates in bad crop years;
- strong reluctance by almost anyone to look critically at the environmental consequences of these measures.

The expansion of the cattle industry was the most environmentally egregious example of how large farmers preempted public resources to finance marginally productive, resource-consuming agriculture.[29] In Costa Rica, for example, about one-third of all state-financed agricultural credit—an extraordinary $1.2 billion between 1969 and 1985—went to finance cattle ranching.[30] Large farmers, who had easy access to the national banking system, received most of these loans.[31] This disproportionate allocation of capital (largely borrowed internationally) produced relatively little foreign exchange and helped drive deforestation at a voracious rate. Between 1950 and 1973 total pasture more than doubled to include almost half of total agricultural land, so that cattle occupied about 1.6 million hectares—approximately one-third of the country's total land mass.[32]

The disproportionate, politically driven investment in cattle ranching was in almost all ways a poor investment. First, the massive extension of public credit was far out of proportion to the relatively modest foreign exchange earnings or the cattle industry's contribution to Costa Rica's domestic agricultural economy. Indeed, the export earnings were not as great as the loans.[33] Second, the loans were consistently in arrears; they required constant rescheduling and moratoria on repayment; and they were defaulted upon by the same farmers who then went back for new loans.[34] Third, they were socially biased. Well-to-do cattle ranchers were among the most powerful lobbies in the country. Not only were loans easier for them to obtain, but they also were easier for them to *not* pay back.[35]

Easy borrowing from the banks accelerated easy "borrowing" from the land. So long as credit was subsidized and land was cheap, ranchers had little incentive to invest in intensified production, much less in long-term measures to protect or restore what was ruined. Instead, they simply borrowed back and forth until external bank credit was exhausted on the one hand, and "environmental credit" was exhausted on the other.

Central America's skewed credit system is only one reflection of this historical pattern of "wrong-way" resource flows.[36] Another example, as John Strasma and Rafael Celis point out in Chapter 5, is the region's maldistribution of land and general ineffectiveness in fairly taxing wealth. And yet a third example, according to Stuart Tucker in Chapter 4, is the two-track, socially biased structure of opportunity in modern, non-traditional agriculture.

Central America's "development model" has been based on international borrowing, environmental consumption, and foreign aid. Running on borrowed time, the economies of the region *did* grow overall during the last 30 years. Yet international borrowing, environmental consumption, and foreign aid are not sustainable. (see Appendix, Figure 4.) The world and Central America have changed. What worked in the past will not work in the future.

AN END TO ENVIRONMENTAL BORROWING

During the 1950s, 1960s, and 1970s, agricultural production more than kept pace with the expanding population. But the strategies and technologies that boosted output over those decades cannot necessarily reproduce the same miracles in the 1990s and beyond.

In the first place, the region's richest, best-watered, and most accessible agricultural zones are all in production. There are no more vast, unused tracts of land. Furthermore, the natural fertility of areas brought under cultivation 20 to 30 years ago is now declining.

Fertilizers, pesticides, and high-yielding seed varieties can offset declining fertility up to a point. Certainly, Green Revolution seeds, combined with relatively inexpensive chemical fertilizers and pesticides, increased the production of such crops as coffee, cotton, and rice, especially in the 1970s. But while commodity prices have declined since the early 1980s,[37] agrochemicals (particularly those that are petroleum-based) have generally become far more costly, both in absolute terms and relative to the value of the commodities they help produce. In addition, the associated health and environmental hazards have reached unacceptable levels in many areas.

Water diversion and gravity-flow irrigation were relatively easy in the 1960s and 1970s, because groundwater was generally abundant where agriculture was expanding. But much of the "easy water" has now been tapped, dammed, used, or polluted. Streams, watersheds, and aquifers have been damaged and retain less water than they used to. Once-fertile lands are now denuded and degraded, initiating a desert-producing cycle that feeds on itself and that has caused long-term changes in the soil, climate, plant and animal life.

Take, for example, Zacapa in Guatemala, Choluteca in Honduras, La Unión in El Salvador, or Nicoya in Costa Rica. These are regions that once absorbed settlers. Today, they are dry, deforested, and worn out. The land cannot support the population, and there are few choices for a new round of outward migration. Economically, the region can scarcely afford to protect critical watersheds in the highlands and best agricultural zones, much less finance irrigation and rehabilitation to restore high productivity in these ecologically devastated lowlands.

In the 1970s a world surplus of easily borrowable "petrodollars" helped fuel the expansion of nonsustainable agriculture in Central America. The Cold War kept dollars flowing through the end of the 1980s. (Between 1978 and 1990 Central America received about $10 billion from the United States in loans and grants.)[38] But today the capacity to borrow is constrained by past debt; and the prospects for extraordinary aid flows, such as the $4.0 billion that El Salvador received during the past 12 years, are negligible.

NEW POLITICS FOR THE 1990s AND BEYOND

There is another reason why the basic development model of the past—in which the elite used politics to convert natural resources to personal wealth and more clout—is no longer sustainable: Central America's politics has also changed. At every level competition is increasing over who has access to fiscal and physical resources. In particular, poor rural majorities constitute an increasingly important element in checks and balances among a gradually widening field of political players.

An underlying theme of this book is that new frameworks must evolve for political bartering and decisionmaking over the allocation of resources. To reverse poverty or environmental degradation, poor majorities must be able to negotiate fairly their needs in relation to those of agricultural exporters, urban professionals, middle-size farmers, tour operators, conservationists, and all the other groups who lay claim to a piece of the pie. Where they do not exist, mechanisms need to be invented for dialogue and deal making among the plethora of competing interests that collectively control the fate of the region's natural resource base.

Each author in this volume hammers home this theme from a slightly different angle:

■ By calling for a "park process" as an extension of the "peace process," former Costa Rican President Oscar Arias and James Nations reinforce the point that parkmaking, like peacemaking, begins by bringing adversaries to the table. Conservation, too, they argue, should focus on recognizing mutual interests and reconciling conflicts.

■ Stephen Cox traces the failure of much of what we call "development" to a bureaucratically driven system that inherently denies citizen participation. The alternative that he proposes, "rigor in process," is an attempt to redress this fundamental weakness.

■ Alvaro Umaña and Katrina Brandon provide an illuminating case study of how Costa Rica struggled to "invent institutions" that would simultaneously reconcile the state's desire to have a unified national strategy for resource management—and at the same time decentralize actual decisionmaking, control, and financial responsibility to a widening network of regional actors.

■ Stuart Tucker argues that emphasis on nontraditional agricultural exports is indeed a good idea for Central America, but that the mainstream development policy reflects and reinforces exclusion of the poor. What is needed, he says, is multilayered reform that widens social access to market opportunities.

■ John Strasma and Rafael Celis dispute conventional wisdom that dismisses taxation as politically impossible in Central America. To the contrary, they argue that site-specific land taxes are possible precisely *because* decisions can be made and enforced by a consensus of local representatives.

NEW COMMUNICATIONS NETWORKS AND THE POOR

Democratization is beginning to penetrate decisionmaking over the allocation of natural resources. In one important respect, time favors democratization. The same extraordinary communications technology that was so crucial in the political upheavals of Eastern Europe and the Soviet Union also has reached Central America. Faxes, videos, telephones, computers, and optical fibers allow previously disconnected people to talk to each other, exchange information, and form new political networks.[39]

Of course, the poor are still poor, and poverty still means powerlessness. But the *informational* environment today is different—in general, improving—and that creates one more building block toward real democracy.

In remote corners, as well as cities, one sees evidence everywhere:

■ In Guatemala *campesinos* who cannot operate typewriters, much less computers, can now fax messages about massacres to foreign journalists and human rights monitors. As reports accumulate, they can set off a chain of international action alerts and generate thousands of protest telegrams to the government within a matter of days. Tomorrow these *campesinos* may still be repressed; but as repression is made visible internationally, it becomes more difficult to sustain locally.

■ In a thin band of jungle running some 200 kilometers along Panama's Atlantic coast, Kuna Indians document their customs and prepare videos. On tape they debate the Columbian quincentennial. More important, they exchange tapes and coordinate strategies long-distance with the Bribri in Costa Rica, the Kekchi Maya in Belize, even the Cherokee in Oklahoma.

■ In Nicaragua a phone-based computer network called Nicarao connects scores of regional environmental activists, journalists, and grassroots organizations to each other. Through Nicarao's link to PeaceNet/EcoNet in the United States, regional users are joined to thousands of counterparts in support organizations and kindred institutions in about a dozen other activist networks throughout the world. In Costa Rica, a new computer network, Huracán, connects disparate nongovernmental organization researchers at the region's five major public universities. In turn, Nicarao and Huracán are linked to each other . . . and to the Internet in the United States, which means they are linked to thousands of individual *networks*, connecting perhaps a million users in universities, corporations, and nonprofit organizations throughout the United States . . . who in turn are newly joined to similar electronics webs in Europe, Australia, and East Asia and to the incipient networks forming in southern Africa, South America, and Eastern Europe.[40]

Of course all communication is not political. Computer conferences and video linkages do not in themselves make powerless people powerful; and information by itself does not translate to power. The rich, too, have access to new technology (indeed, far greater access); so gains by the poor are hardly one-sided, nor are they necessarily equalizing.

Nonetheless, local struggles are becoming visible and more easily incorporated into wider movements. The assumption that the poor always lose is less certain. In general, technology is cheaper, more portable, more durable, and easier to use. If not necessarily accessible to poor individuals, it is at least reaching service organizations and grassroots networks that incorporate the poor.

Take, for example, a group of artisanal fishermen in southern Honduras along the Gulf of Fonseca. This organization has been bitterly struggling with commercial mariculturalists over remaining tracts of mangroves. The fishermen want the estuary mangroves left intact as spawning and fishing grounds and as a source of fuelwood. The commercial growers want to take advantage of the natural hydrology to construct ponds for growing shrimp.[41]

Three years ago the fishermen's group received a camcorder from a foundation grant. At first they used it to record community fiestas and birthday parties. But more recently they have learned to document company-owned bulldozers plowing under mangroves, while a newspaper is held up in the background to verify the date.

These snippets, the fishermen have learned, can be sent to representatives in the Honduran Congress, to newspaper and television journalists, and to international environmental organizations who know that the environmentally sensitive USAID program is helping to finance export-oriented shrimp farming. In effect, the local fisherman have been able to manufacture 15-second sound bites. They may lose their battle anyway; but in taking the fight beyond the local arena, they are improving their odds over the certain loss that they would have faced just a few years ago.

TOWARD A PRO-POOR, PRO-ENVIRONMENTAL POLICY AGENDA

A new politics is indeed in its infancy in Central America. Representative organizations are emerging, links are being forged between previously unconnected groups and social layers, and formal democratic processes are solidifying. But how can this dynamism be translated into public policy that is both pro-poor and pro-environment? Where is the reform agenda that can bring together new political actors, their ideas, and real-world decisionmaking?

The authors of this volume present several difficult and sometimes contradictory policy shifts that must take place. More important, they set forth a series of concrete proposals. They build toward a convergence in poverty and environmental policy, explained in the following pages.

The Softening of Borders

The unification of conservation with development is a challenge that transcends borders. In "A Call for Central American Peace Parks," former President Oscar Arias and James D. Nations propose a regionally managed system of Central American "peace parks" that would reduce stress on the environment and, simultaneously, lessen political tension.

Presently, separate initiatives are under way to establish bi- and tri-national parks along four border zones: the Petén (Guatemala, Mexico, Belize); El Trifínio (El Salvador, Honduras, Guatemala); Sí-a-Paz (Nicaragua, Costa Rica); and La Amistad (Costa Rica, Panama).

All of these areas share common characteristics. They are separated by national borders but joined by ecology; they contain unique wildlife, tropical forests, and archaeological sites; they protect shared watersheds that support agriculture and urban populations; and they are under siege by large numbers of poor people, including many who have been displaced by the region's wars and political conflicts.

As Arias and Nations point out, the problems of wise and just land use are hard enough to address within the boundaries of a single country. These difficulties multiply when administration, cost sharing, and political decisions must straddle borders—particularly borders as contentious as these have been. Moreover, peace parks in these border zones will be meaningless if the needs of the displaced poor are not met.

Yet a park process today is no less improbable than a peace process was yesterday. In 1987 President Arias led an effort—for which he was awarded the Nobel Peace Prize—for all Central American nations to promote dialogue and negotiate solutions to regional warfare and political conflict. In this volume, he and Nations argue that the same process can be applied to conservation—an ambitious proposal to bring poor people into the decisionmaking process over natural resource utilization, while joining sometimes antagonistic parties across sovereign borders.

Aid Reform and "Rigor in Process"

Virtually no one is satisfied with the past decade's multibillion-dollar aid expenditure. In his chapter, Stephen Cox asks, What's wrong? What is it that we don't know about poverty-oriented development assistance? And is there a role for a better kind of development aid in the future?

The problem, Cox maintains, begins with a model of sustainability that is far too narrow. Although development practitioners have begun to worry more explicitly about economic and environmental sustainability, they give far too little thought to social, political, and institutional sustainability.

Cox argues that the conventional practice of development is predicated on mistaken confidence in the degree to which bureaucratic institutions can predict and control what happens in practice. Professional "developers" assume that they influence more than they really do; so, much is planned and little is achieved. In addition, assistance is distorted and driven by the political priorities of governments and donors, not the needs of the poor. And, cutting across all these weaknesses, the model fails to incorporate citizen participation in the management and structuring of development.

Cox calls first for humility. He argues for the downsizing of institutional hubris coupled with greater faith in democratic process. He calls for "rigor in process" rather than for "rigor in design." This means:

■ Securing timely and periodically updated feedback on the actual priorities of the rural poor;

■ Improving the analytical and managerial skills of local and national institutions, both private and public, to ensure continuity after international involvement ceases;

■ Establishing mechanisms for debate over priorities and methods, and "deal cutting" among local and national interests; and

■ Creating "accountability linkages" that give program staff incentives to work flexibly and creatively for results rather than for compliance with workplans.

How might "rigor in process" be introduced into existing and future programs? Cox takes note of several new kinds of "process tools": rapid rural appraisals, multiparty policy dialogues, interagency working groups, horizontal communication among nongovernmental organizations and popular organizations, and training and analytic skills for new participants in development. He discusses these tools in the context of the U.S. bilateral assistance program. Then, he calls for an imaginative new initiative—the creation of a Central American Fund that would provide support specifically for participation-enhancing and process-focused activities.

Creating New Institutions for Conservation and Development

Perhaps the most perplexing environmental challenge facing Central America is how to conserve remaining forests (especially along the Caribbean coast and undeveloped tracts along the Pacific), simultaneously use and restore already overused slope land in the highlands, and at the same time meet legitimate demands for *more* land by a restless, rapidly expanding, rural population.

Nicaragua is a case in point. It supports more standing tropical rainforest on the Atlantic coast than exists in the other Central American countries combined. Although a 2.7-million-acre region known as Bosawas is nominally "protected," the area—which was devastated by Hurricane Juana in 1988—is today beset by lumberers, hunters, land speculators, ranchers, demobilized contras, and Sandinista agrarian reform beneficiaries whose farms were returned to pre-Sandinista owners. Each group is aggressively asserting its political claim by expanding its territorial control. The once seemingly vast rainforest is shrinking with astonishing rapidity.

Management of the inevitable political cross-currents is no easy task; there is no simple right answer. But grappling as best it can, Nicaragua is nevertheless in the process of creating public-sector institutions that can seriously try to address the challenges. There are four basic requirements: research and scientific information as a basis for policymaking; a central authority that can set and adhere to national priorities; financing to make programs work; and participatory mechanisms that can deal with the complexities of local situations.

Neighboring Costa Rica provides at least a partial guidepost. In their chapter on the Costa Rican experience, former Minister of Natural Resources Alvaro Umaña and Katrina Brandon, an expert on parks and development, describe a different, but relevant, set of initiatives to create an institutional basis for conservation. They include:

■ Establishing a high-level, public-sector authority that consolidates responsibility for natural resource management at the national level;

■ Creating decentralized regional authorities that links core protected areas with buffer zones and that institutes channels for local-state dialogue over the management of these zones;

■ Mobilizing public and private funding to support conservation activities and then sharing control over these funds with those at the regional level; and

■ Linking scientific research, especially in tropical forests, to the needs of local development and conservation planning.

Countries such as Costa Rica and Nicaragua are very different of course; and as Umaña and Brandon point out, Costa Rica too has a long way to go to reconcile fully the conflicts between conservation and development and to unite central government authority with grassroots decisionmaking. Yet the institutional experience is nonetheless instructive. It provides Latin America's most fully realized example of a country struggling to link its conservation policies with its development policies.

Rural Development Versus Export Agriculture

It has often been observed that the success of conservation has less to do with what happens inside protected areas and far more to do with the economic activities and agricultural practices of those who are immediately outside. Parks cannot flourish as islands in a sea of rural poverty. No conservation measure, including peace parks, is likely to succeed where development itself fails.

In Central America—with its unanchored modern poor population—the fate of conservation depends directly on the capacity of each country to restore economic vitality to the tattered agrarian social fabric. The rural poor of the 1990s cannot expect to rely solely on subsistence agriculture. The poor too—indeed, the poor *especially*—must make a transition to higher-output cash cropping.

In his chapter on the current orthodoxy of nontraditional agricultural export, Stuart Tucker explains that increased exports and rural development are not the same thing. The new nontraditional crops tend to reinforce rather than reverse the region's maldistribution of wealth. They are neither environmentally nor socially neutral.

Tucker maintains that the shift to these crops is not necessarily wrong. But to rectify unequal access to opportunity, four areas of pro-rich bias must be reversed: financial, infrastructural, institutional, and regulatory. In short, he says:

■ Timely access to reasonably priced credit is necessary before the poor can invest in nontraditional agriculture;

■ Transportation and electrical grids must be extended into hitherto isolated areas, so that the poor also may be assured of getting their produce to market;

■ Reform of ministries of agriculture is required (especially in Guatemala and Honduras) in order to decentralize and strengthen extension activities and improve the effectiveness of government credit to small and landless farmers;

■ Regulation of the competition of export intermediaries and of land acquisitions is necessary to ensure that nontraditional crops do not result in the re-concentration of economic power by the well-to-do.

Tucker argues for reform not only in Central America but in the United States and other developed countries as well. He argues that the United States should provide substantial external assistance for rural infrastructure and education in Central America, increase research on nontraditional production and integrated pest management on tropical soils, search for substitutes for banned pesticides, and end remaining restrictions on freer import to the U.S. market. The goal, he points out, is not just greater overseas sales of new agricultural products; it is an improved structure for agricultural opportunity.

Land and Taxation

Land-extensive, export-oriented farming by the rich coupled with subsistence farming on tiny plots by the poor can only drain the region's remaining physical resources. That may have been a possible "development strategy" in the 1960s and 1970s, when land was available for the taking, especially on the Pacific coast. But now, cheap frontier land is gone.

John Strasma and Rafael Celis argue that land inequity is at the heart of Central America's rural poverty and accelerating deforestation.

Although land reforms have been carried out or attempted in all the countries of the region, they were inevitably underfinanced, paternalistic, and did not reach the majority of the rural poor. Now, the authors say, "It is time for governments to treat the landless as potential small farmers in market economies, rather than as permanent political clients dependent on underfunded, paternalistic government agencies."

How can this be done? One answer is land taxation that is imposed, collected, and spent *locally*.

Strasma and Celis argue that overall tax burdens in Central America are currently relatively light, especially for the very rich. Higher tax burdens are justified. But whether justified or not, with the decline in external aid and with rising pressure to cut fiscal deficits, higher tax burdens are probably also inevitable.

The authors believe that *land* tax, which is generally in disuse, is particularly appropriate for several reasons. First, such taxes make underutilized tracts of land more expensive for rural landowners to hold and, simultaneously, cheaper for the relatively poor to buy or rent. So the taxes are highly redistributive. Second, *locally controlled* land taxes provide an ideal revenue source for rural roads, schools, and other services needed by otherwise impoverished municipalities. They do not directly balance public-sector budget deficits, but they do help finance rural development. And, finally, effective land taxes can be designed to provide incentives for protecting forests and disincentives for cutting them.

One important reason that land taxes are more feasible today than, say, in the 1960s, is because computer-assisted assessment techniques make cadastral surveys and titling less complex than they used to be. Satellite imagery can be used to produce accurate maps. Data from existing land registries can be added to these maps; and the product— Geographic Information Systems (GIS) and Land Registries—are manageable on desktop computers. These sophisticated data bases provide a basis for defining ownership and adjudicating claims. Moreover, open community meetings can and should be held to determine which categories of land are assessed at which rates. These rates are changeable because they require ongoing consensus among competing interest groups; yet they are enforceable and politically feasible for precisely the same reason.

CONCLUSION

Central America is emerging from what will be remembered as an exceptionally dark period. Peace is within reach. And a more prosperous future—at least for some—seems plausible.

Without doubt, continued peace will depend on the region's success in extending prosperity. To that end, increased manufacturing, tourism, diversified international trade, and increased employment in modern urban services are desirable and worth expanding through aggressive policy initiatives. But realistically, these small, poor countries are going to remain highly agrarian in the near future. In the short term, at least, their economic gearing and comparative advantage in the world economy will remain tied to agriculture and resource-based production. Prosperity will depend, in large measure, on how well the region is able to manage its diminishing endowment of natural resources given its high rural population growth.

Managing resources will require more than a commitment to conservation; the issue is not so simple as parks or environmental education. Rather, rural prosperity has to do with shifting away from a development model based on social exploitation, foreign aid, and environmental borrowing to one based on sustainable growth.

The authors of this book offer analyses and concrete proposals on how to move in the right direction. It is of course a truism that Central America presents politically treacherous terrain. Yet these suggestions are offered at a time when political realities everywhere, including those in Central America, are changing rapidly; and for this reason, we offer these ideas in an environment of hope.

Notes

[1] World Bank, *World Bank Debt Tables* (Washington, DC: 1990).

[2] See Appendix, Figure 1.

[3] Benjamin L. Crosby, "Central America," in *After the Wars: Reconstruction in Afghanistan, Indochina, Central America, Southern Africa, and the Horn of Africa*, Anthony Lake (ed.), U.S.-Third World Policy Perspectives, No. 16 (New Brunswick, NJ: Transaction Publishers in cooperation with the Overseas Development Council, 1990), p. 106.

[4] Stringent price stabilizations have now been in place in most of Central America for several years, and, compared to the early 1980s, inflation has significantly decreased. However, all Central American countries, especially Guatemala and Honduras, registered inflation rates in 1990 that were greater than those of 1989. In El Salvador and Costa Rica, inflation increased slightly. In Nicaragua, after a period of hyperinflation and the adoption of a severe adjustment program, inflation was significantly reduced in the later part of the year. See Inter-American Development Bank, *Annual Report 1990* (Washington, DC: 1991) pp. 3-4.

[5] For a discussion of some basic definitions of poverty and alternative indicators, see Appendix, Figure 10.

[6] Inter-American Development Bank, *Annual Report 1990*, op. cit., pp. 3-4.

[7] Inter-American Development Bank, *Economic and Social Progress in Latin America*, 1991 Report (Washington, DC: October 1991), pp. 92-97.

[8] These analyses were derived from a national household and income expenditure survey conducted during the 1979-1981 period and a national sociodemographic survey that was conducted during the 1986-87 period. They are reported in World Bank, *Guatemala: Country Economic Memorandum* (Washington, DC: 1991), Table 8.5; and CEPAL, *Magnitud de la Pobreza en América Latina en los Años Ochenta* (Santiago, Chile: May 1990), Table 12.

[9] Gary S. Fields, "Poverty and Inequality in Latin America: Some New Evidence," in *Urban Poverty in Latin America*, forthcoming, Wilson Center Press, 1992.

[10] Thanks for assistance to Laura Orlando of the ReSource Institute in Boston and Juigalpa, Nicaragua; Michael Stone, University of Texas; William Barbieri and Keith Oberg, Inter-American Foundation; Beatriz Bezmalinovic of DataPro in Guatemala; The Center for Information, Documentation, and Research Support (CIDAI) at the University of Central America (UCA) in San Salvador; and several other colleagues who helped to estimate and confirm the current market wage rate for rural labor. The following mid-1991 exchange rates were used: 4.9 Guatemalan *quetzales*, 5 Nicaraguan *cordobas de oro*, 121 Costa Rican *colones*, 2 Honduran *limpira*, 2 Belizean dollars, 8 Salvadoran *colones*, and 1 Panamanian *balboas* to the U.S. dollar.

[11] William Barbieri, Inter-American Foundation; Beatrice Bezmalinovic, DataPro, personal communication.

[12] Because of high inflation and differences of definition on what constitutes a "minimal food basket," it is difficult to translate precisely the cost of a basket versus daily wages in U.S. dollars. But the larger picture is certainly *no better* than what is reported here. For May 1991, The ReSource Institute reported teacher and nurse salaries at 300 *cordobas de oro* a month in Juigalpa (5 to 1 to the U.S. dollar at that time). A basic basket for a family of four of 32 items was calculated at 960 *cordobas*; for 23 items, 778 *cordobas*. In response to pressure from striking primary teachers, the National Commission on Living Standards tried to calculate the cost of a 53-item "basket" for a family of four. The National Workers' Front calculated $166 a month, the International Foundation for Global Economic Challenge calculated $152, the National Statistical Institute calculated $131, and the Central Bank of Nicaragua calculated $110 (based on USAID food donations). Under terms of the strike settlement, primary teachers' salaries were raised from $45 to $56 a month.

[13] Laura Orlando, ReSource Institute, personal communication.

[14] Price data are from two sources: Michael C. Stone, personal correspondence, 1991; and Belize Enterprise for Sustained Technology/European Economic Community, "Report on the Valley of Peace Socio-Economic Survey," unpublished report (Belmopan, Belize: 1990). The Belize report is a survey of 225 households from a United Nations High Commission for Refugees resettlement community. Most of those surveyed were Salvadoran refugees.

[15] Central American and Panamerican Institute for Nutrition (INCAP), *Análisis de la Situación Alimentaria Nutricional en Centroamérica y Panama* (Guatemala City: INCAP), June 1989, Table 3.

[16] See *Refugees*, No. 62, (March 1989), UN High Commissioner for Refugees, Geneva, which estimates there are about 146,000 "official" refugees, nearly 900,000 undocumented and/or externally displaced persons, about 61,000 returnees, and nearly 872,000 internally displaced persons in Central America (figures include southern Mexico but exclude Panama). The U.S. Committee for Refugees estimates 133,000 "official" refugees, 650,000 to 1.3 million "internally displaced persons," and 200,000 to 1.1 million people living undocumented in Central America under "refugee-like circumstances." For more data, see U.S. Committee for Refugees, *World Refugee Survey 1989* (Washington, DC: 1989). Overall, these estimates are conservative because they probably underestimate the number of persons displaced by endemic poverty and depletion of physical resources. The *World Refugee Survey* estimates as many as 3 million Central American refugees.

[17] *World Refugee Survey 1989*, op. cit.

[18] UNHCR and United Nations Development Programme, *Status Report on Implementation of the Concerted Plan of Action of the International Conference on Central American Refugees* (New York: CIREFCA, March 1991), p. 11.

[19] The 20,000 figure is frequently cited in press reports, e.g., "Battle Over Lands Add New Fuel to Crisis in Nicaragua," *Times of the Americas*, June 24, 1991. See also, U.S. Committee on Refugees, *World Refugee Survey 1991* (Washington, DC: 1991).

[20] *World Refugee Survey 1991*, op. cit., p. 87.

[21] Ibid., pp. 32-33, 88.

[22] Ana Isabel García and Enrique Gomáriz report conservative overall rates of 26.6 percent in El Salvador, 24.3 percent in Nicaragua, 20.4 percent in Honduras, 17.5 percent in Costa Rica, and 15 percent in Guatemala. *Mujeres Centroamericanas: Tomo I, Tendencias Estructurales*, Table 9 (San José, Costa Rica: FLACSO, CSUCA, Universidad de la Paz,

1989), p. 440. Urban rates of women-headed households are much higher, reflecting the fact that impoverished rural women typically migrate to cities to work as domestics. In some Latin American cities, the rate of female-headed households has risen to almost 38 percent; see *La Mujer en el Sector Urbano: America Latina y el Caribe* (Santiago, Chile: United Nations, 1985).

[23] See Mayra Buvinić, "The Vulnerability of Women-Headed Households: Policy Questions and Options for Latin America and the Caribbean," *Serie Mujer y Desarrollo*, No. 8; and Sally W. Yudelman and Michael Paolisso, *Women, Poverty and the Environment in Latin America* (Washington, DC: International Center for Research on Women, September 1991).

[24] The term "street children" encompasses both children "of" the street (no families or homes) and children "on" the street (working on the street but having some kind of family ties or base to which they can regularly return).

[25] G. Baker and F. Knaul, "Exploited Entrepreneurs: Street and Working Children in Developing Countries," Working Paper No. 1 (New York: CHILDHOPE-USA, Inc., 1991), p. 3; and CHILDHOPE-USA, "Guatemalan Street Children Face Death Squads," in *Esperanza*, Vol. 2, October 1990, p. 2.

[26] For a much more detailed discussion of the algorithms of campesino agriculture, see the discussion of "milpa logic" in Sheldon Annis, *God and Production in a Guatemalan Town* (Austin, TX: University of Texas Press, 1987), pp. 31-47; and Gene C. Wilken, *Good Farmers: Traditional Agricultural Resource Management in Mexico and Central America* (Berkeley, CA: University of California Press, 1987).

[27] Centro para Estudias Económicas y Sociales (CEES), *Análisis de la Situación demográfica en al Altiplano* (Guatemala: 1988), unpublished report, Table 12.

[28] This theme is elaborated in Sheldon Annis, "Debt and Wrong-Way Resource Flows in Costa Rica," *Ethics and International Affairs*, Vol. 4, 1990; and Annis, "Costa Rica's Dual Debt: A Story from 'A Little Country That Did Things Right' " (Washington, DC: World Resources Institute, 1987).

[29] For more discussion of the impact of the cattle expansion on Central America's physical environment, see Annis, "Debt and Wrong-Way Resource Flows in Costa Rica," op. cit.; H. Jeffrey Leonard, *Natural Resources and Economic Development in Central America* (International Institute for Environment and Development, 1987), Chapter 4, and Marc Edelman and Joanne Kenen (eds.), *Costa Rica Reader* (New York: Grove Weindenfeld, 1989), pp. 13-19.

[30] Central Bank of Costa Rica, "Crédito y cuentas monetarias 1950-1985" (San José, Costa Rica: 1987).

[31] Sheldon Annis, *(except Costa Rica): A Study in Poverty and National Resource Management*, book manuscript in progress, Chapter 5.

[32] Alonso Ramirez Solera and Tirso Maldonado Ulloa, eds., *Desarrollo Socioeconómico y el Ambiente Natural de Costa Rica: Situación Actual y Perspectivas*, Series Informes sobre el Estado del Ambiente No. 1 (San José, Costa Rica: Costa Rica Fundación Neotrópica, May 1988) p. 41 and 53; Gary Hartshorne, *Costa Rica: A Country Environmental Profile* (San José, Costa Rica: 1984), p. 28.

[33] Data from the Central Bank of Costa Rica, "Crédito y cuentas monetarias 1950-1985," op. cit; and Central Bank of Costa Rica, "Cifras de producción agropecuaria 1957-1984" (San José, Costa Rica: 1986). However, it should be noted that some credit for cattle was also sent to finance dairy production. Dairy revenues are not included in revenues reported for beef.

[34] By early 1987 almost two-thirds of the cattle portfolio was in arrears. It should be noted that to be "in arrears" does not necessarily mean that the borrowers will default. Also, because beef prices are cyclical, rates of default and the proportion of loans in arrears vary from year to year. Available data indicate that, in the early 1980s, cattle growers were poor though somewhat better off than were average borrowers. For example, while about 51 percent of all loans granted by the Banco Nacional in 1983 were nonperforming, about 37 percent of the cattle loans were in this category. See Thais Acosta Rosales, et. al., "Análisis de los factores determinantes de la morosidad de la cartera agropecuaria del Banco Nacional de Costa Rica," thesis prepared for Facultad de Ciencias Económicas (San José, Costa Rica: Universidad de Costa Rica, 1985), p. 30. With widespread default threatened, cattle growers were able to secure concessionary rescheduling from the government in 1985. Moreover, by

early 1987, the cattle growers had one of the *worst* payback rates in the loan portfolio. (Information on loan repayment rates prior to 1980 is not available.)

[35] Accurate data on loan default and arrearage are difficult to obtain, and repayment information is not normally broken down sociologically, i.e., by "large farmer" or "small farmer." However, personal interviews with several knowledgeable high-level Costa Rican banking officials (1987-88) strongly reinforced the conclusion that large farmers were far more problematic borrowers than were small farmers. Even the IMF was unsuccessful in stopping repeated moratoria against the collection of nonperforming loans by large cattle farmers and the extensions of new bridge loans.

[36] Annis, "Debt and Wrong-Way Resource Flows in Costa Rica," op. cit., provides further illustration of pervasive patterns of "wrong-way" resource flows.

[37] For most commodities, these declines are expected to continue. See International Monetary Fund, *World Economic Outlook* (Washington, DC: May 1991).

[38] Congressional Research Service, "Central America: Major Trends in U.S. Foreign Assistance, Fiscal 1978 to 1990," p. 64. The total includes all U.S. bilateral aid, i.e., disaster assistance, development assistance, Economic Support Funds, PL-480 Title I and II, Peace Corps, Inter-American Foundation, and military assistance programs. For regional aid levels, see Annex, Table 5.

[39] This theme is developed more fully in Sheldon Annis, "Latin Democracy: Giving Voice to the Poor," in *Foreign Policy*, Fall 1991; and "Evolving Connectedness of Grassroots Groups and Environmental Organizations in Protected Areas of Central America," *World Development* (Washington, DC: Pergamon Press, April 1992).

[40] For the first systematic attempt to "map" the global spread of computer networks, see John S. Quaterman, *The Matrix: Computer Networks and Conferencing Worldwide* (Bedford, MA: Digital Press, 1990).

[41] Example cited in Annis, "Latin Democracy: Giving Voice to the Poor," op. cit., pp. 97-98.

Summary of Chapter Recommendations

Summary of
Chapter Recommendations

1. A Call for Central American Peace Parks

Oscar Arias and James D. Nations

Far more than war and refugees spill across the borders of Central America's nations—so do poverty and environmental destruction. Not confined by national borders, these problems are shared with, or caused by, one's neighbors. Consequently, Central American leaders are beginning to focus on *regional* approaches to what are *regional*, not purely national, dilemmas.

One concept being implemented to deal with the interrelated problems of poverty and environmental depredation is peace parks. These are binational or multinational protected areas, such as national parks and biosphere reserves, that lie along international borders. Conservationists refer to these lands as peace parks because they promote peace between neighboring nations, ease environmental ills, and help protect biological diversity. First officially proposed in Central America in 1974, these cross-border parks have won major consideration by the region's political leaders during the past decade.

International peace parks already exist along the borders between Costa Rica and Panama, Panama and Colombia, Mexico and Guatemala, and in the trinational areas adjoining Guatemala, Honduras, and El Salvador. New peace parks have also been proposed.

In this chapter, Oscar Arias and James D. Nations discuss the potential political, biological, and economic benefits of Central America's peace parks. In the political arena, the potential for binational or multinational protected areas to neutralize a site of possible conflict has resulted in a proposal to establish parks in at least five zones of past or latent military conflict in Central America. Biological advantages include providing larger habitats for the region's rare and endangered plants and animals, more effectively preserving biological diversity. Coordinating wildlife and watershed protection across borders can save scarce resources for all countries involved and, thus, provides both biological and economic benefits.

Peace parks' design and management emphasize human communities. The people who inhabit the buffer zones of parks frequently depend on natural resources for their livelihood. As a result, improving the agricultural practices of these communities helps the people and should also curb such destructive activities as deforestation and poaching in the parks. Conservationists are increasingly attempting to balance the needs of the poor with the protection of the environment. They realize that the long-term preservation of a natural area depends less on what happens inside the park than outside it—in the lives of the people living nearby. Unless Central Americans protect the natural resources on which their economies are based, they have little hope for making social and political progress.

These internationally protected areas can open the door between nations for talks on issues more controversial than the environment. In doing so, they can provide a mechanism for international attacks on the basic social and environmental problems shared by all the region's countries. The authors suggest that the new Central American Commission on Development and the Environment (CCAD) is the most logical institution to advance such efforts. One of its goals is "to promote coordinated actions . . . for the optimum and wise utilization of the natural resources of the area, the control of pollution, and the establishment of ecological balance." What's more, the CCAD is the obvious vehicle for monitoring the region's efforts in the peace park process. Industrialized nations, as well as multilateral institutions, should support this initiative.

A system of international peace parks in Central America offers great hope for the future of the region and other people of the Western Hemisphere. Peace parks can play a crucial role in reducing conflicts in the region, achieving environmental protection, promoting sustainable development, and alleviating poverty.

2. Citizen Participation and the Reform of Development Assistance in Central America

Stephen B. Cox

Central America has received more than $10 billion in economic aid since 1979 from the United States alone but remains poorer than it was at the beginning of this period. Some 35 percent of the population lives in conditions of extreme poverty, and the region's natural resource base is seriously jeopardized by rapid environmental degradation. The persistence of these problems is due, to a significant degree, to ineffective international development assistance. If Central America is to have a reasonable chance to reduce its endemic poverty and protect its resource base, it must try new modes of channeling development assistance that allow for much broader social participation and that demand more accountable public institutions. Stephen B. Cox proposes practical measures for orchestrating greater public participation and suggests institutional reforms for the more effective delivery of development assistance.

The model of development assistance conventionally employed by national and international agencies and institutions suffers from three basic weaknesses: 1) it characteristically fails to incorporate the social, political, and institutional factors that determine a development project's effective and sustainable outcome; 2) it is premised on mistaken confidence in the capacity of large institutions to predict and control what will happen in complex development programs; and 3) it is distorted by national and international political objectives that may be antithetical to the interests of the poor.

The consequences of the model's weaknesses are the following: 1) large, unwieldy megaprojects that cannot be properly guided once they are launched; 2) inadequate commitment from beneficiaries, bureaucrats, and other key participants who have limited incentive to take the programs seriously; and 3) the reinforcement of undemocratic habits of social and political behavior that are inimical to the evolution of healthy patterns of democratic governance in the region. The antidotes to these ills include paying greater attention to the processes of democratic decisionmaking and problem solving and fundamentally reforming institutions or creating new organizations better suited to address the demanding challenges of sustainable development.

Cox recommends an alternative model to conventional development assistance—one that rigorously assesses the quality of the processes by which program decisions are made and the ways in which projects are chosen, designed, implemented, monitored, and evaluated. He also suggests a number of concrete measures that may be used to manage more broadly participatory and effective development programs.

Novel field research techniques, such as rapid rural appraisal, offer promising new ways for securing concrete and relatively reliable information quickly and regularly, for ensuring that initial program hypotheses ring true, and for helping to keep development programs on target. Multiparty policy dialogues and interagency working groups are consultation mechanisms that can ensure that all relevant decisionmakers and participants are adequately involved before projects are launched. These measures also serve to bring together key players on a regular basis to discuss and solve problems that arise during the course of a complex initiative. Horizontal linkages among nongovernmental organizations (NGOs) and grassroots organizations are promising means for rapidly and effectively disseminating new programs and technological innovations. They also facilitate partnerships involving the NGOs and grassroots groups and development bureaucracies. Last, training in analytical and managerial skills is required to ensure that programs can be sustained after international technical assistance ends.

Cox suggests that the responsibility for promoting more rigorous attention to process in designing and implementing assistance programs must be shared by all. Multilateral and bilateral agencies managing flows of official development aid should encourage broader public participation in setting development agendas. They also should plan for more useful and regular feedback on whether they are accomplishing worthwhile objectives. Nongovernmental organizations and popular groups should become more actively involved in discussions of official development programs and they should undertake aggressive advocacy efforts to demand greater accountability. International private voluntary organizations can play important roles as liaisons in supporting the more direct interaction of indigenous NGOs and grassroots organizations in public policy debates.

Finally, institutional reforms are required to create a more receptive environment for greater attention to process. The U.S. Agency for International Development (USAID)—compromised by political objectives and lacking a clear vision of development—is ill-suited to meet the challenge. U.S. bilateral assistance to Central America should be channeled through alternative mechanisms. The Overseas Development Council's proposal for a new U.S. Sustainable Development Fund (SDF)—as well as an older experiment in development aid, the Inter-American Foundation—merit strong support.

Nevertheless, the complexity of the United States' role in Central America and the demands for efficacy call for serious attention to the search for vastly improved multilateral mechanisms through which an increasing proportion of development assistance can be channeled. Such mechanisms would serve as an alternative to bilateral programs. The author proposes the creation of a multilateral Central American Fund (CAF) as an institutional alternative that could pay greater attention to issues of process. Supported by a number of countries, overseen by a socially diverse and representative board, and staffed by seasoned professionals from a number of countries and disciplines, the fund would make it possible to deliver development assistance in ways that would be more conducive to sound, flexible, and democratically managed development aid.

3. Inventing Institutions for Conservation: Lessons from Costa Rica
Alvaro Umaña and Katrina Brandon

Tremendous worldwide attention has been focused on saving the world's biologically significant ecosystems and on maintaining biological diversity. Toward this end, most countries have established systems of national parks and reserves. Particularly in developing nations, protecting such areas is often impossible—parks and reserves must be integrated into a broader process of sustainable development that links conservation and development. For this connection to occur, it is essential that governments integrate natural resource management and conservation objectives into their economic decisionmaking process. Yet in most Central American countries, agencies responsible for conservation and natural resource management typically are politically weak and have little power to promote reforms that can bring about substantial changes.

Successful management of important conservation lands—subject to increasing development pressure from surrounding communities—will also ultimately depend on the cooperation and support of local populations. People living on the lands that buffer parks and reserves must perceive that the protected areas can contribute to overall economic development. Thus, conservation must be connected to development at the local, as well as the national level.

Alvaro Umaña and Katrina Brandon explain how Costa Rica has attempted to create such linkages. Specifically, the government:

1) Created a new ministry that consolidated disparate environmental agencies and gave greater power and legitimacy to natural resource management. Beyond improving coordination and clarifying jurisdictional boundaries between agencies, the new ministry demonstrated the government's commitment to the environment.

2) Decentralized the management of parks and reserves, and implemented regional conservation units (URCs) that linked "core" protected areas with surrounding buffer lands. These URCs coordinate government agency plans, link public- and private-sector initiatives, and encourage local participation in decisionmaking concerning protected areas.

3) Developed a series of creative financing arrangements and aggressively sought funding for conservation. Costa Rica used debt-for-nature swaps and privatized financing for conservation by turning the control of funding over to the National Parks Foundation.

4) Created the National Biodiversity Institute (INBIO), which catalogues Costa Rica's biological diversity and identifies ways that this natural wealth can be used to generate socio-economic development.

Enormous changes will still have to take place before sustainable development is truly achieved in Costa Rica. Nevertheless, the actions already taken offer substantial insights into how conservation can be furthered elsewhere in Central America. According to the authors, these actions form the social and administrative infrastructure needed to promote change. The authors recommend the following steps to create such an infrastructure in other countries:

1) Increase the legitimacy and power for natural resource management and conservation at the national level by consolidating existing agencies and improving coordination between them.

2) Link protected areas to the lands that surround them by decentralizing decisionmaking authority to the regional levels and increasing local participation in resource planning and use.

3) Use creative mechanisms to finance conservation, such as debt-for-nature swaps, trust funds, endowments, and public- and private-sector ventures. Decentralize control over funding to the regional levels, to better link conservation and development priorities.

4) Understand what biological elements are being protected and how to manage them. Consolidate in-country technical expertise in tropical science, and link the nation's scientific research capacity not only to the management of protected areas and to national development efforts, but to the international scientific community as well.

Other countries stand to learn a great deal from Costa Rica's experience as the country has established a basic structure that reflects the enhanced role of conservation as a necessary component of development.

4. Equity and the Environment in the Promotion of Nontraditional Agricultural Exports

Stuart K. Tucker

Central America is finally pursuing an export-led development strategy. For these largely agrarian societies, new, nontraditional agricultural crops—such as winter fruits and vegetables—must play a key role. The region's five major traditional export crops—coffee, cotton, beef, bananas, and sugar—now face volatile prices, stagnant or declining demand, and a host of competing suppliers. None of these conditions favor continued income growth. Producing corn and beans for domestic consumption offers little hope in alleviating poverty, as the population is growing far faster than is productivity of these crops. In contrast, nontraditional agricultural crops provide large returns on investment and can yield substantial export earnings.

Furthermore, if Central America's rural poor are to play a positive role in sustaining the environment while simultaneously pursuing ways to escape their poverty, they will need alternative sources of income derived from existing agricultural lands. Limited production choices lead the poor to destroy and pollute their surroundings. At the same time, environmental degradation undermines the ability of impoverished people to support themselves. A properly designed nontraditional export strategy offers hope that this vicious cycle can be broken.

Such a strategy requires great changes in current Central American and international public polices. These changes may be expensive, long-term, or even politically difficult, but without them, increasing nontraditional agricultural export production will exacerbate rather than alleviate rural poverty, and thereby indirectly contribute to environmental damage.

In this chapter, the author analyzes existing policies and recommends new ones that are needed to implement a more equitable agricultural development strategy—one that lessens poverty without destroying the environment as much as current production does.

The key policy changes the author suggests for Central American nations are: credit reform; improved agricultural extension; improved rural infrastructure; reformed agricultural ministries; regulated land tenure; and improved access for the poor to education and family planning services.

Major policy reform in Central American countries is fundamental, but the United States and other industrial countries must improve their own policies to support a nontraditional agricultural export strategy that is pro-poor and pro-environment. Some of the major policy changes suggested for industrialized nations are:

- Support credit and public administration reform, the strengthening of agricultural extension, and the improvement of rural infrastructure in Central America;
- Cease U.S. marketing orders and the ban on aid to citrus growers;
- Improve information flow on U.S. pesticide regulations and on integrated pest-management techniques;
- Reduce subsidies to domestic farmers that distort world markets; and
- Support education and family planning in Central America.

Agricultural production in Central America is destroying the very environment on which it depends. Environmentalists and development experts in the region share the task of finding a path to sustainable development, with assistance from external actors. Any policies intended to foster sustainability must be evaluated according to their effects on efficiency, equity, and environmental conservation in the region. To pursue any one of these three objectives and neglect the others will prove destructive to the people and the environment.

The challenge then is to alter public and private practices to overcome the obstacles that presently prevent nontraditional agriculture from being equitable and environmentally sound. Ultimately, success in environmental terms will be achieved when nontraditional agricultural production and exports truly help alleviate poverty.

5. Land Taxation, The Poor, and Sustainable Development
John D. Strasma and Rafael Celis

Land taxes are one of the most effective potential policy measures now available in Central America to reduce poverty and curb the destruction of natural resources in a manner compatible with sustainable development. Land-tax reform, already under way in Costa Rica, is a feasible solution elsewhere. If land values are established with community involvement, and if revenues are earmarked to local governments, infrastructures, and schools, a land tax could promote decentralization and participatory democracy, while increasing production and reducing poverty.

In this chapter, John Strasma and Rafael Celis analyze the present taxation of agricultural lands in Central America, finding it both inadequate and counterproductive. A land tax could encourage landlords to sell some parcels outright, on credit, to their present tenants. The buyers would then pay taxes, but as owners they also would have reason to conserve soil, plant trees, and care about the land they would leave their children.

The authors also examine the potential relationship between agrarian reforms and pressure on fragile land. Existing laws, regulations, and policies largely encourage abuse of the land—not only by squatters but also by those with power (the land owners) who have only short-term profits in mind. For example, forest lands are often regarded as unimproved and underutilized. Agrarian law defines the clearing of forests as an improvement, because it prepares the land for "productive" pursuits, such as raising crops or grazing cattle. Laws that do take a long-term view are seldom implemented.

A new strategy that favors both the poor and natural resources would have a modern land survey and tax as key components. As a first major step, a cadastral survey or inventory of land would more clearly define the rights to land and would demarcate holdings (e.g., state lands, protected and not, and private holdings of all sizes, cooperatively or individually held). Next, the participants in state land programs should have clearly defined terms on which they could buy full, negotiable, legal rights to the land they till. The next step is to determine unit values of land, preferably with broad citizen participation, and then to merge the cadastral survey with the tables of unit values to create a tax roll.

For the authors' strategy to protect tropical forests and also be pro-poor, it must enable unemployed, landless laborers to see a future for themselves in saving, rather than destroying, the forests. Therefore, for instance, part of the revenues from an effective land tax could be used to hire the poor as forest guards. In short, policies need to make protecting trees more attractive than stealing them.

Among the numerous other benefits of a modern land tax and its revenues are:

■ A modern land tax would define rights more clearly and could easily support a system under which the tax rate is lower when the forest is managed in a sustainable way, and much higher when it is pillaged.

■ A land tax can provide powerful incentives for better land management and accurate information about land rights.

■ Land-tax revenues could help finance community infrastructure or support a land bank to provide the landless and small farmers with mortgage loans to purchase land.

■ Land-tax proceeds could leverage significant external resources to finance conservation plans for environmentally threatened lands.

Land taxation can contribute greatly to protecting the environment by requiring an inventory of natural resources, defining rights, and identifying occupants and owners. And when the tax is high enough to be noticeable to owners, exemptions from it for environmentally sound practices will become valuable incentives.

Land taxes are no panacea; more direct land distribution programs are also needed. But taxation is a significant policy tool to help solve the problems of poverty, underdevelopment, and environmental destruction.

Part III
Poverty,
Natural Resources,
and Public Policy
in Central America

Chapter One

A Call for
Central American Peace Parks

Oscar Arias and James D. Nations

INTRODUCTION

During the past five years, the Central American republics have successfully ended most of the civil wars that have marred the region for so many decades. As these conflicts subside, Central Americans are turning their attention toward the equally serious issues of poverty and environmental degradation, which are now widely recognized throughout the region as interrelated problems. How to resolve them, however, remains a matter of ongoing investigation and activity.

Central American leaders have also begun to realize that all of these ills—warfare, poverty, and environmental decay—bleed across national borders into the lives and territories of their neighbors. Thus, these leaders are beginning to focus on *regional* approaches for *regional* problems.

One concept being increasingly implemented is peace parks—binational or multinational protected areas, such as national parks, wildlife reserves, and other conservation areas that lie along international borders and create tracts of forested wilderness in zones of political or environmental conflict. Conservationists refer to these lands as peace parks because they promote peace between neighboring countries, ease environmental problems, and help protect biological diversity. First officially proposed in Central America in 1974, cross-border parks have gained major consideration by political leaders in the region during the past decade.

Today, Central American conservation workers, frequently assisted by international colleagues, are struggling to keep these few existing peace parks alive and to create new ones throughout the region. International peace parks already exist along the borders between Costa Rica and Panama, Panama and Colombia, Mexico and Guatemala, and in the trinational area that joins Guatemala, Honduras, and El Salvador (Map 1). New peace parks are proposed for establishment between Guatemala and Belize, Honduras and Nicaragua, and Nicaragua and Costa Rica.

The potential benefits of Central America's peace parks go far beyond the biological advantages of having larger territories for the endangered animals and plants that inhabit these areas. Peace parks also bring economic and political benefits. Coordinating wildlife and watershed protection across borders can save scarce resources for all countries involved. Peace parks also reduce stress along historically tense borders by providing governments with an agenda for mutual action on issues of common concern. Moreover, the most promising aspects of establishing these peace parks in Central America is the movement to include rural families in the planning and development of the parks and the buffer zones that surround them.

A REGIONAL APPROACH

Central America was the focus of intense geopolitical conflicts in the 1980s, sparked by the aftermath of the Sandinista revolution in Nicaragua, the persistent armed struggle in El Salvador, and considerable tensions between several countries in the isthmus. These disputes were leaning dangerously toward military actions—influenced by external forces in both Nicaragua and El Salvador—when Costa Rica submitted its Central American peace plan in early 1987.

More than 200,000 displaced Central Americans had fled to Costa Rica across the Nicaraguan-Costa Rican border to escape civil wars in Nicaragua and El Salvador. Armed conflicts not only threatened peace and security in the region, but also were ecologically devastating to many Central American nations. The peace process aimed to end the war as well as its negative human and environmental impacts. The five Central American presidents realized that if the massive migration of Central Americans from one country to another persisted, the regional crisis could not be fully settled.

The problems of Central America extended beyond national borders and, therefore, could be resolved only with the cooperation of all parties concerned. Thus, the five Central American presidents had to make their new regional approach prevail over ingrained and pervasive nationalistic sentiments. The countries of the isthmus had to exclude the use of force as a means of persuading others to follow a particular course of action. They had to respect their neighbors' territorial integrity and political independence and enhance peaceful dialogue and negotiation.

LEARNING FROM THE PEACE PROCESS

The peace process—also known as Esquipulas II—assumed that when legal standards of conduct, negotiation, and implementation procedures are clear and straightforward, mutual confidence among participants may grow to exclude nationalistic attitudes. When problems are international and mutual confidence prevails over nationalistic behavior, governments willingly cooperate because they perceive no threat to their sovereignty or political independence. To build confidence among the five presidents, negotiations had to incorporate clear and determinate principles, rules, and procedures that most participants shared and accepted as valid.

Esquipulas II set the stage for further cooperation among the Central American countries by diminishing nationalistic policies and border tensions and by paving the way for significant increases of mutual confidence. It is now possible to extend the spirit of the peace process to confront the most urgent challenges in the region: increasing economic development and arresting environmental destruction.

In response to this need for sustainable development, the Central American presidents created a regional commission on the environment and development at the summit in Costa del Sol, El Salvador, in February 1989. Later that year in Costa Rica, the presidents signed the Comisión Centroamericana de Ambiente y Desarrollo (CCAD), thus formalizing a new institution. The first regional effort of its kind in the world, the CCAD illustrates how the peace process led directly to a higher priority on environmental issues.

Central America's economic, social, and political progress depends on the sustainable use of natural resources. Moreover, environmental degradation can provoke civil strife. Growing unemployment, large-scale emigration, economic stagnation, and the inability to feed expanding populations often lead to revolutions. Just as the Central American national economies are tied to the global economy, their individual ecological systems are inextricably linked to one another.

Events in other parts of the world have underscored these environmental interdependencies. For example, the accident at the Soviet Union's Chernobyl nuclear power plant destroyed agricultural crops and

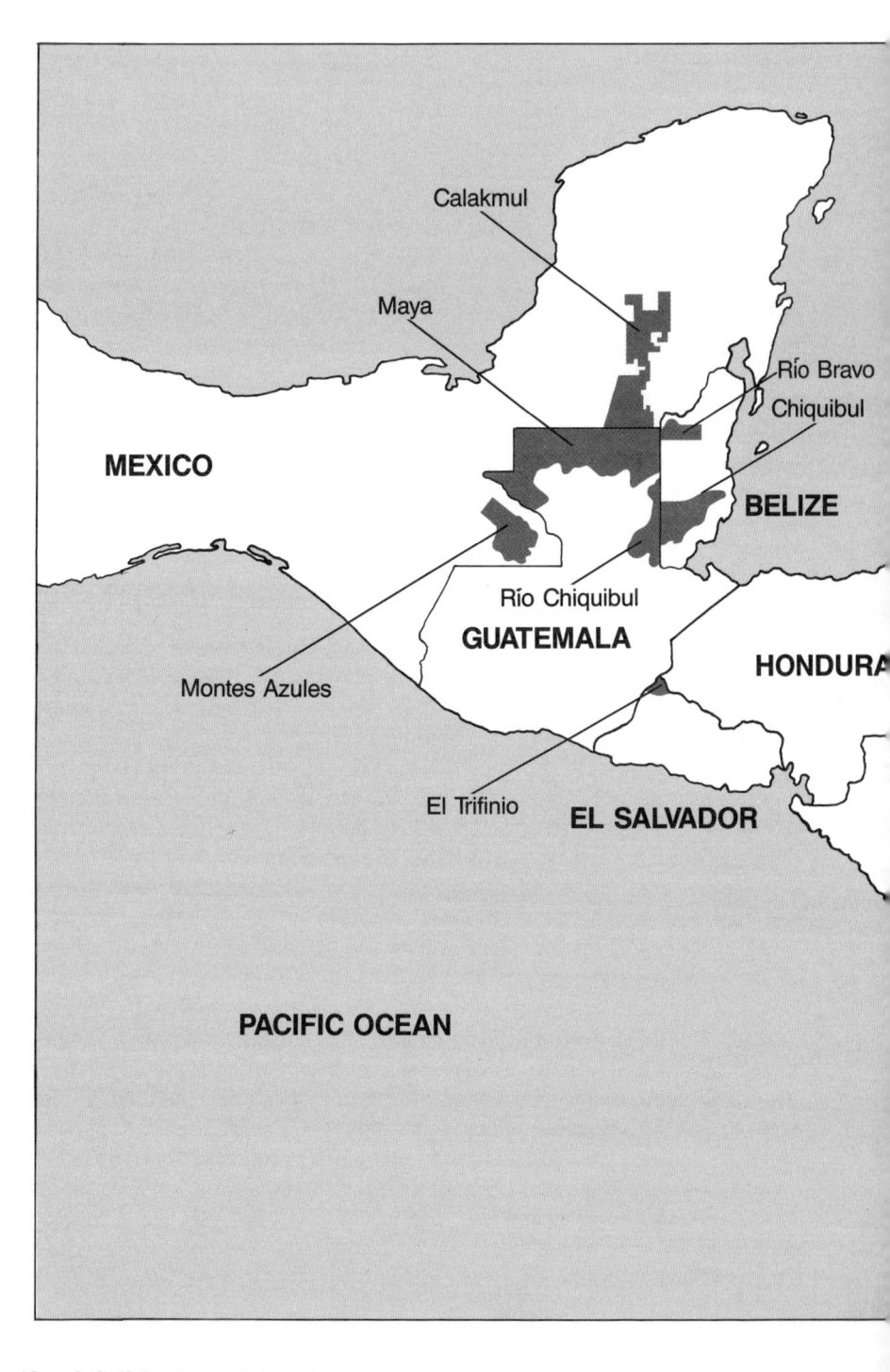

Calakmul

Maya

Río Bravo

Chiquibul

MEXICO

BELIZE

Río Chiquibul

GUATEMALA

HONDURA

Montes Azules

El Trifinio   **EL SALVADOR**

PACIFIC OCEAN

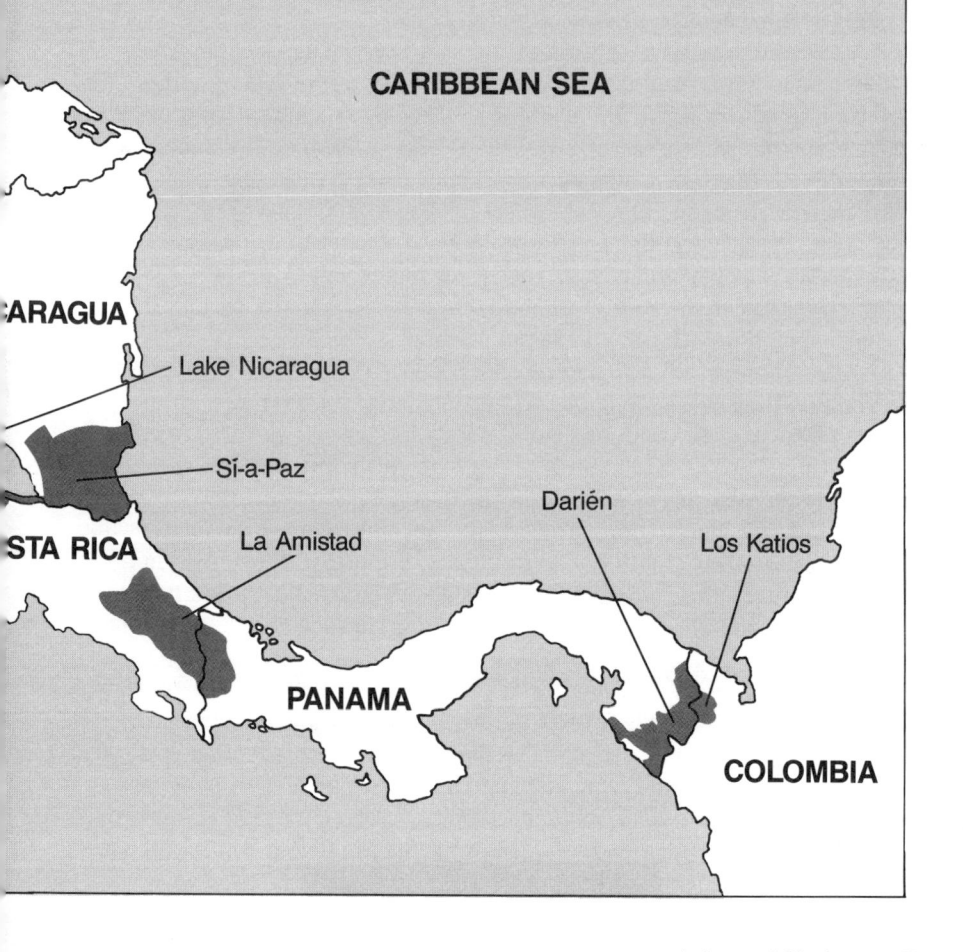

MAP 1. INTERNATIONAL PEACE PARKS IN CENTRAL AMERICA

CARIBBEAN SEA

ARAGUA

Lake Nicaragua

Sí-a-Paz

Darién

Los Katios

STA RICA

La Amistad

PANAMA

COLOMBIA

threatened water supplies in several European nations. U.S.-Canadian relations have been strained by acid rain produced by U.S. industry that is contaminating parts of Canada. New copper smelters in northern Mexico are jeopardizing clean-air standards in neighboring Arizona. And U.S. agriculture along the Río Grande may be adversely affecting water supplies in northern Mexico.

SEEKING SOLUTIONS TO REGIONAL ENVIRONMENTAL PROBLEMS

The Central American political agenda is increasingly confronting environmental threats in the region that could be ameliorated through the negotiating approach of Esquipulas II. All too frequently, environmental problems are not confined by national borders; they are either shared with, or caused by, one's neighbors.

Let us mention some examples:

■ Environmental refugees are flowing across Central America's borders on a dozen fronts: Guatemalan and Salvadoran farm families fleeing lands made infertile by overuse in their own countries are clearing tropical forests in neighboring Belize. Mexicans from deforested areas in the states of Tabasco, Chiapas, and Campeche are poaching wildlife and mahogany trees in the tropical forests of Guatemala.

■ Pesticide pollution in one Central American country contaminates water supplies and coastal resources in another.

■ Erosion caused by Guatemalan hillside farmers results in sedimentation on downstream Honduran farms.

■ Deforested slopes in southern Belize create flash floods in Kekchi Indian villages in Guatemala's Department of the Petén.

■ Acid rain produced by Mexico's Coatzacoalcos oil refineries is threatening tropical forests and ancient Mayan ruins in the Guatemalan Petén and on Mexico's own Yucatan Peninsula.[1]

At the same time, protecting the environment is inextricably linked to improving the living conditions of the poor. Many rural families trying to provide for their basic needs are driven to destroy gradually the very natural resources their lives depend on because they lack economic alternatives.

As a result, managers of protected lands are increasingly attempting to balance the needs of the poor with the conservation of the environment. They understand that the long-term preservation of a natural area depends less on what happens inside the area than on what happens outside—in the lives and communities of people living on the lands that border parks and reserves. These people are either important allies or enemies of protected areas.

The "parks and people" movement in conservation is a new focus on the link between wilderness lands and human needs that attempts to ease poverty by helping rural families to exist in economic and ecological balance with their natural environments. Thus, international conservation increasingly promotes agroforestry and reforestation efforts. Higher crop yields and more equitable distribution of land that is already developed reduce rural families' need to clear additional forests.

The most farsighted expression of the parks and people movement is the biosphere reserve concept first promoted by the United Nations Educational, Scientific, and Cultural Organization (UNESCO). Biosphere reserves combine wildlands conservation with the needs of nearby human communities by merging economic development and biological preservation.

As the latest expression of the parks and people movement, the proposed and existing binational peace parks (many of which are biosphere reserves) concentrate as much on the buffer zones that fringe protected areas as they do on the inner core areas that safeguard a park's biological diversity. Map 2 shows the Sí-a-Paz peace park and its buffer zones.

BENEFITS OF PARKS FOR PEACE

In the early 1980s, Mexico and France proposed the creation of a demilitarized zone on the Nicaraguan-Costa Rican border. Costa Rica rejected the plan because it might have given unlimited authority to the Sandinista army to operate in Costa Rican territory and possibly endangered the safety and lives of Costa Ricans living on the Nicaraguan border. The tension surrounding this proposal did not permit serious consideration for either a demilitarized zone or a peace park.

Since the Esquipulas II accords were signed, however, peace and democracy have been restored in Nicaragua and border tensions diminished in number and intensity. Peace parks in Central America now seem possible. Binational protected areas are emerging as part of a broader change in Central American relations, a change that could be called a "Central American Peace Park Process."

A peace park process can only flourish under what former Swedish Prime Minister Olof Palme called "common security"—that is, one nation seeking security not against its neighbors, but *with* them. Recent, major democratic accomplishments in Central America constitute a significant leap forward toward peace and common security in the region, thereby increasing the feasibility of creating peace parks. The benefits of such an international process can be divided into three categories: political, economic, and biological.

NICARAGUA

MAP 2:
SI-A-PAZ:
PROPOSED
SYSTEM OF
PROTECTED
AREAS FOR
PEACE

Lake Nicaragua

Agricultural Buffer Zone

Forestry Buffer Zone

Proposed
Wildlife Refuge
Indio-Maiz

Barro de Colorado Wildlife Refuge

Proposal Corridor

Tortuguero National Park

SAN JUAN RIVER

Proposed
Los Guatusos
Wildlife Refuge

Proposed Extension of Canos Negros

Canos Negros Wildlife Refuge

COSTA RICA

Source: Environmental Project on Central America (EPOCA), Costa Rica, 1989.

Political Benefits

Peace parks require and promote peace, as the term implies. With this in mind, the United States and the Soviet Union proposed the creation of an international peace park along the Bering Strait, a sensitive border area. Covering millions of hectares, the Beringian Heritage International Peace Park would ease barriers to transportation and communications between these countries.

The potential for binational or multinational protected areas to neutralize an area of possible conflict has resulted in a proposal to create parks in at least five zones of past or latent military conflict in Central America: along the Belize-Guatemalan border; in the mountainous area where El Salvador, Guatemala, and Honduras meet; on the border between Nicaragua and Honduras; on the Nicaragua-Costa Rica boundary; and in the Gulf of Fonseca, where El Salvador, Honduras, and Nicaragua squeeze together on their Pacific coasts. The Nicaraguan initiative— along the southern San Juan River—would be called "Sí-a-Paz," International System of Protected Areas for Peace. Thus, the concept of international peace parks creates a link between environmental protection, international cooperation, and the struggle against poverty in developing countries.

A BELIZE-GUATEMALA PEACE PARK. Peace parks provide governments with cooperative areas of agreement that can lead to discussions of points of political conflict. For instance, Belize and Guatemala have long been at odds over a decades' old claim by Guatemala on its neighbor's territory. Guatemala's former military governments often proclaimed publicly that all or part of Belize belonged to Guatemala. Claims on Belizean lands have not been pressed since a democratically elected president took power in Guatemala in 1986, and President Jorge Serrano Elías recently recognized Belize's sovereignty and independence. Tensions still exist, however.

The possibility of armed struggle is made less likely because Belizean and Guatemalan conservationists are now planning a binational peace park along their common border. In 1988, the Guatemalan Congress declared 44 new conservation areas. Three of these lie on Guatemala's boundary with Belize. One of the three, Guatemala's Maya Biosphere Reserve, shares 60 kilometers of frontier with northern Belize, where conservationists have created a second site—the Río Bravo conservation area. To the south is the third expanse, Guatemala's Río Chiquibul conservation area, which runs for 50 kilometers along Belize's Chiquibul National Park. It, too, is being proposed as a biosphere reserve.

The Río Chiquibul region seems an especially appropriate place to tie together these two Central American nations. The Chiquibul River runs through Guatemala for almost half of its total length. Yet, it is also the principal water supply for Belize's San Ignacio Valley—the country's breadbasket, additionally serving both the country's capital and its largest city. Thus, protection of the Río Chiquibul on both sides of the international border emerges as a major point for discussion between these two countries. Politicians in both Belize and Guatemala have indicated that cooperating on seemingly neutral subjects such as binatioñal parks opens a dialogue for other more sensitive territorial issues. What's more, the two nations consider the topic of peace parks significant enough to have initiated discussions of it at ministry and vice-presidential levels.

SI-A-PAZ: THE NICARAGUA-COSTA RICA BORDER. Similar benefits may come from a proposed binational park lying between Nicaragua and Costa Rica. The Río San Juan defines Nicaragua's border to the south and Costa Rica's to the north. Former Nicaraguan President Daniel Ortega established the 2,900-square-kilometer Sí-a-Paz Biological Reserve in early 1990. On Costa Rica's side, Sí-a-Paz would complement the existing Barra del Colorado Wildlife Refuge and the Tortuguero National Park—a 190-square-kilometer area that protects endangered sea turtles, mangrove forest, and lowland moist tropical forest.

This rainforest was the scene of serious border tensions during the Sandinista-Contra war, but its transformation into a peace park—Sí-a-Paz—is currently being proposed by Nicaraguan and Costa Rican conservationists. To underscore the area's importance in dampening military conflict, the Nicaraguan government has agreed to settle returning ex-contra fighters in communities outside the park and away from the border.

EL TRIFINIO: EL SALVADOR, GUATEMALA, AND HONDURAS. In another site of past conflict in Central America, the Organization of American States and the governments of El Salvador, Guatemala, and Honduras have joined forces to create the international conservation and development area, El Trifínio, or La Fraternidad. At the junction of these three republics, a 7,584-square-kilometer expanse is being transformed through a trinational development plan that includes the protection of a core forest area and the restoration of surrounding ecosystems. The restored land will, in turn, be encircled by a large multiple-use zone aimed at improving the region's economic and social conditions. This multiple-use zone will incorporate such infrastructure projects as roads, health and education programs, and improved electric service.

The El Trifínio development project encompasses territory in all three nations: 45 percent in Guatemala, 40 percent in Honduras, and 15 percent in El Salvador.[2] Today, forests cover only 20 percent of the region, although reforestation and ecosystem recovery are planned where appropriate. Three areas will be developed for tourism: the spectacular Mayan ruins at Copán in Honduras; Esquipulas, Guatemala, where the peace plan was signed; and the mountain peak of Montecristo—El Salvador's last forestland.

Biological Benefits

When conservationists discuss international protected areas with politicians, they are likely to focus on the benefits of diminishing military threats in areas of potential conflict. Nevertheless, their primary goal is the protection of biological diversity—that is, the planet's immense variety of irreplaceable living organisms. Here, the benefits of international peace parks are many: they improve the survival rates of plant and animal populations, prevent the spread of animal diseases, and allow genetic material of plants and wildlife to pass between protected populations.

Joining protected areas across borders expands the size of the preserved habitat. A single, large secure area in the same biological region is more effective in preserving biological diversity than are several unconnected, small sites. The reason for this is simple: other factors being equal, the larger the habitat, the larger the population of wild animals. And large populations, in general, are less likely to become extinct than are small ones.

A binational peace park that straddles almost the entire frontier between eastern Panama and the South American country of Colombia, the Darién-Los Katios, points to yet another biological benefit of transborder park complexes. Since 1960, the Panamanian government has been actively attempting to prevent the spread of aftosa (commonly called hoof-and-mouth disease) into Central America, where beef exports to the United States earn millions of dollars each year. U.S. law prohibits beef imports from countries infected with hoof-and-mouth disease.

Chiefly in response to this economic threat, Panama established the Darién National Park in 1980. Covering 5,790 square kilometers, it contains different zones intended for a variety of uses. For eight kilometers edging the border, and eight kilometers along the path of the Pan-American Highway, a zone of absolute conservation protects rainforest resources from any form of exploitation. Sections of land along the park's rivers and major tributaries are designated "cultural conservation zones," where indigenous families are allowed to fish, farm, and build settlements. On the Colombian side lies the other half of the peace park—Los Katios National Park, created in 1973. It encompasses the area between the Panamanian border near the headwaters of the Río Paya in Panama and the left bank of the Río Atrato, which runs through northwestern Colombia on its way to the Golfo de Uraba. Accordingly, Los Katios fronts on some 30 kilometers of the Panamanian frontier.

The Darién National Park serves four purposes: ecosystem conservation, watershed protection, preservation of indigenous lifestyles and archaeological sites, and prevention of the spread of aftosa from South America into Central and North America.[3] In 1983, the Darién was accepted as an internationally recognized biosphere reserve, under the aegis of the United Nations Man and the Biosphere Programme.

Economic Benefits

Peace parks also provide important economic benefits to neighboring nations. For instance, internationally protected areas frequently conserve crucial watersheds. The Río San Juan, which forms the border between Nicaragua and Costa Rica, drains a watershed that reaches north into Nicaragua and south into Costa Rica. Since 1879, the river has been considered a potential site for a lock canal connecting the Atlantic and Pacific Oceans. At the very least, the San Juan seems a likely candidate for generating hydroelectric power.

A similar justification for an international park—protecting the watershed to produce electricity—exists at La Amistad National Park, on the Costa Rica-Panama frontier. Costa Rica's Institute of Electricity has proposed hydroelectric dams on at least one major river flowing through this park—the Sixaola, which serves as the border between the two countries. It is possible to develop no fewer than 10 hydroelectric projects in the Río Sixaola watershed. Although several sites have been identified for similar potential projects on the Costa Rican side of La Amistad alone, most will not be seriously considered until at least the year 2050.

However, such projects in protected forest areas can have negative, as well as positive, consequences. Reservoirs can inundate vast expanses of land, wiping out human communities, wildlife habitat, and—in some regions—archaeological remains. Large construction projects also bring roads, which can open primary forest to colonization and destruction.

And yet, the need for hydroelectric power can also be a primary justification for conserving forests. Because large protected areas in Central America—especially multinational parks—usually embrace immense forestlands, they sustain the watersheds that supply water to reservoirs.

Finally, there is a further, more immediate economic advantage to binational parks: The involvement of two or more nations increases the financial resources available for creating and protecting the parks.

PEACE PARKS AND PEOPLE

Faced with growing populations and increasing poverty in Central America, conservationists realize that the most effective way to safeguard natural resources is to use them, in sustainable ways, in the fight against poverty. As a result, conservation efforts in peace parks also focus on buffer zones—the regions that surround the nucleus, or core protected area, of a park. Frequently, communities in these zones depend on natural resources for their livelihood. Improving the agricultural practices of families who live on the buffer lands should help prevent such destructive activities as deforestation and poaching in the park's nucleus.

One of the most promising facets of this new conservation movement is the emphasis on human communities in park design and management. As mentioned earlier, several of Central America's peace parks are, or are proposed as, biosphere reserves. In the buffer zones of La Amistad Biosphere Reserve, for example, conservation organizations work with the Guaymi and Bribri Indians living in both Panama and Costa Rica. The residents of the Bribri Indian reserve of Ujarrás are being taught agroforestry techniques that will enable them to produce the food and income they need on land they have already cleared.

THE CHALLENGE AHEAD

Despite the many benefits of international peace parks in Central America, the concept is not without a problem—the implied threat to national sovereignty. Ways are being found to overcome this problem, but some political leaders have expressed hesitancy at promoting binational parks for fear that they are somehow relinquishing control of national territory.

Mexico, Guatemala, and Belize: Forging Bonds Beyond Borders

Early attempts by Guatemalan conservation leaders to engage Mexican government officials in talks about Guatemala's Maya Biosphere Reserve and Mexico's adjoining Calakmul Biosphere Reserve and Montes Azules Biosphere Reserve were met coldly. Until mid-1991, Mexican government officials were reluctant to even attend meetings addressing the concept of international protected areas, apparently feeling that any discussion of the issue would open the door to proposals for binational control of border areas.

Despite reluctance to deal with the issue at the policy level, control along shared national park boundaries came to a head in the field in February 1991, when Guatemalan soldiers and park officials seized a half dozen Mexican trucks and 70 Mexican loggers poaching mahogany and cedar trees from Guatemala's Maya Biosphere Reserve. Documents seized during two raids on Mexican logging camps inside Guatemala's reserve showed that Guatemalan forestry officials had issued bogus logging extraction contracts to eager Mexican companies.

Finally, in August 1991, Mexico's Secretary for Urban Development and Ecology (SEDUE) accepted an invitation from the Central American Commission for Environment and Development to attend the first trinational workshop on frontier parks in the Maya region. Representatives of SEDUE and Mexico's Ministry of Foreign Relations were joined in Belize City by their counterparts from Guatemala and Belize to confer on both the political and technical aspects of cooperation in existing and potential protected areas along borders shared by the three nations. The discussions produced an exciting sense of confidence and congeniality among the representatives of the three countries. Further meetings were planned for early 1992. Still, all three nations have been careful to remind each other that they are seeking cooperation—not joint control—along their border areas, and that all of their activities will be carried out with complete respect for national sovereignty.

Successful Binational Management: La Amistad Reserve

A Central American protected area over which binational control *is* being considered is La Amistad Reserve of Costa Rica and Panama. Discussions during a series of meetings sponsored by Conservation International (an international, nonprofit conservation organization based in Washington, D.C.) and the Organization of American States have been leading toward the use of joint guard patrols inside both countries' territories. Although participating nations do worry that their neighbors might use protected areas to take military action against them, steps are being taken to alleviate this concern.

Furthermore, the two countries have plans for cooperation on various levels in regard to the park. Citizens' ecology groups formed on both sides of La Amistad to support the binational park have also agreed to cooperate on a variety of projects—ranging from visiting each others' communities to exchange ideas and information, to working together on economic development projects. The Panamanian and Costa Rican groups plan to produce a shared document on their joint activities. These events indicate that Panama and Costa Rica are making significant advances in cooperatively managing La Amistad Biosphere Reserve.

No one has proposed that international peace parks in Central America should blur the borders between the region's republics. Peace parks are not designed to threaten national sovereignty. Rather, by seeking to protect resources along their common boundaries, Central American nations are seeking *regional* solutions to their environmental problems. The existence of international peace parks indicates that these countries can coordinate their national activities for mutual environmental, economic, and political benefits.

TOWARD A PROCESS FOR CREATING PEACE PARKS

Central America continues to depend on natural resource-based activities, such as agriculture, forestry, and fishing, so the region's most important long-term goal is to ensure the continuing existence of these natural resources. Unless Central Americans protect the resources on which their economies are based, they have little hope for making social and political progress. Peace parks can play a crucial role in reducing conflicts, achieving environmental protection, and alleviating human poverty.

In addition, peace parks can facilitate Central America's slow climb toward social and economic justice. These internationally protected areas can open the door between nations for talks on issues more controversial than the environment. In doing so, they can provide a mechanism for international attacks on the basic social and environmental problems shared by all the region's countries.

The new Central American Commission for Environment and Development is the most logical institution to advance such efforts. One of its specific goals is "to promote coordinated actions by governmental, non-governmental, and international organizations, for the optimum and wise utilization of the natural resources of the area, the control of pollution, and the establishment of ecological balance."

Because the CCAD brings together government officials from each Central American country to discuss regional solutions to regional problems, it is the obvious vehicle for monitoring the region's efforts in the peace parks process. Already, the CCAD appears to be assuming this role. During late August 1991, it sponsored the first in a series of meetings among the environment ministries of Mexico, Guatemala, and Belize in the frontier parks of the Maya tropical forest region. This gathering was also a model for discussions on other sensitive Central American issues.

To serve as the vital mediator in the peace parks process, the CCAD will require financial and technical assistance. Aid from some non-profit international groups has already been forthcoming for Costa Rica and for the Maya region. But additional support could come from the recently created Global Environment Facility administered by the World Bank, the United Nations Development Programme, and the United Nations Environment Programme. If the CCAD is to oversee a successful process for creating and maintaining peace parks in Central America, the institution will need investments of millions of dollars over the next decade.

Bilateral aid for this park process would be a positive step, as well. The new emphasis that the U.S. Agency for International Development is placing on protected areas and sound natural resource management fits well into the Central American peace park process. Ongoing support from the agency's Regional Office for Central America and Panama to the CCAD provides a solid start.

A system of international peace parks in Central America offers great hope for the future of Central Americans and other peoples of the Western Hemisphere. As both a political concept and physical reality, peace parks simultaneously sow regional harmony, promote sustainable development, and protect biological diversity. The industrialized nations—as well as multilateral institutions—would do well to support this initiative.

Notes

[1] John Noble Wilford, "New Threat to Maya Ruins: Acid Rain," *The New York Times*, August 8, 1989.

[2] "Three-Country Development Project Inaugurated," *Central America Report*, Vol. 14, No. 46 (November), 1987, p. 368 (Guatemala: Inforpress Centroamericana). More than 572,000 people live in the area, 60 percent of them in extreme poverty. Two-thirds of the residents depend on agriculture for their livelihood; more than 250,000 are unemployed or underemployed.

[3] Roger Morales and Craig MacFarland (eds.), *The Joint Management of the Frontier Zone of the Darién*, First Colombian-Panamanian Technical Meeting, November 1979, Turrialba, Costa Rica, Tropical Agricultural Research and Training Centre, Technical Report No. 5.

Chapter Two

Citizen Participation and the Reform of Development Assistance in Central America

Stephen B. Cox

Between 1979 and 1991, Central America received more than $10 billion in bilateral assistance from the United States alone, yet the region is now poorer than it was in 1980. An estimated 9 million Central Americans (35 percent of the population) live in conditions of extreme poverty, and the incomes of 65 percent of all Central Americans are insufficient to meet basic needs. One child in every 10 dies before reaching age five, and two-thirds of those who survive suffer from malnutrition.[1] Equally alarming is that the natural resources upon which all hopes for future growth and recovery must be based are in serious jeopardy. Watersheds, forests, fisheries, and agricultural lands are becoming polluted or disappearing at a rate that, in many cases, threatens irreversible degradation of natural resources.

The persistence of endemic poverty and the rapid pace of environmental destruction are particularly ominous given the magnitude of the efforts that have been launched to counter them. This chapter discusses some of the causes of these failed efforts and suggests new ways for confronting the related priorities of reducing poverty and increasing environmental protection.

OBSTACLES TO EFFECTIVE DEVELOPMENT ASSISTANCE

The central proposition of this chapter is that attempts to address these priorities often fail because the approach to development assistance commonly used by national and international agencies is flawed. The model suffers from three fundamental weaknesses:

1) It is based on a definition of "sustainable development" that is far too narrow to be effective.

2) Conventional development assistance is premised on a mistaken confidence in the extent to which institutions can predict and control the evolution of development programs.

3) It is distorted by international and domestic political priorities that may be inconsistent with the best interests of the poor.

All three of these weaknesses are exacerbated by the failure of institutions to offer adequate opportunities for broader citizen participation in their nation's development decisions. Greater involvement is essential, first, for implementing an appropriately broad definition of sustainability and, second, for generating the information needed to stay on top of complicated and rapidly changing development programs. Similarly, increased citizen participation is crucial not only for creating control mechanisms that allow complex development programs to adapt to new conditions, but also for critiquing and altering political objectives that may actually work against a program's objectives of alleviating poverty.

Fortunately, there is a growing body of experience on methods for correcting some of the weaknesses that hamper conventional development assistance. This chapter offers an analysis of some of those shortcomings and describes approaches for promoting greater citizen involvement and more effective management of the development process.

Pitfalls of a Narrow Definition of Sustainability

In recent years, environmentalists seeking to protect fragile ecosystems have come to recognize that those very ecosystems often coexist with poor people who are more concerned about surviving the coming year than they are with preserving rare environments. At the same time, some of the developing world's more enlightened economic planners are realizing that development strategies often jeopardize the natural resources on which the strategies depend. To their credit, environmentalists and economists alike are beginning to incorporate economic and environmental variables, respectively, into their thinking.

Although the recent efforts to integrate economic and environmental considerations represent an important step forward, sustainable development, as commonly conceived, is still too narrowly defined. A vague term, it seems to mean something like this: economic development that is environmentally sustainable because it does not destroy the natural resources needed to produce benefits in the fifth and fiftieth years, and environmental protection that is economically sustainable because it does not necessarily require people to forgo too much current income for environmental objectives they may deem a luxury.

Yet, environmental and economic sustainability encompass only a few of the factors that diverse human populations and institutions worry about and compete over in regard to any given policy initiative. A successful working definition of sustainable development must incorporate *social, political,* and *institutional* sustainability if it is to be useful in generating feasible options for the future.

A few examples illustrate the point:

■ Poor farmers, or *campesinos,* who are struggling to get by are usually more concerned about keeping a portion of their land in subsistence crops or in securing title to their land (or both) than they are about developing a potentially lucrative new tree crop with its attendant environmental benefits.

■ Leaders of small farmer associations are often more anxious to negotiate better prices for basic grain crops—an issue on which those who elected them will judge their performance—than they are to rationalize land use.

■ And government planners may be under enormous pressure to produce more export income from mineral sales or to develop hydroelectric plants to reduce payments for increasingly expensive oil imports. Such goals cause the environmental impacts of the mines and dams to slip off the policy agenda.

To achieve *social sustainability,* a development program must engage everyone affected, particularly the beneficiaries, to such a degree that they will choose to remain involved over time. Lacking such broad social support, programs must rely on unsustainably expensive subsidized incentives or, worse, on coercive or punitive means to force compliance with unpopular measures.

Initiatives promote *political sustainability* only if they can be implemented without undermining the existing political agreements and understandings that make it possible for public officials and other political actors to work together effectively. Little is accomplished in designing a streamlined regional decisionmaking structure for resource planning if local and municipal governments refuse to cooperate because they perceive the new structure as an unwarranted encroachment on their traditional authority. Similarly, few elected officials will spend much political capital supporting conservation schemes that ask their constituents to tighten their belts unless they are convinced that the constituents believe the conservation to be worth the cost.

Institutional sustainability means the capacity and willingness of national and local institutions to sustain political and economic support for a development program after the conclusion of the intensive initial phase of international assistance. In addition, institutional sustainability requires serious efforts to train local or national staff in the professional skills needed to adapt a project to ever-changing needs and circumstances.

Problems of Information and Control

Central America's attempts to alleviate poverty, stimulate growth, and—more recently—to curb environmental degradation read like a demonstration of Murphy's Law: "If something can go wrong, it will." Development programs often fail because they are vulnerable to factors that fall beyond the scope of the plans and analyses on which they are based. For example, reforestation efforts may falter because rising international beef prices create more compelling economic incentives for clearing forest lands to raise cattle, or because the rural poor cannot maintain their incomes while waiting for sustainably exploitable forest crops to mature. Similarly, reserves established to protect unique ecosystems may be threatened by export development schemes that turn small farms into plantations for new export crops, thereby forcing displaced subsistence farmers to clear virgin forest to plant corn and beans. It sometimes seems that every attempt to find a solution either encounters or actually generates unanticipated problems that pose obstacles to a project's success.

Such problems should not surprise us. Efforts undertaken in the simplest environments invariably run into unforeseen complications. In international development programs, the potential for stumbling across the unexpected is magnified many times by inadequate planning data on dozens of key technical and economic variables, as well as by the enormous social and cultural gaps that separate international technical experts and host government bureaucrats from extension agents, community leaders, and the poor.

Even with access to reasonably reliable information on rainfall, soil characteristics, crop yields, market prices, and the infrastructural requirements of a proposed program, expert planners have no guarantee that their goals will be acceptable—much less compelling—to the intended beneficiaries. More often, program designers cavalierly assume that beneficiaries will cooperate. It is equally common to find public officials planning and spending huge sums of scarce international aid on projects that are then negated by similarly well-intentioned efforts of other bureaucrats working on another floor in the same ministry.

In conventional development assistance, program designers implicitly follow a linear, mechanistic model that assumes established and knowable relationships between a program's inputs and outputs. Programs are characterized by huge initial investments of highly paid professional staff and consultants, who plan large-scale solutions to pressing problems and detail anticipated actions and outcomes with great specificity. Consequently, projects tend to be large and complex, perhaps to justify the enormous expenditures for the planning phase. Implementation is then governed by fixed, a priori specifications of who will do what and when; little room is left for flexible responses to the exigencies of a program's evolution.[2]

In using this model to provide development assistance, planners run the risk of assuming that we know too much about how the world works. As Neil Jamieson of the East-West Center has noted, despite the fundamental ideological and methodological conflicts that have typified discussions of development during the past several decades, "Marxists, socialists, and capitalists have shared [a set of] evolutionary,. . . universalistic, positivistic, and utilitarian assumptions. They have shared a common faith in the capacity of techno-scientific bureaucracies to shape the world in desirable ways, based upon these assumptions."[3]

In fact, development processes are not particularly predictable. The prescriptions for one set of problems inevitably generate new difficulties that need to be evaluated and addressed in a different context, which itself has been shaped by the attempt to solve the original dilemma. Bound to an inflexible model of development, project planners are, in effect, attempting to aim heavy artillery at moving targets in the dark. Drawing on cybernetic theory, Jamieson observes that ". . . achieving or maintaining some desired state of a system is now recognized to be dependent upon feedback. What is minimally required is a communications network that produces action in response to an input of information and then includes the results of its own action in the new information by which it modifies its subsequent behavior."[4]

Such feedback is absent in conventional, over-engineered development efforts. True, mid-course evaluations are a commonly accepted tool in project management, but those evaluations are seldom designed to be more than reflections on whether or not a project is being executed as planned, and as measured by the highly structured and often quantitative indicators of progress set forth in the original design. Mid-course evaluations are seldom intended to ask the tougher and far more important questions: Do the objectives still make sense? Do fundamental assumptions about how the system works appear to hold true? Do the intended beneficiaries seem to be interested in or committed to the outcome?

Nevertheless, these deficient mid-course evaluations are often the only formal mechanism available to project managers who need information about their progress. Few programs include explicit plans for systematically soliciting and using feedback from project beneficiaries and other involved people, although routine feedback is essential to effective development assistance.

Preeminence of Political Priorities

During the last four years of the 1980s, approximately 70 percent of total U.S. aid to the Western Hemisphere went to four countries (Costa Rica, El Salvador, Guatemala, and Honduras) whose combined population accounts for only about 5 percent of Latin America's total population. Such a curious distribution raises obvious questions. U.S. bilateral assistance—like the official development assistance programs of many other countries—is allocated to objectives that are primarily political in nature. For example, aid is offered to political or military allies, to countries hosting U.S. military bases, and to nations seen as key in Washington's efforts to interdict the flow of illegal drugs to the United States. These purposes may or may not be worthwhile, but they are not developmental.

Incentives to evaluate a project's effectiveness in development terms do not materialize because such effectiveness is often not the fundamental goal of the donor institution. Although usually staffed by dedicated and competent development professionals, government agencies are typically charged with executing political, military, or other nondevelopmental objectives. Staff members are not encouraged to ask potentially embarrassing questions about the efficacy of programs as measured in developmental, environmental, or poverty-reduction terms. Instead, the preeminence of political concerns creates an environment in which an official must find a recipient-country agency best suited to use politically meaningful sums of money in a politically determined time frame.

The emphasis on political interests also contributes to the large and unwieldy scale and scope of many official development assistance programs. When the objective is to "move money" quickly to show support for a friendly government, bilateral aid bureaucracies—notoriously understaffed and overworked—have a clear incentive to allocate funds on a scale that exacerbates the problems of insufficient information and control discussed earlier.

At the same time, bureaucrats in recipient countries avoid basic questions about the justification and feasibility of a development project so as not to bite the hand that feeds. Too often, a recipient government is more likely to use resources to extend patronage or gain political control. In countries with limited democratic participation in selecting those who govern, public employees are seldom pressured to ensure that international assistance is used effectively to respond to the interests of the intended beneficiaries. Putting politics first also tends to limit the choice of institutional partners. When the objective of a development program is to support a friendly government, the selected counterpart agency is normally a governmental entity or a politically acceptable nongovernmental organization (NGO).

Consequences of Limited Participation

Broader citizen participation is essential to making sound development decisions. Fortunately, by the late 1980s, all Central American countries had elected civilian heads of state. As the region struggles to build democratic institutions, it confronts the reality that policymaking authority has long been vested in small, unrepresentative elites. A large and increasingly active community of popular organizations and development- focused nongovernmental organizations has been a much-neglected governing partner. The durability of democracy in Central America depends on offering these and other citizen representatives a greater voice in setting priorities, in making decisions, and in holding elected leaders and public institutions accountable.

Restricting citizen involvement also reduces the effectiveness of development assistance programs. In most instances, only highly selective feedback is allowed to influence decisions on adapting a project to changing circumstances. Thus, information on whether key participants and beneficiaries are acting as expected is limited and often useless.

Moreover, if fewer people are allowed to participate in designing and managing a project, fewer people will be committed to the project's success. Consequently, when unanticipated obstacles require inter-institutional cooperation, the relationships on which cooperation must be built are often too weak to effect a solution.

Finally, in healthy democracies, as well as in established authoritarian states, the influence of any given public official may be short-lived. Sudden changes of staff in key positions expose the continuity of complex projects to the vagaries of political processes. Even when such appointments are made largely on the basis of merit, the chances of finding the best person quickly are remote, given endemic shortages of skilled professionals. No competent corporate executive would strike an important business deal with partners who are likely to vanish from the scene during the course of the enterprise, taking with them control over institutions and resources that are essential to the partnership. Yet it is common for development program designers to vest tremendous authority in a handful of people whose power may have been unacceptably limited or tenuous from the outset. Without the broad community commitment to a project that greater participation can offer, an initiative is extremely vulnerable to inevitable changes of personnel.

Reducing poverty and protecting Central America's natural resource base will require substantial, continued investments of international development assistance. The International Commission for Central American Recovery and Development (also known as the Sanford Commission) estimated in 1989 that international aid flows of $2 billion a year will be required to underwrite the region's basic recovery and development priorities in the immediate future.[5] And the Central American Commission for Environment and Development (CCAD)—created by the presidents of the Central American republics to coordinate regional sustainable development efforts—estimates that the region will need $1 billion of new capital in the first half of the 1990s for environmental projects alone. Given the magnitude of these requirements and the region's own financial distress, some mechanism for managing large-scale transfers of resources from abroad is crucial. But greatly increased aid following conventional approaches is likely to yield disappointing results. A new model for the way in which development assistance is delivered is now essential.

In sum, given the multiple challenges of more broadly defined sustainability, the time has come to adopt a humbler epistemology of development. The complex challenge of promoting effective development requires more complete knowledge of a wider array of variables than any organization can hope to command, particularly at the outset of a proposed enterprise. Moreover, it is impossible to know with confidence in advance how all the participants in a proposed program or policy change will react during the life of the project and beyond; yet, sustainability requires a greater focus on the "thereafter" phase of projects than in the past. To achieve more effective programming, we must pay greater attention to the issues of feedback, incentives, and participation. The following pages present some suggestions for an alternative, process-focused approach to development assistance along with concrete proposals for effecting such an approach.

AN ALTERNATIVE: RIGOR IN PROCESS

In the traditional models of development assistance, a tremendous premium is placed on planning ahead—determining all the tasks and specifications at the outset of a project. Such "design rigor" may be useful when one can predict with some reliability how a program will unfold, but it cannot be applied to countries where unpredictability is the rule rather than the exception.

What is needed instead is "rigor in process." Social science researchers pay attention to research methodologies without assuming at the outset of their studies that they know what they are going to discover. Reasonable hypotheses lend structure and direction to their inquiries, but honest investigators remain open to the possibility that their hypotheses may need to be discarded; they design workplans that take into account the need for such changes. This "process rigor" is essential to the integrity and effectiveness of the research itself.

Even greater process rigor is required for effective development assistance. We should not assume at the start that we know how citizens, bureaucrats, business interests, and technical innovations are going to come together in our programs. To compensate for our limited understanding, we need to include in our plans feedback mechanisms—ways to ensure a steady flow of updated information on how the project is unfolding and how our initial assumptions about the ways of the world may need to be altered to accommodate the changing realities of developing societies.[6]

Specifically, process rigor calls for greater attention to:

1) Periodically gathering feedback on the actual priorities of beneficiaries and of other key participants during all stages of the proposed project.

2) Collecting and using information on what systems and tasks the local and national institutions will accept and can manage, and on changes in the institutions' willingness and ability to do so over time.

3) Improving the analytical and managerial skills of local and national institutions (private and public) to ensure continuity after international involvement ceases.

4) Establishing effective linkages and mechanisms for public debate over priorities and methods, as well as for negotiation among a variety of participants at both local and national levels.

5) Creating accountability links that give program staff concrete incentives to work flexibly and creatively to achieve tangible results as opposed to merely complying with the original workplans.

6) Arbitrating and managing conflicting interests within the host government itself, and coordinating policies that originate or must be implemented in different bureaucratic milieus.

In a sense, process rigor is to design rigor what a good software package is to a piece of computer hardware. Without the advantages that an effective software program can offer for flexibility and adaptability to changing needs and applications, an expensive and well-designed computer is useless. The suggested tools and techniques that follow— although not a comprehensive list—can help to ensure adequate process rigor. None used alone is a panacea for the problems that limit project efficiency, but attention to the process, strengthened by these techniques, can do a great deal to enhance program effectiveness.

Rapid Rural Appraisal

In the late 1970s, rural development workers in South and Southeast Asia began to develop methods for generating practical and timely information to improve their projects. Rapid rural appraisal (RRA), as this technique has come to be called, has spread quickly in Asia but has only recently been applied to programs in Latin America.

In essence, RRA is an exercise undertaken in the field by a multi-disciplinary team that quickly collects and evaluates new information and new hypotheses about rural life and development programs. The insights are then used to generate and update plans and hypotheses about what development interventions are expected to accomplish and how.[7] In contrast to more formal survey research methods, RRA is a systematic but loosely structured approach to data collection that places a premium on obtaining a sufficient amount of useful information rapidly, without spending a lot of time and expense studying irrelevant details.

A key to the utility of RRA is what Gordon Conway of The Ford Foundation and Edward Barbier of the International Institute for Environment and Development call the "diversity of analysis," which is gathering information in many different ways from many different sources. Each aspect of a situation under study—be it planting methods, rainfall patterns, or seasonal allocations of labor—is examined by "triangulating," or by questioning a number of sources (for example, poor farmers, local extensionists, homemakers, and others). "Truth" is approached through the rapid buildup of diverse information rather than via statistical replication. Secondary data, direct observation in the field, semi-structured interviews, and the preparation of diagrams all contribute to a progressively more accurate analysis of the situation under investigation.[8]

Well-done appraisals offer a flexible but systematic way to collect useful data throughout the life of a project at a cost, in both time and money, that is modest enough to permit repeated use of the method. The objectives of a study are not inflexible but can be adjusted as the team learns more about what it needs to know. No simple standardized methodology is prescribed. Instead, new techniques are improvised in the field to secure information that appears important. Team members work together to produce interdisciplinary insights and hypotheses.

Most important, perhaps, the appraisal is based in the beneficiary community. Most of the learning takes place in the field, in short, intensive discussions with farmers and other beneficiaries whose perspectives are systematically incorporated into the emerging diagnosis of the situation.

The potential importance of rapid rural appraisal and related techniques for improving process rigor is considerable. Such methods may be used in program design to develop a more realistic and textured appreciation of the problems to be addressed. They also are useful for monitoring and generating evaluative feedback on a project's progress and for ascertaining the continued viability of a project's hypotheses about beneficiary priorities and behavior. Furthermore, RRAs can help policymakers to think more critically about policy formulation and planning. Used correctly, they permit "reality checks" on whether or not development assistance efforts are having their intended impact. Just as important, RRAs can generate practical, detailed information on how to correct misperceptions and to target efforts more successfully.

Multiparty Policy Dialogues

Multiparty policy dialogues enable participants from diverse and representative institutions and social settings to meet on neutral ground to discuss common problems and alternative responses. Such exchanges can be particularly useful for program planning, as they offer a means to develop a broad, plural consensus about goals and methods among people whose cooperation will be crucial to a program's success. Like rapid rural appraisals, dialogues of this sort are iterative, interdisciplinary, interactive, and informal. In contrast with RRAs, however, they need not necessarily occur in the field or in rural communities, and organizers may rely to a greater extent on more conventional modes of policy analysis in preparing the agendas for subsequent discussions.[9]

By bringing together policymakers, business leaders, rural activists, community promoters, environmentalists, and popular organizations, multiparty policy dialogues offer an opportunity for constructive discussions of specific policy issues. Participants can listen to and learn from each other's views of common problems and look for ways to arrange deals from which all may benefit. Dialogues of this sort may be especially helpful in addressing issues of national policy that set the stages in which development initiatives must play themselves out. Such a method may also aid in identifying some of the underlying institutional and political constraints that can later threaten the implementation of a project. Finally, multiparty policy dialogues can point out some of the influences of other sectoral and macroeconomic policies that may fall beyond the original scope of a development program or of problems being discussed.

Although far too few attempts have been made to promote broadly participatory dialogues on specific development issues, three recent experiences, all in Costa Rica, may help to illustrate how such an approach can work. Development Alternatives (a private policy research center in the United States) and the Center for Development Training (CECADE, a nongovernmental organization that offers training and technical assistance to rural communities and groups of small farmers) are cooperating on a series of dialogues that bring together grassroots groups, nongovernmental development organizations, and policymakers to discuss the impacts of national structural adjustment strategies on rural communities. The Organization for Tropical Studies (OTS) has begun a program that combines rapid rural appraisal with multiparty policy dialogues. The RRA teams work with municipal leaders to analyze local issues, while the dialogues involve national legislators and policymakers to address priorities identified during the initial municipal RRA exercises. Finally, the Environmental Law and Natural Resources Center (CEDARENA, a nongovernmental organization) has had great success in using a similar approach to convene broadly participatory discussions of land use and land tenure laws.

A few practical lessons may be drawn from the experiences of these nongovernmental organizations. First, dialogue organizers must have credibility and legitimacy in the eyes of all of the proposed participants. Where no single institution has a sufficiently broad network of relationships, it may be appropriate to attempt a collaborative project involving more than one institution, each with different constituencies (as in the collaboration just described between Development Alternatives and CECADE).

Second, careful attention must be paid to developing any documents used as the basis for discussion. It helps to consult first with all of the prospective participants, to talk over their chief concerns about the topic or topics of the dialogue, to learn about their own implicit hypotheses and biases, and to discover areas in which they may be operating under different assumptions or using different language. The prior consultations also serve to engage everyone in the process—to awaken their interest in a debate to which they have contributed and from which they can expect practical results.

Some leveling of the playing field is appropriate. If a dialogue is to address, for example, the impact of export agriculture on rural communities, then subsistence farmers and rural development workers should be trained to use the economic policy language of national policymakers. Conversely, policymakers and other elites should learn how to communicate with local people to understand their points of view. Without these steps, disenfranchised groups may feel that they have been taken advantage of once again—used as window dressing in a lopsided "dialogue." Policymakers, meanwhile, may come away with reinforced notions of the futility of discussing serious issues with people who do not speak their language.

Once the groundwork is completed, all parties should be afforded a series of opportunities to meet and debate the issues. Successive issue papers, which incorporate consensus and discussion from previous dialogues and new research to clarify points of information, should be prepared for each event. Smaller representative working groups may be convened to deal with key ancillary concerns.

The objective of multiparty policy dialogues is to begin a process of pluralistic communication in which diverse elements of civil society have an opportunity to develop working relationships. Once communication begins, the prospects for constructive agreements are greatly enhanced. More important, the process can also increase the probability that resulting policy initiatives will enjoy broad support from a number of institutions, thereby enabling one to make flexible and creative adjustments as new programs and policies evolve.

Interagency Working Groups

Often, the efforts of one government agency are undermined by others within the same government. For example, initiatives to slow the rate of deforestation have been commonly frustrated by land-titling regulations that recognize the clearing of forest as an "improvement" or by banking regulations that assign no value to uncleared forest, offering perverse incentives for small farmers who need collateral for a production loan. In Costa Rica, the Ministry of Natural Resources, Energy, and Mines was created in 1987 to ensure greater coordination among policymakers in its three vice ministries. Four years later, there was still no operational mechanism for the routine coordination of policies and programs among the ministry's diverse executive authorities, each of which has its own enabling legislation. As a consequence, environmentally unsound electrification and mining projects could still be undertaken with little input from the vice ministry of natural resources.

Interagency conflicts are partially a consequence of the pressure in donor organizations to program large sums of development assistance quickly. In such an environment, one is deterred from involving institutional representatives who might not agree on a project's goals and methods. One way to minimize the propensity of public agencies to undermine each other's efforts is to use interagency working groups to discuss issues that involve the jurisdiction of several agencies. Chosen for their interest and expertise, the members of such gatherings may negotiate solutions to thorny institutional disputes that are unlikely to be resolved by stroke-of-the-pen mandates from senior decisionmakers. The working groups need not be formal decisionmaking bodies, nor must they involve an unwieldy number of participants from a wide array of institutions to be effective, as do the multiparty policy dialogues. Often, it would be enough just to bring together a handful of mid-level managers on a regular basis to discuss how they can better collaborate. A focused, goal-oriented working group can be very useful in promoting institutional and political sustainability.[10]

Horizontal Communication Among Nongovernmental Organizations

The literature on rural extension programs in developing countries is replete with references to the obstacles to communication posed by the social and cultural differences between extensionists and the rural poor. In many cases, the barriers to communication are compounded by a history of flawed extension offerings. There is a well-founded skepticism among the poor about the utility of production packages and strategies developed and promoted by outsiders who have inadequate information from prospective users on such issues as farmers' attitudes toward risk, capital availability, and market access.

In Central America, a large and growing network of hundreds of community organizations and nongovernmental organizations has been working hard for decades, communicating directly with local communities to develop and introduce appropriate ideas for sustainable development in the region. Promoting more effective horizontal communication among these organizations offers one of the simplest and most cost-effective ways to disseminate valuable development practices.

The efforts of World Neighbors, a U.S.-based nongovernmental organization, offer an interesting example of horizontal communication. In the 1970s, the World Neighbors staff in Guatemala worked closely with poor farmers in indigenous communities to develop an approach to culturally and technologically appropriate agricultural changes that have produced impressive results. In dozens of applications, these techniques have more than doubled yields of subsistence crops in the span of a season or two, while halting erosion and substantially restoring soil fertility on environmentally fragile hillside farms. Described in Roland Bunch's *Two Ears of Corn*, the methodology relies on simple, direct communication with *campesinos* to identify factors that limit increased yields and to develop low-cost, environmentally sound technologies for removing those barriers.[11] The resulting lessons are then passed on by word of mouth, from farmer to farmer. Field staff recruited from the involved communities oversee a straightforward extension process in which locals using the new techniques demonstrate their gains to interested members of neighboring communities.

In recent years, World Neighbors and other independent nongovernmental organizations have begun to disseminate more aggressively this approach to innovation and extension, by sending small teams of trained local people to visit and talk with other community associations and nongovernmental groups in a number of countries. They rely on the simple eloquence of the methodology's proven effectiveness to persuade others to try it. In 1988, a partnership involving World Neighbors' team in Honduras and the Development and Peace Service (SEDEPAC, a prominent Mexican nongovernmental organization) introduced the approach to rural communities affiliated with the National Union of Small Farmers and Cattle Ranchers (UNAG, a popular organization then representing some 125,000 farming families in Nicaragua). With very modest donor resources, this partnership has resulted in the rapid diffusion of this sustainable development success story among thousands of the rural poor.

World Neighbors' experience is one of the many examples of how successful ideas developed by Central America's burgeoning network of nongovernmental organizations and other groups can be effectively and inexpensively disseminated throughout the region. In recent years, the Central American nongovernmental organization community has made progress in establishing national and regional associations of NGOs and community groups, which enhances the prospects for this sort of communication. For example, the Regional Network of Nongovernmental Conservation Organizations for the Sustainable Development of Central America (REDES) has recently begun to coordinate exchanges of information and technologies among the region's NGOs. The Central American Alliance of Development Organizations (Concertación) has emerged as an insistent questioner of many fundamental assumptions of foreign aid and public policy. Support for enhanced communication among these associations and for efforts to integrate them into the policy process may be the most cost-effective way to promote popular participation in the management of sustainable development in Central America.

Training in Analytical and Managerial Skills

Many development projects display impressive initial success and then founder after their highly paid managers move on when international support ends. Institutional sustainability requires the training of local professionals with the analytical and managerial skills necessary to design, monitor, direct, and evaluate sustainable development programs. Instruction in such key areas as public administration, resource economics, program management and evaluation, strategic planning, and environmental impact analysis is critically needed.

One hopeful advancement is the recent venture by the Central American Institute of Business Administration (INCAE) to develop professional training programs in resource management. Arguably Latin America's best institution for training in private and public administration, INCAE now offers a series of seminars and executive training programs that will also be incorporated into its master's programs in business, economics, and public management. Beginning in 1992, it will offer a master's program in resource management for professionals from all over Latin America.

In addition to formal programs such as INCAE's, other efforts are needed. Once the Organization for Tropical Studies has completed its pilot program of teaching municipal leaders to use rapid rural appraisal in assessing their own sustainable development options, it may continue to work with REDES and other nongovernmental organizations to make instruction in these techniques more broadly available throughout Central America. Training programs in business analysis and administration also are needed for NGOs and popular organizations to enhance their abilities to prepare solid business appraisals of proposed development projects and to manage the projects effectively.

Finally, more support is needed in the areas of strategic planning and institutional development for Central American nongovernmental organizations. Most of these groups were founded by highly dedicated and enthusiastic promoters and activists. Such qualities are indispensable for organizations that operate on shoestring budgets and that are obliged to change their programs in response to the often capricious shifts in the interests of the international donor community. But all too often, NGOs lack fundamental skills for strategic planning and institutional development. In the United States, analogous nonprofit associations have access to a growing network of service groups that offer instruction in strategic planning, advocacy, fund raising, board governance, staff training, and a number of other institutional development skills. The time has come to establish similar training services for Central America's critically important development institutions.

Who Should Promote Rigor in Process?

Every institution genuinely interested in providing more effective development assistance is responsible for emphasizing process rigor in designing and implementing its programs. Still, it may be useful to think of a division of labor that assigns different tasks to different types of institutions to promote greater rigor in process.

Bilateral and multilateral organizations, and their host government counterpart agencies, can do a great deal to set the stage for more effective attention to process. Donors could make a difference by acknowledging the complex relationships within governments and societies that fix the parameters for project success. This may be done by using rapid rural appraisals or similar methods to obtain more regular and helpful monitoring information, by establishing interagency working groups to plan and monitor programs, and by using multiparty policy dialogues to engage all interested parties before erecting elaborate program designs.

Architects of development assistance programs must also consider whether the manner in which they specify program designs and objectives is conducive to greater effectiveness. An excessive preoccupation with and confidence in prior design rigor—closely specifying outcomes, benchmarks, cost parameters, and timetables—may cause the formal design to become more important than the search for workable solutions. Evaluations and monitoring will focus on the official benchmarks instead of asking difficult questions about effectiveness, beneficiary interest, and sustainability.

More flexible measures of achievement that are not specified in terms of rigidly quantified targets may be more realistic tools for monitoring effectiveness. For example, a process-oriented evaluation might concentrate on *qualitative* appraisals of the ability and creativity of interagency working groups in anticipating and resolving obstacles and be less preoccupied with meeting formal targets for the number of seedlings planted or the volume of credit administered.

Bilateral and multilateral donors can also make a serious contribution by working more closely with and providing greater support to nongovernmental organizations in Central America. The NGOs can help to diversify the social reference points of development bureaucracies and provide more and better information on whether efforts are achieving useful results. In many cases, they may also prove to be more competent managers of development assistance funds than are public institutions.

Development organizations must make far greater attempts to consult with the public before, during, and after launching projects. Nevertheless, as long as politics looms so large among the considerations of development institutions, it is naive to expect that official development assistance agencies will be able to address the problems of process on their own. Greater accountability requires that citizens actively and effectively demand more responsive government programs. A strong and competent nongovernmental organization sector is essential for this task.

In the past, the Central American nongovernmental organization community often shied away from visible involvement in advocating policy reforms and government accountability. More recently, NGOs and popular organizations increasingly include policy-related issues on their agendas. These groups should continue to work constructively with the public sector, without losing their capacity to be objective. Toward this end, support from private donors (foundations, international private voluntary organizations, and others) will be essential. Governments and their official international contributors cannot be expected to underwrite critiques and independent monitoring of their own efforts, particularly when those efforts are motivated by political interests.

Private donors active in Central America should consider the extent to which their programs are explicitly addressing salient public-policy issues. Private contributors can support nongovernmental organizations' efforts to press governments for greater accountability and reforms that would be too sensitive for official aid agencies to finance. Direct support for policy dialogues, program monitoring, and other activities managed by independent NGOs and grassroots organizations can provide the sort of "bottom-up" pressure for accountability that is required for more responsible and effective development assistance programming.

INSTITUTIONAL REFORMS IN DELIVERING DEVELOPMENT ASSISTANCE

As this chapter has discussed, one of the principal problems with official development assistance is the pressure to program large sums of aid to conform with fundamentally political objectives. The "obligation to obligate"—to move the money out the door before the end of the fiscal period—also leads to the funding of ineffective megaprojects.[12] Such pressures place a premium on design rigor and naturally tend to diminish the participation of contrary or dissenting voices in the planning and implementation of an aid program. The narrowly defined government-to-government mode of most bilateral assistance, and the similarly poor relationships of multilateral development finance institutions, have greatly limited the prospects for more creative efforts that pay appropriate attention to feedback and participation. If we are to focus adequately on process rigor, we must reform the delivery of bilateral and multilateral development assistance to the region.

U.S. Bilateral Assistance

Much of the public discussion about reforming development assistance focuses on ideas for improving the effectiveness of regional cooperation and multilateral aid. This concentration on multilateralism is particularly appropriate in regions, such as Central America, that have recently suffered from military conflicts in which one or more of the principal bilateral aid providers has been involved. As Anthony Lake of Mount Holyoke College has observed: "By definition, societies emerging from internal military conflict are highly charged politically. Assistance from multilateral agencies is much less likely to run afoul of lingering resentments than is aid from the former patrons of one side or another."[13] Accordingly, the reform of U.S. assistance to Central America should include a search for ways to channel more of the aid through multilateral channels.

Multilateral institutions have their own limitations, however, and cannot bear the entire burden of managing the aid flows that should be directed toward Central America. Moreover, the United States continues to have legitimate national interests (as well as distinctive strengths) that do not always coincide with those of multilateral institutions. Indeed, there is a strong case to be made that more diversity is needed in approaches to development assistance, rather than the potentially homogenizing effect of processing all aid through a handful of multilateral organizations.

Nevertheless, a growing chorus of critics is justifiably concerned about the effectiveness of current U.S. assistance to the region.[14] The U.S. Agency for International Development (USAID), in particular, deserves thorough and critical scrutiny. Increasingly, it is guided by short-term political concerns, lacks a coherent long-range vision of development, and is subordinated in policy discussions to the U.S. State Department, the National Security Council, and other executive bodies. With its hands tied by legislative earmarks and other procedural shackles, the agency is ill-suited to monopolize the management of U.S. bilateral development assistance as it has in the past.

An interesting alternative proposed by the Overseas Development Council would be to establish a Sustainable Development Fund (SDF). The fund would distribute U.S. bilateral monies to a diverse community of recipients working on development priorities jointly chosen by the Congress and the Executive Branch.[15] A donor, rather than an operational agency, the fund would be able to support directly the activities of recipient governments, national and international nongovernmental organizations, private profit-making firms, international organizations, and USAID itself. As the fund became established with a solid professional staff and a known track record, its share of U.S. bilateral funding would increase, while the share allocated through the agency would diminish.

The Sustainable Development Fund represents an important conceptual advance in the structuring of U.S. bilateral assistance. Staffed by experienced professionals, who respond to a limited set of developmental priorities and are given the latitude to deal with a more varied set of grantees, the fund would be able to act more creatively than USAID does. It would also have greater independence from short-term foreign policy interests. Prospective grantees would be called upon to compete for U.S. bilateral assistance in a more open marketplace of ideas and initiatives. Freed from some of the political and bureaucratic constraints that limit USAID's scope, relationships, and effectiveness, the fund would be far better qualified to support the type of creative, process-oriented experiments discussed earlier in this chapter.

An older, time-proven idea may also merit increased support. The Inter-American Foundation (IAF) is a U.S. government agency founded in 1969 as an alternative "people-to-people" model for delivering development assistance. Staffed largely by field representatives with hands-on, grassroots development experience, the foundation specializes in making relatively small grants directly to nongovernmental organizations and popular organizations. Over the past 20 years, it has funded a large number of the more productive innovations generated by the Latin American NGO community. In recent years, its board and senior management have on occasion shown themselves to be unfortunately vulnerable to the influence of narrow U.S. foreign policy thinking. Nonetheless, the foundation's solid and experienced professional field staff has maintained the institution's credibility as a good-faith partner in grassroots development experiments. If it can continue to resist pressures to subordinate its program to short-term foreign policy interests, the Inter-American Foundation will merit a substantial increase in staff levels and financial support in any restructuring of U.S. foreign aid to Central America.

Finally, some aspects of the debt-for-nature elements of the Enterprise for the Americas Initiative (EAI) announced by President George Bush in mid-1990 represent an important step forward in U.S. assistance for sustainable development activities in Central America. If they comply with specified economic policy prescriptions, Latin American countries may negotiate to reduce their bilateral debt with the United States through debt-swap mechanisms. The proceeds can then be applied to capitalize environmental trust funds in the debtor countries. Resources from these trust funds would then be used to support initiatives that link resource conservation with economic development. Grants may be made from the funds to local, national, or regional nongovernmental organizations, to community organizations, and—"in exceptional circumstances"—to agencies of the national government.

Significantly, the Enterprise for the Americas Initiative specifies that a majority of the members of the trust funds' governing boards must represent environmental and community development nongovernmental organizations of the recipient country. Properly implemented, this requirement could improve process rigor in the region's sustainable development efforts. If the funding decisions are made by a genuinely representative body, the grantees will have clear incentives to respond to public interests. To ensure appropriately plural representation, EAI administrators should allow existing national associations of environmental and development nongovernmental organizations to help name the nongovernmental organization members to these boards, and they should resist the temptation to select only participants who are politically acceptable to the U.S. government.

The Enterprise for the Americas Initiative is notable for linking two fundamental development priorities in Latin America: debt reduction and the generation of capital for sustainable development investments. Although the macroeconomic significance of the EAI-based debt reduction should not be exaggerated (current service payments on all of Latin America's bilateral debts to all creditors amount to only 10 percent of the region's annual payments of principal and interest), it is a step in the right direction. Economist Richard Feinberg has noted that the impact of this measure could be greatly increased if other bilateral creditors, particularly those in the Paris Club, chose to match the terms of the initiative's debt-reduction scheme.[16] Forgiveness of Central America's P.L. 480 debt to the United States as of October 1990 under current EAI provisions could generate nearly $250 million worth of capital for national environmental trusts in Costa Rica, El Salvador, Guatemala, Honduras, and Nicaragua.

Nevertheless, as a bilateral program, the Enterprise for the Americas Initiative is heir to all the shortcomings and the concomitant risks of politicization of this type of aid. One amendment to the current EAI proposal might improve its effectiveness and demonstrate the United States' good faith and interest in promoting multilateral approaches to Central American development. The United States should amend the initiative to specify that a substantial proportion of the debt-for-nature revenues, now earmarked for the national trusts, be allocated to a new multilaterally supported Central American Fund.

A New Proposal: The Central American Fund

Many of the thorniest problems of environmental protection in Central America transcend national boundaries (see Arias and Nations, Chapter 1), and there is a growing constituency for approaching reconstruction and development in the region in a multilateral fashion. Moreover, many essential tasks—such as professional training programs—are best done on a regional basis, to exploit economies of scale, to optimize the use of scarce human resources, and to promote greater interaction among individuals from different countries. In its 1989 report, the International Commission for Central American Recovery and Development urged the adoption of ". . . the principle of symmetrical multilateralism, where donor and recipient countries and international organizations can coordinate aid policies and programs."[17] To this end, the governments of Central America, the international nongovernmental organization community, and official development assistance institutions (bilateral and multilateral) should work together to establish a multilateral Central American Fund (CAF) that would be designed to avoid the pitfalls of many other development assistance efforts.

The Central American Fund would receive aid from public and private sources in a number of countries and channel it to development projects in Central America. As with the EAI's trust funds, grants could be made to local, national, or regional nongovernmental organizations, as well as to community organizations and government agencies. A central priority of the fund would be to promote initiatives that reflect an appropriate measure of concern for the process rigor defined earlier. It might also make investments in more conventional projects (rural credit schemes, national park development, production programs, etc.), providing that these ventures were designed to include suitable mechanisms for feedback and citizen participation.

But, as a funding institution, the Central American Fund's most compelling priority would be to provide support specifically for participation-enhancing and process-focused activities. It should function as a clearinghouse and financial resource for promoting creative thinking about development assistance effectiveness and not attempt to replicate the missions of other institutions better suited for supporting more conventional development projects.

The Central American Fund should be governed by an international board of directors that represents participating nations and different elements of civil society. Some representation of donor governments and multilateral financial institutions may be inevitable, but their numbers should be kept to a minimum. Delegates or nominees of donor governments and multilateral institutions should never make up more than a third of the board's membership. On the other hand, representatives of national governments in Central America are both desirable and inevitable. Their involvement would help to engage those governments in the fund's process-oriented program. Nevertheless, the mission of the Central American Fund requires that a much broader voice be given to interests not traditionally considered. Accordingly, the majority of the members of its governing board should represent nongovernmental groups in the region, including NGOs, businesses, cooperatives, and community and producers' organizations. The initial nongovernmental representatives should be chosen through broad and open consultative processes.

The staff of the Central American Fund should be an interdisciplinary group of experienced professionals who broadly reflect the interests of the nations participating in the fund. A majority of staff members should be Central American nationals, although the CAF should draw as much as possible on existing expertise, regardless of nationality. To the maximum extent feasible, they should have hands-on development experience.

To ensure accountability to its represented interests, the Central American Fund board should oversee and authorize staff selection. To safeguard program coherence, however, responsibility for all but the largest grants (for example, those of more than $500,000) should be delegated to the fund's chief executive officer. The board should restrict its direct involvement in program decisions to defining missions and values and to periodically reviewing and approving staff-proposed strategies and grants.

Several options exist for underwriting the Central American Fund's initially modest financial requirements. Earmarking part of the necessary funds that may result from the EAI debt-swap mechanisms may be one source. The allocation of a mere 10 percent of the $250 million projected, matched by funds from other sources, would provide adequate start-up capital.

Debt-swap programs with other bilateral and multilateral donors could also generate substantial additional capital. As of October 1990, the Central American Bank for Economic Integration (BCIE) held a portfolio of more than $700 million in foreign debt, of which 63 percent stemmed from bilateral loans from the United States, Germany, Mexico, and Venezuela, and another 19.5 percent came from multilateral loans. Extension of debt-swap opportunities for some or all of this BCIE-held debt could create a substantial pool for supporting the Central American Fund and other regional development programs.

Debt-swap proceeds, however, should not be the Central American Fund's sole financial source, as they do not really offer much-needed inflows of new capital to the region. Such monies ultimately come from the coffers of debtor governments. In addition, national legislatures are often not consulted when portions of national budgets are allocated directly from central banks to debt-swap programs. Although the uses of the funds thus created may be laudable, it would be ironic to place too much confidence in such a nondemocratic fiscal process precisely at a time when Central America is attempting to build accountable democratic institutions.

To increase and diversify the donor base, new capital should also be solicited from multilateral and bilateral aid programs, private foundations, and international nongovernmental organizations. Special efforts should be made to persuade the Japanese and Europeans to contribute to the Central American Fund.

CONCLUSION

During the last few years, the people of Central America have dared to hope that peace will soon return to their region. The imminence of a Central America without war offers the prospect that these societies at last can begin to focus their skills and resources on building both democratic institutions and healthier, more equitable economies. Nevertheless, the hopeful signs of peace are accompanied by the prospect of a disturbing decline in the levels of international development assistance available for the region in the 1990s. It would appear that the diminishing importance of Central America on the geopolitical agendas of major donor nations may be all too promptly reflected in the allocation of fewer development assistance funds.

More aid, not less, is needed now as the region rebuilds and as its fledgling democracies attempt to consolidate their early gains. The levels of international assistance, however, are ultimately far less important than the manner in which that aid is bestowed and managed. Conventional approaches to development assistance—with their narrow focus on the technical tasks at hand, their mistaken assumptions about how much they can know and control, their distorting overlay of political objectives, and their limitations on participation—will not meet the challenge. Predictably, conventional programs will continue to fail in achieving their developmental objectives. More important, at this moment in history, if such programs do not promote greater accountability and broader citizen participation in decisions about development aid, they will also fail to take advantage of the window of political opportunity now open for the growth of democracy in the region.

One of the criticisms made by many serious development professionals has been that broader citizen participation is 1) difficult to achieve, and 2) not cost-effective. Although it may indeed be hard to achieve, the tools for greater process rigor presented in this chapter offer some promising ways to start. However, limiting participation in the interests of cost-effectiveness ranks as one of the most egregious examples of false economy in the history of social thought and public policy. The question is not whether development programs can afford the luxury of full citizen representation, but whether—given the track record of conventional, nonparticipatory approaches—we can afford *not* to promote greater participation.

The task of increasing citizen involvement is a daunting one that will require immense effort and even greater political will. Some improvements can be made by existing development institutions as they think critically about how they operate. Other solutions will require institutional reforms and even new institutions that are designed to call upon ideas, efforts, and resources from a more representative array of citizen interests. Bilateral ventures such as the Sustainable Development Fund and the Enterprise for the Americas Initiative are sorely needed to improve the effectiveness of the United States' bilateral assistance to the region.

Even more important, however, are creative, new attempts to develop better multilateral approaches to the delivery of development aid. The Central American Fund proposed in this chapter offers one such option. Supported by a number of nations, overseen by a socially diverse and representative board, and staffed by seasoned professionals from different countries and disciplines, the fund would make it possible to deliver increasing flows of assistance in ways that would be more conducive to sound, flexible, and democratically managed development.

Notes

[1] The International Commission for Central American Recovery and Development, *Poverty, Conflict and Hope: A Turning Point in Central America* (Durham, NC: Duke University Press, 1989).

[2] For an interesting critique of the conventional model, see Norman Uphoff, "Paraprojects as New Modes of International Development Assistance," *World Development*, Vol. 18, No. 10, 1990, pp. 1401-11.

[3] Neil Jamieson, "The Paradigmatic Significance of Rapid Rural Appraisal," Proceedings of the 1985 International Conference on Rapid Rural Appraisal (Thailand: Khon Kaen University, 1987), pp. 88-102.

[4] Ibid, p. 95.

[5] *Poverty, Conflict and Hope*, op. cit.

[6] The concept of rigor in process has much in common with David Korten's "learning process approach," which may be familiar to many readers. For more on his ideas, see David Korten, "Community Organization and Rural Development: A Learning Process Approach," *Public Administration Review*, Vol. 40, No. 5 (September-October 1980), pp. 480-511.

[7] This description of RRA is adapted from Gordon R. Conway and Edward B. Barbier, *After The Green Revolution: Sustainable Agriculture for Development* (London: Earthscan Publications, Ltd., 1990), pp. 177ff. Also see Jennifer A. McCracken, Jules N. Pretty, and Gordon R. Conway, *An Introduction to Rapid Rural Appraisal for Agricultural Development* [London: International Institute for Environment and Development (IIED), 1988] for a general introduction and an annotated bibliography. The IIED has established an international network to disseminate information on RRA and its cousin, participatory rural appraisal. Finally, a helpful how-to-do-it review is presented in *Participatory Rural Appraisal Handbook: Conducting PRAs in Kenya*, jointly prepared by the National Environment Secretariat of the Government of Kenya, Clark University, Egerton University, and the Center for International Development and Environment of the World Resources Institute, Natural Resources Management Support Series, Vol. 1 (February 1990).

[8] Korten, op cit., pp. 480-511.

[9] L. David Brown of the Institute for Development Research and the Boston University School of Management presents examples of organizations attempting to promote such interactions and an interesting analysis of these organizations' functions and dynamics. See L. David Brown, "Bridging Organizations and Sustainable Development," paper prepared for the Conference on Social Innovations and Global Management, Case Western Reserve University, November 13-15, 1989.

[10] For an illuminating discussion of an effective working group in action, see Frances F. Korten, "The Working Group as a Catalyst for Organization Change," in *Transforming a Bureaucracy: The Experience of the Philippine National Irrigation Association*, ed. Frances F. Korten and Robert Y. Siy, Jr. (West Hartford, CT: Kumarian Press, 1988). Another source for examples and discussion of working groups is Barbara Gray, *Collaborating: Finding Common Ground for Multiparty Problems* (San Francisco, CA: Jossey-Bass, 1989).

[11] Roland Bunch, *Two Ears of Corn: A Guide to People-Centered Agricultural Improvement* (Oklahoma City: World Neighbors, 1982).

[12] Uphoff, op. cit.

[13] Anthony Lake, "Overview: After the Wars—What Kind of Peace?" *After the Wars: Reconstruction in Afghanistan, Indochina, Central America, Southern Africa, and the Horn of Africa*, U.S.-Third World Policy Perspectives, No. 16 (New Brunswick, NJ: Transaction Publishers in cooperation with the Overseas Development Council, 1990), p. 23.

[14] For an interesting discussion of some alternatives, to which the analysis in this section is indebted, see John W. Sewell and Peter M. Storm, "United States Budget for a New World Order: Promoting National Security and Advancing America's Interests Abroad" (Washington, DC: Overseas Development Council, 1991).

[15] Ibid, pp. 6, 23-24.

[16] Richard E. Feinberg, "The Enterprise for the Americas Initiative," Testimony presented to the Subcommittee on Western Hemisphere Affairs and the Subcommittee on International Economic Policy and Trade, Committee on Foreign Affairs, U.S. House of Representatives, Washington, DC, February 27, 1991.

[17] *Poverty, Conflict, and Hope*, op. cit., p. 84.

Chapter Three

Inventing Institutions for Conservation: Lessons from Costa Rica

Alvaro Umaña and Katrina Brandon

INTRODUCTION

Costa Rica has a worldwide reputation as a leader in conservation—a reputation that is attributable, in part, to the nation's immense array of protected areas. Nearly 27 percent of Costa Rica is safeguarded to some degree. Areas having absolute protection, such as national parks and biological reserves, encompass more than 6,000 square kilometers, or 12 percent of the entire country. These lands constitute the core of the nation's system of protected areas, and they are generally thought to be the most biologically diverse.[1] To a large degree, the system is patterned on the U.S. model of national parks.[2]

Protected areas other than parks, such as forest reserves, protected zones, wildlife refuges, and Indian reserves, make up nearly 15 percent of the country's landmass. They are mostly privately owned (or communally owned in the case of Indian reserves) and are generally classified as multiple-use areas that are protected by law and can be used only subject to certain restrictions. In addition, they are often populated and have both a high forestry development and conservation potential.

All of these wilderness areas combined shelter most of the nation's 208 species of mammals, 850 species of birds, 160 species of amphibians, 200 species of reptiles, and 130 species of freshwater fish, as well as an estimated 25,000 species of insects. It is estimated that if Costa Rica succeeds in protecting these lands, it will preserve nearly 95 percent of its flora and fauna, which represents about 5 percent of all the plant and animal species currently known to exist on the planet.

By the mid-1980s, Costa Rica had taken steps to establish a framework that would link the protected areas with both national- and local-level needs. The first initiatives centered around creating and adapting institutions, both public and private, that would administer the processes needed to improve the existing parks system. Among the basic changes needed were consolidating and protecting the national parks system, enhancing the national significance of conservation, integrating park management with the needs of the surrounding communities, and developing funding mechanisms for conservation and natural resource management.

These measures were essential to reshaping conservation and to establishing a new framework that would support "sustainable development" throughout Costa Rica. This chapter describes how that nation adapted existing institutions and created new ones to integrate conservation with the development process. In light of the Costa Rican experience, each country should invent its own institutional structures for conservation. These new institutions must link conservation and development at national and regional levels, as well as in the minds of the rural poor, who often bear the ultimate costs of conserving their nation's resource base.

COSTA RICA'S SYSTEM OF PROTECTED AREAS

Starting in 1969, Costa Rica began developing a system of protected areas that today encompasses more than 70 sites, including national parks, biological reserves, wildlife refuges, protected zones, and forest reserves. They include both public and private lands that embrace more than one-quarter of Costa Rica. For the first decade, Costa Rica's government emphasized the creation of parks and protected areas. This period was characterized by a rapid increase in the system's number and size of areas, and by increased support to the National Park Service, especially in the late 1970s. The creation of this system was not without problems. Costa Rican law requires that once an area is declared a national park it must be expropriated, and the government must pay the owner fair-market value. Yet, in many cases, the government lacked the funds to pay landowners, and the process of expropriation and payment lagged far behind park declarations. For example, it took nearly 20 years for the government to reimburse landowners whose properties were expropriated to create Cahuita National Park. The lack of prompt settlement for expropriated lands created high levels of mistrust toward park officials and a resentment of government policies in much of the country.

One institution created in 1978 to support the parks was the National Parks Foundation (NPF), which was initiated by the government but is an independent and private nonprofit foundation. The NPF is dedicated to planning, managing, protecting, and developing national parks and reserves. During the 1969-1979 period, it began playing an important role by supporting the government in the acquisition and management of protected areas as well as by attracting international resources from other governments and conservation organizations. One of the NPF's most significant undertakings was its successful campaign to extend Braulio Carrillo Park. Sponsored by the NPF, this international fund-raising activity was a joint effort with the Organization for Tropical Studies (a consortium of U.S. universities that conducts research in Costa Rica) and The Nature Conservancy (a U.S.-based nongovernmental conservation organization).

Despite the rapid increase in the number of parks and reserves during the 1970s, the Costa Rican government lacked the resources to protect them. Colonization and deforestation were widespread in wildlands adjacent to parks and reserves, often the results of roads built to reach previously inaccessible areas. In some parts of Costa Rica, such as the Talamanca region, local populations that had been there for centuries began clearing lands to prove ownership, as squatters rapidly moved in following road construction.

After its initial expansion, the parks system entered a period of relative decline in the early 1980s, which was attributable to many interrelated factors. First, although the parks existed on paper, little money was available to manage or protect them, in large part because of the concurrent economic crisis. Second, there were absolutely no budgetary allocations for land purchases. A high inflation rate meant that, although there were the same nominal financial resources, the buying power was substantially reduced. Finally, staff levels fell after Costa Rica imposed a government-wide hiring freeze as part of its structural adjustment loans with the International Monetary Fund (IMF). Coordination among government agencies responsible for managing these areas was historically poor, and it diminished further with fewer funds and lower staff morale.

The country's fiscal strain—which reduced social programs and business expansion, and increased poverty—also exacerbated the threats to protected areas from development and logging pressures. For example, gold miners invaded Corcovado National Park in 1985. Many of these people were actually displaced workers from abandoned banana plantations. As the government was unable to stop the invasion, several hundred people began panning for gold, a process that severely damages rivers through sedimentation and mercury pollution. For several months, both the National Park Service and the central government were unable to control the park. Finally, a court order forced the police to evict the gold miners, after compensatory benefits were negotiated between the outgoing government and the nearly 800 miners and their families. Because the government was unable to deter such actions, its ability to manage the parks was diminished in the eyes of the public. This led to increased encroachment.

During the 1980s, serious land-tenure and management problems were evident in many of the protected areas not designated as parks. For example, forest reserves, which are 80 percent privately owned and account for almost 4,000 square kilometers, began rapidly deteriorating because of poor timber-extraction techniques. In addition, the park system did not provide for replanting and forest regeneration, which would ensure replacement of the portions harvested or maintain the forest close to its natural conditions. Coordination between the forest service, which manages most of the remaining conservation areas, and the National Park Service was relatively poor.

Many of these multiple-use protected areas served as "buffer zones" between developed areas and parks and reserves. As destructive forest exploitation and unsustainable development patterns increased in these areas, their value as buffers to the national parks declined. Land-tenure problems particularly affected La Amistad, Tortuguero, Braulio Carrillo, Corcovado, and Arenal National Parks. Land-tenure and management problems also plagued much of the 2,800 square kilometers of Indian reserves.

By 1986, when Oscar Arias was elected president, protected areas exceeded 12,000 square kilometers—equivalent to 24 percent of the country's landmass. The Costa Rican government had expropriated and paid for nearly 80 percent of the land for all parks and biological reserves. However, if deforestation rates in Costa Rica (among Latin America's highest) remained constant, only forests within protected areas would still exist by the year 2000. There was no working management system to maintain the parks and other protected areas, and fixed costs of managing existing resources consumed 90 percent of the funds for conservation. At $4.4 billion, the country's foreign debt was one of the world's highest in per capita terms, so prospects of attracting new resources to expand or improve conservation were limited. In short, the incoming administration was confronted with serious problems in the natural resource sector. In addition, the gold-miners problem had started to attract considerable press attention, which added an element of urgency and crisis to the situation.

REORGANIZATION OF CONSERVATION MANAGEMENT

The Arias administration's tenure marked the revitalization of conservation in Costa Rica, which was characterized by consolidation of efforts and managerial reforms. One of its most important challenges was to slow the nationwide deforestation rate and improve park management while providing economic benefits to local populations. The guiding concept for reorganizing the management of protected areas was the need to give meaning to the rhetoric of sustainable development, especially for the people living in buffer zones. This meant developing a link between absolutely protected government-held lands (12 percent of the country) and privately held protected areas (15 percent). Providing options for people to sustain themselves in the buffer zones was seen as the key; if local populations learned that they could survive and prosper from the existence of parks and protected areas, they would stop destroying the forests. The government wanted to support these buffer-area populations to turn them into frontline defenders of the parks.

It was clear that both the government and the public would have to perceive natural resource management and conservation as higher priorities than had previously been the case. A management system to oversee the protected areas was required, as was a means of linking all the areas. The Costa Rican government needed greater credibility in its protection efforts. In addition, new funds would be required to pay for the process of consolidation and sustainable development.

Prior to the election, Oscar Arias and his advisors (including Alvaro Umaña, co-author of this chapter) developed a plan to accomplish these objectives. The plan 1) consolidated power for conservation into a new ministry; 2) developed a new system that was decentralized and that would serve to link and manage both the protected areas and the buffer zones; 3) created new financing mechanisms so that objectives could be met without draining scarce economic resources; and 4) developed the technical capacity to describe and catalogue the species (and their potential uses) that compose Costa Rica's tremendous biological diversity. These steps are described in the following section.

Consolidating Power for Conservation

The Ministry of Natural Resources, Energy, and Mines (MIRENEM) was established one month after the Arias administration took office. The new bureaucracy gave greater power and legitimacy to natural resource management, raising it to the level of other economic sectors. It also fulfilled the need for an integrated approach that would improve the stewardship of all of Costa Rica's natural assets, including parks and reserves, watersheds, hydroelectric generating capacity, and such nonrenewable resources as hydrocarbons and minerals. MIRENEM was charged with developing integrated policies for the sustainable management of all the nation's natural wealth.

At the policy level the ministry developed key strategies to:
- promote an integrated approach to the management of protected areas and buffer zones;

- single out biological diversity as a key management objective; and
- start the process of defining a national strategy for sustainable development with a long-term perspective that would highlight the role of renewable resources and biological diversity.

The functions that were consolidated within the new ministry had previously been split between the Ministry of Energy and Mines and the Ministry of Agriculture. Two units of the Ministry of Agriculture (MAG)—the National Park Service (NPS) and the General Forestry Directorate (DGF)—were transferred to MIRENEM.[3] The agriculture ministry felt that the forestry department was politically important since the authority to grant or refuse forestry permits and to distribute fiscal incentives for reforestation served as a strong power base. Those who benefited from the permits and incentives were often among the most economically powerful people in Costa Rica. They could act as advocates for, as well as a pressure group on, the Ministry of Agriculture when necessary. Despite opposition, the forestry department became part of MIRENEM. This transfer was of great importance for conservation.

The consolidation gave MIRENEM authority over all of the country's protected areas. Although the new ministry began operations after Arias was elected, it did not have formal approval from the Costa Rican Congress until the administration changed four years later. (President Arias's direct support for the creation of MIRENEM was not matched by support from the opposition-controlled Congress, which did not formally approve its establishment until eight days after Oscar Arias left office in 1990.)

Could an "unofficial" ministry affect changes? The answer is an unequivocal yes. Although the authority to formally *create* MIRENEM rested with the Congress, the Arias administration was still able to establish a completely legitimate, functioning ministry through the exercise of power. The authority for creating the new ministry, and for declaring a minister, was legally valid because the Energy and Mines segment of MIRENEM was previously a ministry. And the control of the park service and the forestry department was possible because their budgets were transferred to MIRENEM. In short, although there was no law approving the establishment of MIRENEM, everyone knew that the new ministry had the direct support of the president. The remaining challenge was to strengthen the role of conservation in the absence of new legislation.

REACHING BEYOND THE BORDER. One of the primary concerns of MIRENEM was how to manage a mosaic of more than 60 different protected areas, including national parks, Indian and forest reserves, biological reserves, wildlife refuges, and protected zones as well as their adjoining buffer lands. The system was badly underfunded, threats to all of the protected areas were serious, and the gold-mining problem continued to deteriorate.

Shortly after the creation of MIRENEM, the gold miners threatened to reinvade the park if they were not compensated immediately. In an unprecedented action, the Costa Rican Congress approved compensation, both in-kind and cash payments. This eventually cost the Costa Rican government almost $3 million and nearly tripled the yearly budget of the National Park Service. It also diverted sorely needed resources away from park management.

This second incident with the gold miners reminded MIRENEM that borders were not enough to defend the parks and that, at least conceptually, the current boundaries had to be extended. MIRENEM felt it had to create structures that, first, would make local populations sympathetic to the existence of parks and protected areas and, second, would help them see the direct potential benefits of such lands. The result hoped for was the wiser use of protected areas. MIRENEM began developing new programs that reached beyond park boundaries. For example, it created gold-miners co-ops outside parks to stop the miners' invasions.

Although both the forestry department and the park service were housed in MIRENEM, the new minister lacked the authority to combine them, in part because of the unusual status of MIRENEM itself. The two agencies were subject to different governing laws, so they could not be fused. However, no law stated that personnel from the two agencies could not be united. MIRENEM began urging regional personnel from the two divisions to work together to start the integration process.

MIRENEM also developed a National Conservation Strategy (NCS) for sustainable development nationwide, not just in conservation but in all sectors—including energy, agriculture, education, and industry. The NCS could not be implemented solely by governmental fiat. Instead, it required agreement—both legal and in terms of public support—at all levels of society through hundreds of different decisions both at the national and local level. The NCS laid out a process to achieve that official and popular ratification. The successful outcome of the process demonstrated that the Arias administration did assign major importance to implementing sustainable development principles through a wholly democratic process.

Decentralized Management of Protected Areas

The new vision espoused by MIRENEM stressed that protected areas could best be conserved if they were part of the strategy for integrated, sustainable development of rural areas.

In 1987, MIRENEM proposed the creation of a National System of Conservation Areas (SINAC) to begin a process that would integrate protected areas' management and decentralize much of the decisionmak-, ing power to regional levels. Under SINAC, nine Regional Conservation Units (URCs), sometimes called "megaparks," were established throughout the country: Guanacaste, Arenal, Bajo Tempisque, Sí-a-Paz, Cordillera Volcánica Central, Pacífico Central, La Amistad, Península de Osa, and Parques Marinos (see Map 1).

Each URC was composed of areas in one of three land-use categories. First, the "core" areas were those that were subject to absolute protection, such as national parks. Then there were buffer zones—often forests or indigenous reserves—that were multiple-use areas. In some cases, the buffer zones were biologically significant lands under extreme threat, often from new settlement pressures. In other cases, the buffers were already highly populated or had already been converted to agriculture. Finally, lands already in production, such as agricultural areas, also were included in the URCs (see Map 2).

Each URC was headed by a director, who was responsible not only for park management but also for community outreach. To meet outreach objectives, each URC undertook a planning process to define how ecologically and economically sustainable activities could be initiated. Local participation was promoted to ensure that the communities had a voice in the management of protected areas. Thus, committees composed of local leaders and government officials were organized for each region. Scientific and tourism interests were also integrated into the planning process.

The horizontal integration proposed under the URC system emphasized conservation. It was an attempt to respond, at least initially, to the lack of coordination between the forestry department and the park service. It also served to address the more serious and frequent problem of insufficient intergovernmental coordination, leading different national government agencies to unintentionally undermine conservation efforts on a regular basis. For example, the Ministry of Public Works and Transport often built roads near protected areas. New settlers and illegal loggers usually followed; in a short time deforestation near the new roads was significant.

Each URC director was responsible for coordinating the plans of other government agencies within the region, as well as the potential environmental impacts of those actions. For the first time, there was a way to identify and mitigate potentially adverse impacts. The different agencies also began to develop new activities that were responsive to the needs of the local populations and addressed rural poverty. Although low by Central American standards, the existing level of poverty in Costa Rica made it essential that management of protected areas be linked with income-generating activities outside the core protected areas of the URCs.[4]

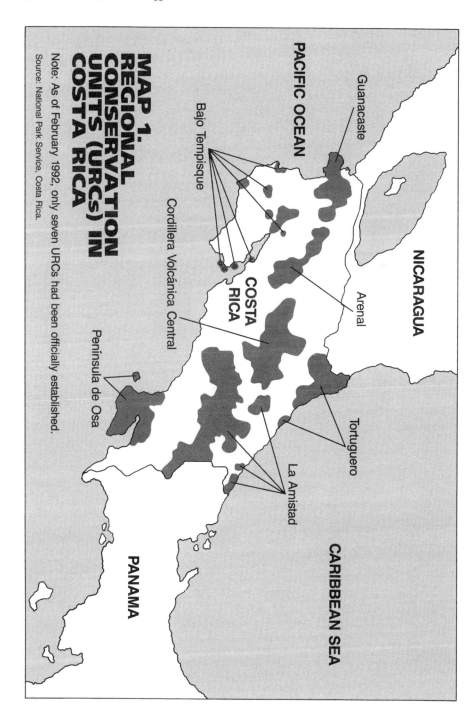

MAP 1.
REGIONAL
CONSERVATION
UNITS (URCs) IN
COSTA RICA

Note: As of February 1992, only seven URCs had been officially established.

Source: National Park Service, Costa Rica.

NICARAGUA

CARIBBEAN SEA

PANAMA

PACIFIC OCEAN

COSTA
RICA

Guanacaste

Bajo Tempisque

Cordillera Volcánica Central

Península de Osa

Arenal

Tortuguero

La Amistad

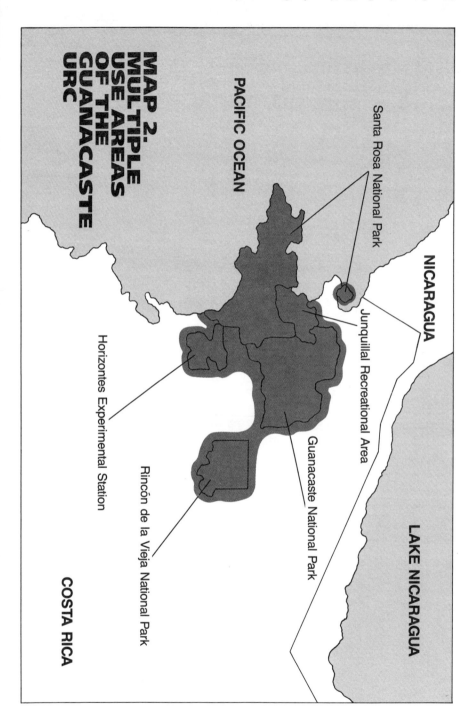

MAP 2.
MULTIPLE
USE AREAS
OF THE
GUANACASTE
URC

PACIFIC OCEAN

Santa Rosa National Park

Junquillal Recreational Area

Horizontes Experimental Station

Rincón de la Vieja National Park

Guanacaste National Park

NICARAGUA

LAKE NICARAGUA

COSTA RICA

Staff of each URC was responsible for developing plans for its region that would not only identify or integrate local community views, but also coordinate regional and national budgets, scientific research plans, and government actions. URC directors began working with local conservation groups, community organizations, and both international and local nongovernmental organizations to incorporate local initiatives, scientists, nature tourism interests, and private conservation efforts in the planning process of the regional units. Government agencies having jurisdiction in each URC began identifying mechanisms to coordinate their activities with one another and with local populations.

Involving local people in the planning process was viewed as essential. For URCs to work over the long term, they had to offer something to nearby communities. In addition, it was hoped that local participation would help to identify what potential economic benefits the protected areas could provide to each URC. Local involvement also developed a new generation of advocates for the environment—at the local level. In many cases, it was difficult to identify appropriate groups to work with or how to work with them. Neither the park service nor the forestry department had a great amount of experience in dealing with rural people.

Potential avenues for participation differed in each URC. Some, such as Arenal and Tortuguero, had well-defined local organizations that were able to identify clearly the priorities in their regions. In other areas, such as the Talamanca region, there was no single group that represented all the interests of the population. Including them in the participatory process was difficult, because it meant coordinating numerous groups with differing views.

Although the creation of the URC system was well received by many international organizations, it was seriously criticized within the Costa Rican government. Objections from the Ministry of Planning (MIDEPLAN), which is officially charged with all national economic planning, were the most significant. This ministry felt that the URC system instituted a regional process that bypassed MIDEPLAN's administrative and planning divisions. MIRENEM successfully argued that the URCs were not "planning" areas but "implementation" units, and it retained management of the protected areas.

As explained earlier, oversight of the URC system was delegated by MIRENEM to the National System of Conservation Areas (SINAC), which is made up of the directors of each URC, and the executive director of the National Biodiversity Institute, as well as representatives from MIRENEM, MIDEPLAN, and the National Parks Foundation. However, SINAC was responsible for reviewing the progress in each of the URCs. It controlled the planning and budgeting process and set priorities for the URC system. SINAC was sometimes criticized for not decentralizing to the extent anticipated.

Following the creation of MIRENEM, it took almost three years to implement the URC system. The planning process for the URCs was ongoing. By the third year, committees in each URC were established and were meeting regularly. When the Arias administration left office, the structure for a unified management system that attempted to reconcile the needs of local people with a national goal of preserving biological diversity was in place.[5] Since 1988, the system has adjusted to changing priorities in both conservation and development but the structure remains essentially unchanged.[6]

New Financing Mechanisms

Without a fresh infusion of funds, MIRENEM and the URC system would have accomplished little. The economic crisis of the 1980s left insufficient money to improve the management of protected areas. While the crisis with the gold miners increased the need to protect other areas from potential invasions, it also drained scarce economic resources even further when the Costa Rican Congress ordered the National Park Service to compensate the miners. In addition, the terms of the structural adjustment loans that Costa Rica had negotiated with the International Monetary Fund (IMF) had led to cutbacks in public-sector employment. As a result, there were fewer people to implement anything—particularly an ambitious and labor-intensive undertaking such as establishment of the URCs.

Furthermore, the government still needed to pay landowners whose properties had been expropriated and converted into parks or reserves. Thus, a major effort was started to reduce the number of "inholdings" (i.e., expropriated lands within parks for which compensation is still due to the owners) and to avoid creating new parks without providing financing for land purchases.[7] Between 1986 and 1990, more than 1 billion colones (some $12 million) was paid for land purchases from budgeted funds, donations, and debt swaps. The number of inholdings was reduced to 10 percent of parklands.

New parks—such as Guanacaste and Arenal—were established using financing mechanisms proposed by MIRENEM: a debt-for-nature program, and, as part of this, an intensive international fund-raising effort, as well as privatizing the financing.

DEBT-FOR-NATURE SWAPS. In 1986, informal negotiations between MIRENEM and the Central Bank of Costa Rica led to agreement on a debt swap mechanism. Over the next two years, the Central Bank approved five different swap agreements or quotas.

In 1987, MIRENEM proposed a debt-for-nature program for which the Central Bank approved the first of these quotas.[8] Various donors contributed over $900,000—equivalent to $5.4 million of Costa

Rica's debt—which generated $4 million in local currency bonds which could be used for conservation projects.[9]

In 1988 Costa Rica proposed the second quota, a specific debt-for-nature swap, to be used for sustainable development activities. In this case, the government of the Netherlands provided financial support and a swap was completed that generated $9.9 million in local currency.[10]

Shortly after negotiations started with the Dutch, a parallel effort was undertaken with the Swedish government to complete and endow Guanacaste National Park—a major conservation project in northern Costa Rica. Swedish students and private conservation groups actively supported the project; the swap supported by the Swedish public and private sources generated over $17 million in local currency that could be used for conservation. Two subsequent swaps generated additional funds for conservation.

In all, over $12 million in grants and donations were used to purchase nearly $80 million of Costa Rica's debt and generate over $42 million in local currency bonds for conservation. The net result was that the Central Bank provided three colones in bonds for each colon donated to Costa Rica.[11]

Costa Rica worked aggressively to obtain donations from friendly governments that would be increased through debt-swap mechanisms. With the active participation of MIRENEM and the Ministry of Planning, as well as the personal support of President Arias, debt swaps elicited strong support in Europe. Additional funds from a variety of donors, primarily U.S. environmental groups and foundations, were converted into local currency bonds from other swaps.

PRIVATIZING URC FINANCING. Another unique feature in the financing of the URC system was that Costa Rica moved control of the funding to the National Parks Foundation (NPF), which is legally a private institution. The Central Bank approved a program that was to be authorized by MIRENEM and carried out through the NPF. All of the money except the Dutch donation was channeled to the URCs through the foundation, which is responsible for receiving contributions and assuring responsible financial accounting and management. Donors were encouraged to identify a specific URC they wished to fund. MIRENEM believed that contributors would be more likely to make long-term commitments to specific lands, where they could see both the challenges and the yearly progress, rather than to a general, country-wide conservation fund. And it was obvious that long-term funding would be needed before sustainable development activities could be implemented in particular URCs. Whenever possible, endowments were created with debt-swap monies to ensure long-term funding for a variety of projects. Another unique feature of the program was that a wide variety of activities could be supported in each URC with the funds: management of protected areas, environmental education, ecological and scientific tourism, and sustainable forestry, as well as purchases made purely for land preservation.

The basic advantage in having the funds channeled through the National Parks Foundation was that it offered increased flexibility and responsiveness. Under Costa Rican law, MIRENEM would have had to budget all expenditures prior to receiving funds or else all donations would have gone to the government's general fund. But, as a private organization, the NPF could receive funds from external sources and then decide, with the URCs, how best to allocate the monies. The intent was to allow URC committees to decide, in conjunction with local communities, what the most urgent needs were at any given point in time.[12]

Using these financing mechanisms, MIRENEM was able to attract substantial resources and thus generate some $100 million for natural resource management, energy, and mines. The debt swaps were worth about $40 million in local currency alone. No other government ministry attracted as much external funding or technical assistance during the period.

However, there have been some problems with the privatization of the URC system. So far, it has not been possible to identify major donors for all of the URCs. In some cases, substantial delays have occurred in securing approval for funds promised by multinational and binational donors. But, overall, the mechanisms for attracting major funding were put into place and successfully captured substantial amounts of money for conservation.

Assessing Costa Rica's Biological Diversity

A final critical element in the policy reform was the adoption of scientific criteria and their integration in the URC planning process—a process that included the participation of specialized technical and scientific groups. The country has a prodigious number of organizations and individuals interested in tropical science, all of whom are keenly interested in improved management of the country's protected areas. This could eventually prove vital to maintaining biological diversity (biodiversity).

Costa Rica is probably the world's largest center of tropical research, with hundreds of scientists carrying on research programs there every year. For example, the Organization for Tropical Studies (OTS)—a prominent scientific research and tropical educational center—represents a consortium of more than 40 U.S. and Costa Rican universities. Each year visiting researchers and students spend more than 30,000 person-days in Costa Rica participating in the organization's programs. In a sense, OTS is one of the largest tourist agencies in the country. But beyond the economic benefits OTS generates through nature tourism, its researchers produce a wealth of scientific information. Yet the results of most scientific research were leaving the country along with the researchers.

To capture as much information as possible, a biological diversity program was formally established within MIRENEM. The local and international scientific communities were incorporated both at the national level, through this program, and at the regional level, through participation in the URC planning process. Thus, Costa Rica was able to base many of its decisions about protected areas on specialized scientific knowledge.

President Arias established a planning commission to explore how a national center for biological diversity could be established. Based on the commission's recommendations, the National Biodiversity Institute (INBIO) was created by presidential decree as a private, nonprofit organization in the fall of 1989. Its objectives are to conduct an inventory of the diversity of the nation's life forms and to analyze the central and potential contributions of biodiversity to society and development. In addition to collecting and identifying Costa Rica's species, INBIO has begun determining the distribution, abundance, habits, and habitats of the species. Because of Costa Rica's small size and enormous variety of habitats, it may be possible to succeed in this task of assessing the country's biodiversity. Beyond simply cataloguing species, INBIO will be analyzing various ways in which this biological wealth can be used to generate socio-economic development.

The creation of INBIO is intended to benefit the country at all levels—from local to national. As part of the data-collection process, INBIO is training people who live in the buffer zones as parataxonomists (people taught to identify species, but lacking the formal education). It eventually hopes to train almost 200 people as parataxonomists throughout Costa Rica. The products ultimately identified because of these efforts are expected to create employment for rural people and to provide economic justification for keeping wildlands intact. At the national level, the discovery of a single major pharmaceutical product could generate enough income for Costa Rica to pay for the management of all the nation's protected areas.

INTEGRATING CONSERVATION INTO THE DEVELOPMENT PROCESS

Costa Rica faced many of the problems common to developing countries trying to manage its natural resource base and develop a system of parks and reserves. In 1986, the country's ability to manage the existing system of parks and protected areas was limited. Overlapping and unclear jurisdictions, serious funding and personnel shortages, an inability of environmental agencies to coordinate with each other or with other agencies, and environmental agencies with insufficient power (compared to that of other government ministries) were major factors inhibiting the government's ability to manage protected areas. Because of clashes between local people and park management agencies, there was a serious "image problem"; people did not expect effective management. As a result, encroaching into and logging of protected areas were increasing.

If anything, Costa Rica's international reputation as a country committed to preserving biological diversity through its parks system made solving these problems more urgent and more difficult. Although the international community held the parks system in high regard, within the country—and especially in rural areas—there was a feeling that the parks served only the "gringo tourists," at the expense of local needs. Any strategy had to solve the system's real problems in a way that would win both international and local approval.

This would not be possible unless new administrative structures were created that would give greater importance to the role of conservation in, rather than apart from, the development process. It meant altering the way decisions were made about natural resources, at both national and local levels, which in turn required significant bureaucratic changes to integrate conservation more effectively into development planning.

Latin America encompasses more than 70 million hectares of protected areas that offer an uncommon challenge to prove that conservation and development can be combined. Costa Rica provides one example of how a country is trying to do this. The key actions (the establishment of MIRENEM, INBIO, and the URC system, as well as creative financing) all result from Costa Rica's unique needs and circumstances. As such, these particular institutions are not necessarily transferable to other countries. But these *kinds* of institutions and their underlying conservation objectives are necessary to further conservation in other Central American countries. The table lists the actions undertaken in Costa Rica to attain specific conservation objectives.

The *actions* and the *processes* that other countries will need to follow may be very different from those followed by Costa Rica. Yet many countries have the same *objectives*. Thus, Costa Rica can serve as a model by demonstrating one way of implementing much-needed reforms that can help create institutions for conservation.

Consolidation and Coordination of Institutions

Costa Rica's first step—the creation of MIRENEM—served to put conservation on a par with other government agencies, thereby giving greater power and credibility to natural resource management. It allowed

TABLE 1. ACTIONS AND THEIR IMPLICIT CONSERVATION OBJECTIVES

1) Consolidation and coordination of institutions: creation of MIRENEM
   - increase legitimacy and power for natural resource management and conservation
   - consolidate natural resource and conservation agencies
   - clarify jurisdictional boundaries
   - improve governmental coordination and planning of natural resource use
   - initiate sector-wide planning linking conservation and development through the National Conservation Strategy

2) Decentralization of park management: development of the URC system
   - improve intersectoral coordination for each region
   - increase local participation in resource planning and use
   - create vertical linkages between local people and government within each region
   - decentralize decisionmaking authority to regional levels
   - demonstrate the direct links between conservation and natural resource use and development practices and policies at local levels

3) New financing mechanisms launched
   - attract funds for conservation through creative mechanisms (e.g., debt swap)
   - align donors with a particular region to ensure long-term funding commitment
   - decentralize control of funds to regional levels to improve the quality of decisionmaking; and
   - privatize overall debt-swap funding through the National Parks Foundation to ensure greater participation

4) Linking tropical science to conservation planning: creation of the National Biodiversity Institute (INBIO)
   - systematize and capture research and development activities under way nationwide
   - link tropical research to protected areas system and its management
   - identify economically valuable species and ways to generate rural income
   - provide an official mechanism for public/private sector collaboration on research and development

the government to consolidate management functions scattered among different agencies into one ministry. Although the legal integration of these agencies (e.g., the forestry department and the National Park Service) was not possible, President Arias's support made creative solutions to these obstacles possible. MIRENEM could keep separate budgets to meet legal requirements but integrate staff to meet practical needs with authority.

The same problems and needs with respect to natural resource management exist in many other countries. What Costa Rica did—consolidating and enhancing the power given to natural resource management—is possible, and needed, in many other nations. The *way* Costa

Rica did it, and the speed with which such changes were made, may be difficult to achieve in other countries. However, to the extent it is possible, the establishment of strong natural resource management and environmental agencies should be encouraged.

Nicaragua has recently transformed its natural resource management agency into a ministry. It hopes that, as was the case in Costa Rica, 1) a minister can more effectively represent the case for natural resource management than can an agency head, and that 2) the consolidation of different management agencies into one ministry will lead to improved coordination. Other Central American countries are moving in this direction and beginning to combine wildlife and park agencies, for example. But the kind of sweeping reform achieved in Costa Rica—linking the park management agency, the wildlife service, the forestry department, the mining sector, and the energy department—has yet to be made elsewhere.

Decentralization of Park Management

Many Latin American countries have acted to protect their natural heritage by establishing a system of protected areas. Some countries, such as Costa Rica, started the process a few decades ago, while others have moved more recently. Throughout Central America "officially gazetted protected areas have increased from only 30 in 1970 to more than 230 by 1990."[13] Many of these newly established parks and equivalent reserves rival those of some developed nations in their ecological representation and the percentage of land protected. However, in most countries it is easier to legally guarantee park protection on paper than to guard against encroachment by loggers, ranchers, poachers, farmers, and squatters. It is estimated that nearly three-quarters of the protected areas in Latin America are not effectively safeguarded, and that an even larger percentage lack long-term management plans and financial resources needed to guarantee their perpetuity.

In many nations, parks and reserves are administered by a central bureaucracy, often without adequate knowledge of local conditions or sensitivity to local cultures. The parks are policed by rangers who distrust local people and perceive them as threats. Far from being sympathetic to conservation objectives, rural communities often see national parks and reserves as enemies or threats to their future. The fact that governments have had to evict poor people living in or near biologically significant areas to create parks only ensures that relations between parks and local communities are seldom positive.

Creating the URC system in Costa Rica required careful balancing of many competing interests. The system was intended to ensure that conservation policies give priority to rural development and to the basic needs of neighboring communities. This was seen as essential for the long-term survival of the URC units. Within the units, projects that provide *multiple benefits*—social, economic, and ecological—and encourage the protection of irreplaceable natural resources were given high priority, followed by efforts that would promote sustainable solutions to rural problems. The vision was that the URCs would allow the entire spectrum of needs to be addressed—from consolidating national parks and reserves to providing sustainable livelihoods for local people.

The URC system was designed to forge links between government agencies and sectors such as planning, health, and public works. It was also created to encourage an interchange between the government and local communities. It decentralized the decisionmaking power to these communities in the hope that local people would become better managers of the resources in their URC if they participated in an inclusive decisionmaking process that involved diverse interest groups in each region. Although the system was in place by 1990, the processes that will make "sustainable development" work—such as local participation, actual decentralization of decisionmaking, integration and coordination of government programs, and integration of conservation and development needs—will not function at maximum effectiveness for years. It is too early to see clear results from such an ambitious undertaking. However, linking conservation and development in biologically significant areas through participatory approaches is now being seen as one of a very few options for preserving biological diversity.[14]

Costa Ricans are literate and comfortable expressing strong opinions to the government without fear of reprisals. The URC system, at least in theory, could open the floodgates for endless citizen demands for the government to act on a host of sensitive issues: land tenure, services, and the generation of rural employment. Because the rural poor are unafraid to make such requests and the government is willing to listen, there is reason to hope that the system could be successful. As the URC system begins to function, the government may be unable to respond to all of the demands that arise across the country. But to achieve change, local populations must articulate their needs. And, at the same time, the ways in which protected areas can meet or hinder these needs must be determined.

A number of limited experiments, resembling individual URC units, are under way elsewhere in Central America. No *system* for an entire nation has been adopted; in most countries, the closest parallels to the URCs are cases in which governments have turned over responsibility for a specific protected area to a nongovernmental organization (NGO). For example, in Guatemala, an NGO called Defensores de la Naturaleza (Defenders of Nature) took over management of the Sierras de las Minas Biosphere Reserve in 1990. The Guatemalan government is likely to relinquish management of other protected areas to different NGOs. In principle, these groups may begin encouraging not only increased local participation in the management process, but improved coordination between government and private sectors as well. The Honduran government also has turned over management of protected areas to two different nongovernmental organizations.

Conservation initiatives under way in Guatemala and Honduras—if pushed beyond the protection of single sites—could lead to the creation of a URC system similar to that of Costa Rica. In other nations, a national system could be established by the government. Costa Rica's URCs will provide a great deal of information to countries on both the effectiveness and inherent limitations of such a system. The essential ingredient will be persuading nations to move beyond the rhetoric of encouragement to actually beginning the processes of participation and decisionmaking. The URC system highlights the need for improved intergovernmental coordination and simultaneous planning for protected areas and buffer zones.

New Financing Mechanisms

Financing to support conservation is needed in virtually all countries. Few nations will be able to attract the levels of external resources that Costa Rica has. But securing additional funds for conservation through mechanisms such as debt swaps could be greatly expanded throughout Central America.[15] The barriers to these arrangements—their inflationary potential, the difficulty in defining an acceptable "package" of financial terms for swaps, the scarcity of donors, finding local and international nongovernmental organizations able and willing to participate, and the limited capacity of many organizations to absorb large amounts of additional financing—can be surmounted in most cases.

The extent to which other Central American governments would be willing to create regionally based endowments for conservation is unknown, but there is a clear indication that many are interested. In Nicaragua, the government established the National Commission for the Environment and Land-Use Planning (CONAMOR), an interinstitutional commission on the environment and land use that is housed in the economics ministry. Among its responsibilities are developing priorities for foreign-aid assistance and soliciting debt-for-nature swaps.[16]

The Costa Rican government encouraged the "privatization" of funds to finance conservation in the country. To follow suit, other governments must be willing to lose direct control of substantial amounts of money generated through debt swaps by helping to secure and then turn over management of these funds to a freestanding nongovernmental organization, such as the National Parks Foundation. It is uncertain that other governments will be willing to follow Costa Rica's example. But lack of government initiative does not mean that innovative financing mechanisms cannot be developed.

For example, World Wildlife Fund-United States and three Guatemalan NGOs have agreed to establish the Trust Fund for Conservation in Guatemala. The fund would be endowed with an initial debt swap of $1 million, to be increased up to $5 million. Interest from the fund will be used to endow permanently a variety of projects throughout Guatemala, from technical studies to site-specific projects. The trust's board is composed of representatives from World Wildlife Fund and from the Guatemalan NGOs. It also includes a nonvoting government representative. The board may be increased to nine voting members.

In Costa Rica, this money is administered by regionally based committees, which greatly enhances the opportunity for local groups to act on their own decisions. Such a system limits the transferability of the Costa Rican experience to countries willing to delegate decisionmaking authority below national levels. But it is possible that the initiatives under way in Guatemala and Honduras aimed at decentralizing park management will lead to greater local and regional control over financing.

Linking Tropical Science to Conservation Planning

The creation of the National Biodiversity Institute (INBIO) in Costa Rica resulted from the need to consolidate in-country technical expertise in tropical science, as well as to stop the loss of scientific research and knowledge. Through INBIO, Costa Rica has embarked on an unprecedented systematics and ecological exercise with the expectation that the findings will 1) augment national pride and knowledge, and 2) bring substantial revenues that will help link conservation and economic development. But with a largely literate population, good universities, and in-country scientific groups, Costa Rica begins this exercise from a position of strength, relative to many developing nations. It also has long been a magnet for tropical research.

The creation of INBIO is the one aspect of reorganization of natural resource management that could most easily be replicated in other countries. Although its implementation depends on locating large amounts of outside support, it is the least "political" of the initiatives that Costa Rica undertook. At present, no other institution comparable to this institute exists elsewhere in the world. Thus, Costa Rica's experience in establishing INBIO, gathering biological data, training parataxonomists, and working with private-sector companies could be transferred elsewhere.

CONCLUSION

Costa Rica's efforts demonstrate that sustainable development will require creativity, innovation, and the capacity to implement new programs and policies. In many cases, this will mean adapting or establishing the institutional structures to implement new processes, reforms, and laws that link conservation and development. These institutions should be flexible, yet able to control effectively natural resource use. They should be able to forge bonds between different government sectors and create new alliances within regions. And, finally, they should be willing to encourage widespread local participation and decentralize decisionmaking to local and regional levels.

Costa Rica made a variety of changes in *how* natural resources and conservation are administered within the country. All of these reforms were designed to decentralize decisionmaking. Only a small part of what ultimately will be required for the nation to match the "sustainable development vision" set forth in the National Conservation Strategy has been accomplished thus far. But the fact that such a vision exists, and that a national government has embraced it and set out goals for achieving it, is significant. The Costa Rican government has set a standard by which others can be judged in the future. It is also noteworthy that Costa Rica has shown the creativity and initiative to promote actively a system that will lead to change. The basic structure is in place to reflect the enhanced role of conservation as a necessary component of development.

Notes

[1] These strictly protected areas will be called "parks" throughout the chapter; other protected mixed-use areas, and parks generally, will be referred to as protected areas.

[2] These protected areas are significant because of the unique ecosystems and flora and fauna that they contain, which in many cases, are found nowhere else in the world. Enforcement of regulations regarding permissible uses is strongest in these areas, and in most cases, the only types of uses allowed are controlled tourism and scientific research.

[3] Although the Ministry of Agriculture did not lose the park service, it did not want to part with the forestry department. There were also discussions about transferring the Fisheries Agency from the Ministry of Agriculture to MIRENEM. But in the ensuing bargaining process that was needed to create MIRENEM, fisheries remained in the agriculture ministry.

[4] Although Costa Rica's rural quality of life is above that of other Central America countries, estimates for the 1980s suggested that 20 percent of the rural population lived in absolute poverty, over half lived in poverty. See H. Jeffrey Leonard, *Natural Resources and Economic Development in Central America* (Washington, DC: International Institute for Environment and Development, 1987), p. 76.

[5] In May 1991, MIRENEM sent a draft law to congress to reform the National Parks and Forestry laws and to consolidate legally the National System of Conservation Areas.

[6] The Calderon government did, however, change the name to Regional Conservation Areas (ARCs).

[7] In June 1991, the Costa Rican Supreme Court ruled that land expropriated by the government and converted to parks without payment to the owners would revert to the people who owned it prior to its expropriation.

[8] In this arrangement foreign-currency-denominated obligations are to be repaid to their holders in local currency, or with local-currency-denominated instruments, on the condition that the proceeds *will* be used to purchase equity in some predefined domestic investment project.

[9] Debt-for-nature swaps are similar to debt-for-equity swaps. Typically, an international organization purchases a country's foreign debt at its disounted market value. The title for this debt is exchanged for new domestic currency obligations that are used to finance conservation programs. The specific terms of this program were 75 percent of face value, 25 percent average interest, and five-year maturity.

[10] These were converted by Costa Rica's Central Bank at 33 percent of face value, but with a maturation of four years maximum and interest rates at 15 percent per annum.

[11] The alchemy of debt-for-nature swaps means that the colones injected into the economy by local currency bonds can have a significant inflationary effect. To minimize the inflationary impact, the bonds are non-negotiable and only interest and principal payments are monetized bonds, or less than 50 percent of face value. From this perspective, the Central Bank of Costa Rica and the orginal donor have shared the discount obtained in the purchase of debt titles in secondary markets. If titles are purchased for close to 15 cents on the dollar, the Central Bank can match the grant on a three to one basis and still pay less than 50 percent of the face value of the title, thereby reducing future interest payments on this amount.

[12] Another example of the use of debt-swap funds was the Dutch Sustainable Development Debt Swap, described elsewhere. The purpose of the swap was to create an endowment for reforestation and sustainable development with social interest groups such as cooperatives and farmers' organizations throughout Costa Rica. From 1989 to 1990 nearly 4,000 hectares were planted by these groups using funds generated by interest payments on the local currency bonds. The bonds are held in an escrow account, and the utilization of interest payments was determined jointly by MIRENEM and MIDEPLAN, in consultation with the Dutch Government. These local resources have also been used to strengthen a variety of local nongovernmental organizations. The endowment has also created employment for more than 500 individual beneficiaries.

[13] Steve Cornelius, "Wildlife Conservation in Central America: Will it Survive the 90's?" Proceedings of the North American Wildlife and Natural Resource Conference, *Transactions*, Vol. 56, pp. 40-49.

[14] M. Wells and K. Brandon, *People and Parks: Linking Protected Area Management with Local Communities* (Washington, DC: World Bank, 1992).

[15] The Costa Rican experience has already served as a model for debt swaps in Ecuador, the Dominican Republic, and most recently in Mexico and Brazil.

[16] Cornelius, op. cit., p. 12.

Chapter Four

Equity and the Environment in the Promotion of Nontraditional Agricultural Exports

Stuart K. Tucker

INTRODUCTION

In the field of development, diversification of exports is today's rallying cry, and Central America has finally responded by pursuing an export-led development strategy.[1] One thrust of this approach is rapid expansion of labor-intensive manufacturing exports, especially clothing, footwear, handbags, handicrafts, and wood products.[2] Yet, for these largely agrarian societies, new, nontraditional agricultural exports not only must play the primary role but also are now touted by aid donors and recipients as pivotal to the region's development strategy for the rest of the century. Most of the efforts of external aid donors will be aimed at assisting this approach.[3]

Central America's five major traditional export crops (coffee, cotton, beef, bananas, and sugar) face volatile world prices, stagnation in demand, and a world of foreign competitors. Meanwhile, other Central American agricultural crops, particularly fruits and vegetables, offer the prospect of growing markets and fewer competitors. Because the five traditional export crops dominated the economy for many decades, the new-comers are being called "nontraditionals." They mainly include winter vegetables and fruits, nuts, exotic tropical fruits, and ornamental plants and flowers, most of which are shipped overseas fresh or chilled.

This chapter argues that diversification into nontraditional agricultural exports can be good for development, in theory. However, if current policies continue, such exports will tend to intensify both existing income inequities and environmental damage.

The export of nontraditional crops is a necessary element of a successful medium-term development strategy for Central American countries. Producing corn and beans for domestic consumption offers little chance of alleviating poverty, as the population is growing far faster than is the productivity of these crops.[4] Commercial cash crops may offer the kind of economic opportunities needed to improve the human condition, but only if global supply and demand favor continued production growth. On the other hand, nontraditional agricultural exports provide large returns on investments and can yield high earnings in the future. Certainly, a community's income from producing export crops would far exceed what is required to buy food for those people who once grew the food crops but have switched to cultivating nontraditionals.

If Central America's rural poor are to sustain the environment, while simultaneously escaping their poverty, they will need alternative sources of income that are derived from existing agricultural lands. Limited production choices lead the poor to destroy and pollute their surroundings. At the same time, environmental degradation undermines the ability of impoverished people to support themselves. If properly designed, a nontraditional export strategy offers hope that this vicious cycle can be broken.

There are pitfalls to this strategy. The production and export of nontraditional agricultural crops is neither environmentally nor socially neutral. The so-called new panacea could be a pandora's box, releasing numerous ills into developing societies: food-import dependency, uncertain export markets for producers of the new crops, environmental damage from new cropping patterns, income inequities, concentration of land holdings as well-to-do farmers acquire property for growing nontraditional products, over delegation of government-agency authority to private actors, and diversion of U.S. foreign aid away from the social needs of the many and toward commercial profits for the few.

Unless current policies are dramatically altered, the pressure to increase nontraditional agricultural exports may exacerbate rural poverty and thereby indirectly contribute to environmental degradation. Central Americans and their aid donors need to implement policies that will strike a balance between efficiency, equity, and environmental conservation. To pursue any one of them and neglect the others will lead to nonviable production choices. The challenge is to alter public and private practices to overcome the obstacles that currently prevent nontraditional agriculture from benefiting everyone and being environmentally sound.

This chapter discusses the social and environmental concerns surrounding nontraditional agricultural exports, particularly in Costa Rica,

Guatemala, and Honduras. Policies are analyzed and recommended to establishing a strategy for the export of nontraditional agricultural crops that includes the alleviation of poverty.

THE PROMISE OF NONTRADITIONAL CROPS

When viewed from the perspective of reducing rural poverty, nontraditional agricultural exports seem to be ideal. A large number of crops are being investigated for their potential as exports.[5] The varying climate and seasonal requirements of these products give farmers many choices of what to cultivate. Consequently, for poor farmers with scarce capital and little resources, nontraditional alternatives hold the promise of a higher income than do the domestic food crops they have previously grown. In fact, the number of new crops being developed in Costa Rica, Guatemala, and Honduras is impressive (see Table 1).

The majority of nontraditional agricultural exports are off-season fruits and vegetables that sell well in the United States from October to March. In industrial countries the primary markets for this produce are airlines, luxury hotels and restaurants, and upper-income families in major cities (although the growth in U.S. demand for many of these products appears to be broadening because of rising health consciousness).

Tropical fruits, such as pineapples, passion fruits, melons, limes, and oranges, have been exported for decades. However, winter fruits grown in the highlands, such as strawberries, blackberries, raspberries, and boysenberries, are relatively new exports, as are off-season vegetables—mainly snow peas, broccoli, squash, and brussel sprouts. Even some of the farmers in remote sections of western Honduras are growing apples and pears for shipment to neighboring El Salvador. In efforts to diversify from coffee trees to a similar type of crop, nut trees (macadamia, for instance) have been introduced throughout Central America. Costa Rica has capitalized on its biological diversity by entering the business of shipping flower seeds and live plants to American and European plant markets.

In Costa Rica, where nontraditional agricultural crops are being most rapidly adopted, export success has been striking. Although production started from a small base, Costa Rican vegetable and fruit exports (excluding bananas) to the United States achieved a growth rate of 31.5 percent annually from 1983 to 1990 (see Table 2). If current trends prevail in Costa Rica's trade with the United States, in 1996 the country's fruit and vegetable exports alone will surpass the combined total for its major traditional agricultural exports of coffee, sugar, bananas, and beef. In addition, Costa Rican ornamental plant shipments to the United States

TABLE 1. NONTRADITIONAL AGRICULTURAL EXPORT PRODUCTS IN CENTRAL AMERICA 1990

	Costa Rica	Guatemala	Honduras
Vegetables			
Asparagus	●	●	●
Black pepper	●		●
Broccoli	●	●	
Brussel sprouts		●	
Cabbage		●	
Cauliflower	●	●	
Chayotes (vegetable pears)	●	●	●
Chile peppers	●		
Cucumbers		●	●
Endive and lettuce		●	
Garlic		●	
Miniature squash		●	○
Miniature corn		●	○
Onions		●	
Parsley		●	
Small cucumbers		●	
Snow peas		●	○
Spinach		●	
Tomatoes	●	●	●
Fruits			
Apples			●
Aromatic fruit trees			●
Avocados			●
Blackberries and blueberries		●	○
Citrus fruits, including oranges	●	●	●
Coconuts	●		
Grapes		●	
Mangoes	●	●	●
Melons	●	●	●
Peaches			●
Pears			●
Persimmon		●	
Pineapples	●		●
Plums			●
Strawberries	●	●	●
Watermelons	●	●	●
Other			
Cacao	●		●
Cashews			○
Cut flowers	●	●	●
Macadamias	●	●	
Ornamental ferns	●		
Rice		●	
Vanilla		●	
Yucca	●		

Note: ● = established; ○ = being investigated or developed
Source: Author's survey of literature, interviews, and field observations.

TABLE 2. CENTRAL AMERICAN NONTRADITIONAL AGRICULTURAL EXPORTS TO THE UNITED STATES

Export Values	1983 ($ millions)	1983 (percent of all exports)	1990 ($ millions)	1990 (percent of all exports)	Annual Average Percentage Change[a] 1983-1990
Costa Rica	14.5	3.2	98.5	9.8	31.5
Guatemala	16.0	4.0	53.8	6.8	18.9
Honduras	12.3	2.8	23.8	4.8	9.9
Total, Above	42.8	3.3	176.1	7.7	22.4
Total, Central America	49.6	2.8	208.2	8.0	22.3

Physical Volume	1983 ('000 cwt)	1983 (percent of which pineapples)	1989 ('000 cwt)	1989 (percent of which pineapples)	Annual Average Percentage Change[a] 1983-89
Costa Rica	95	88.4	2147	55.5	68.1
Guatemala	145	2.8	938	0.0	36.5
Honduras	742	89.8	1425	21.2	11.5
Total, Above	982	76.8	4510	33.1	28.9
Total, Central America	1007	74.9	4827	31.0	29.8

Note: Data do not include bananas.

Source: U.S. Department of Commerce and U.S. Department of Agriculture, unpublished data.

rose at a rate of 17.3 percent annually from 1983 to 1989. The growth rates for all of these nontraditional products far exceed the 3.6 percent annual growth achieved by the nation's primary traditional export crops.[6]

Advantages of Nontraditional Crops for the Poor

In theory, nontraditional agricultural products assist in alleviating rural poverty in three significant ways. First, and most valuable, is that such crops can be produced where the poor live—in the highlands and transitional watershed areas—and most can be grown on small plots. Because of the varying seasons, it is possible to rotate different crops throughout the year, thus helping to preserve soil nutrients and reduce erosion. In this way poor people may be able to intercrop nontraditionals with their usual corn and beans. The extra income helps them to stay on their parcels of land, despite economic and environmental pressures to leave.

Second, nontraditional agricultural production provides employment for the landless during harvest time, as pickers and packers. Delicate fruits, vegetables, and flowers are not as amenable to mechanical harvesting as traditional crops are, and picking is labor-intensive work. Women also can play a greater role in this stage of production, because manual dexterity, not strength, is the necessary attribute. As more women have numbered among the landless poor since 1980, nontraditional agriculture fulfills a crucial socioeconomic role by providing much-needed employment.

Third, many of these new crops mature relatively quickly. Unlike coffee trees, most nontraditional plants do not require years of growth before a significant harvest allows farmers to recover their initial investments. Production experiments can be conducted involving only a short-term gamble, thereby encouraging even hesitant poor farmers to investigate export crops. Thus, entrance into international production entails less risk than do other cash crops.

OBSTACLES TO EASING POVERTY THROUGH NONTRADITIONAL AGRICULTURE

Despite the potential benefits for Central America of cultivating nontraditional crops, there are a number of problems associated with their production, marketing, and export that create doubts about the likelihood that such agriculture will help reduce poverty. Businessmen throughout the region cite transportation, credit, and pesticide residue regulations in foreign markets as the most significant problems, but no one's list stops with these three. Rich producers can afford to find ways past such bottlenecks, but for the poor the problems may be insurmountable. In the near term the focus on nontraditional crops may actually exacerbate poverty. The role of U.S. and regional public policy will be crucial in overcoming these problems.

Adopting New Crops

Making the decision to gamble on new and different crops is certainly the first obstacle to switching to nontraditional agriculture. Farmers need to know about the available seed varieties and their cultivation requirements. Worldwide agricultural studies generally concentrate on food crops or on temperate zone crops, devoting scant resources to nontraditional cash crops, especially those that can be grown in the tropics by poor people. Most agricultural research is conducted within universities of the industrialized world, where the major concerns are not productivity on volcanic hillsides in Central America. Moreover, research efforts of the region's institutes and governments are frequently underfunded. Although there has been progress in Central America to encourage greater investigation of nontraditional plants [for example, at the Tropical Agricultural Research and Training Centre (CATIE) in Costa Rica], dissemination of these efforts into rural areas has been slow; benefits extend primarily to farmers with large holdings.

Throughout the region agricultural extension services are inadequately funded and irrelevant to the needs of most poor farmers. In practice, "extension information" is frequently offered by local store owners who convey self-serving data provided by manufacturers of agricultural inputs such as fertilizers. Too few lessons have been widely taught regarding successful low-input or traditional production techniques (i.e., using little water, fertilizer, or other chemicals). Programs such as *Campesino a Campesino* in Nicaragua, in which small farmers disseminate information and teach others how to experiment with low-input farming, have not been replicated on a larger scale. Although these programs emphasize subsistence crops, they also provide small-scale farmers with a basis upon which to expand into nontraditional cash crops.

The most successful producers of nontraditional crops are those who have access to appropriate information on such crops. Often large exporters aided by foreign investors assist growers. The pattern developing throughout Central America is that production information originates abroad and gradually reaches the villages—but only when large growers and intermediate shippers find that such knowledge sharing can be useful to establishing supplier networks. The U.S. Agency for International Development (USAID) has attempted to finance the dissemination of such information, but efforts in the 1980s largely bypassed rural subsistence farmers. Farmers' cooperatives exist in some places, meeting the needs of small-scale cultivators for appropriate information. However, even co-ops are heavily dependent on help from exporters.

Even if farmers are aware of production methods for a nontraditional crop, market timing is crucial. For example, until recently Guatemalan growers of winter vegetables were highly dependent on the price and quantity estimates of a handful of shippers (who for the most part did not make up a "competitive" market). Small farmers' ignorance of prices in Miami led to frequent cases of price fraud in winter vegetable sales. However, by establishing their own export cooperative, a group of farmers in the central highlands near Guatemala City was able to improve competition when its crops were purchased by intermediaries. The group's efforts forced commercial middlemen to give growers better prices (and not just to the co-op). This phenomenon—of imperfect competition among middlemen—is repeated for virtually every type of nontraditional agricultural export. Yet there are also too few "success stories" about introducing real competition for the products of small growers.

Another problem concerns estimating the quantity that the market will demand. Generally, farmers take all the risks during the growing season and then must find exporters to purchase their produce at harvest time. The volatility and risk in nontraditional production creates a chaotic situation for growers; they have no guarantees that they will locate a buyer who will export. Because the local market demands very low amounts of nontraditional crops, it can absorb only large quantities of such produce at a fraction of the price an exporter will pay. Growers will incur large losses if the export buyers cannot sell their crops and, consequently, decide not to purchase their crops. Poor farmers have the least access to information to make judgements about market demand for nontraditional produce.

With the most sought-after export crops, such uncertainties can be reduced through guaranteed purchase agreements between exporters (who supply the production inputs) and farmers (who promise to deliver the harvest to them). However, in an imperfectly competitive market, this innovation has been distorted by pricing schemes that discriminate against the small farmer. Exporters claim that these purchase agreements are the only way to ensure the quality and quantity controls necessary for export shipments, but the result is that they exclude the poorest farmers from export sales opportunities.

Production Problems

The need for capital and for information on cultivating nontraditional crops presents all but insurmountable obstacles to significant increases in the production of nontraditional exports by poor farmers in Central America.

INITIAL CAPITAL REQUIREMENTS. There is a striking contrast between the initial capital investment needs of traditional and nontraditional crops. Using traditional methods, a Honduran grower of corn or beans requires about $130-160 per hectare annually.[7] Using more modern techniques to produce corn or beans, the farmer needs about $190 per hectare—an increment within the range of an innovative small-scale farmer. The jump to nontraditional crops, however, is a quantum leap. For example, the cost of growing cucumbers, grapefruits, pineapples, and cantaloupes under traditional methods is about $1,000 per hectare. In contrast, high-yielding, high-quality technological techniques for cultivating pineapples and cantaloupe can require $2,000 to $4,000 per hectare. Guatemalan growers of raspberries and blackberries must invest about $1,000 per hectare, if they plant a minimum of 10 hectares. Strawberries cost about $3,000. Asparagus is considered a "starter" crop by Guatemalan export promoters. Yet, the minimum requirements are estimated to be 20 hectares and $520 per hectare (and the rate of return is much smaller than that for the more capital-intensive crops). These high initial investments may not daunt medium-sized coffee growers, who typically expect to spend close to $2,000 per hectare in initial capital and need more than $700 per hectare in annual working capital. (And they then must wait several years before the coffee trees reach maturity.) However, investments of this magnitude are beyond the reach of poor farmers accustomed to raising corn and beans.

Such large capital requirements have not impeded relatively well-do-to investors in Costa Rica (foreigners and banks account for about half the investments in the nation's production of nontraditional crops). Elsewhere, growers seek dependable credit. In fact, in Honduras and Guatemala the primary problem for farmers is the failure of credit markets. The high rates of return that growers can reasonably anticipate should be sufficient to garner investor or banker support. Nevertheless, governmental credit institutions in these two countries have been unable to respond adequately. They have cumbersome loan authorization processes; they are too centralized to be available to farmers in most of the countryside; they do not have the information necessary to assess the risks that growers encounter; and they are short of funds. In some cases corruption and theft in the national agricultural institutions are privately acknowledged to be rampant. The result is that loan approval can take up to a year (arriving too late for the short growing cycles associated with nontraditional crops), and most of the recipients are not the small, poor farmers who most need the credit.

LAND REQUIREMENTS. In addition to capital scarcity, a major obstacle for poor farmers is the inequitable distribution of land and the difficulties of acquiring or renting land. Most nontraditional agricultural exports need little land, but some of the crops that require the least amount of initial capital unfortunately do require large areas of land. For example, the Honduran honeydew melon industry has one of the lowest capital per hectare investment requirements (about $250) and one of the highest rates of return. However, a minimum of 500 hectares of land must be sown for the crop to be financially viable. Farms of such size are not typical. To avoid this problem, the melon exporters have actively sought to finance large numbers of neighboring, small-scale growers, binding them into two-way contracts covering supplies and purchasing of output.

OTHER INPUT PROBLEMS. Other production components can be costly as well. For instance, the cost of seed and seedlings is higher for nontraditional crops. However, much of the working capital costs are for technology-intensive inputs (such as irrigation, fertilizers, pesticides, and refrigerated storage) and labor-intensive harvesting and packing.

Nontraditional vegetable crops need more water than do corn and beans and some traditional cash crops, such as cattle and coffee. However, where water is plentiful, transportation often is a problem. As a result, most Guatemalan nontraditional production is being developed near ports and airports, far from low-cost water sources. And Guatemala's remote, water-rich western highlands have yet to see the introduction of more than a few nontraditional exports. Micro-irrigation and roads are expensive, and often infeasible, solutions for the poor.

The lack of reliable electricity is another infrastructural limitation. Many nontraditional exports must be refrigerated. Rural areas in Guatemala and Honduras are exceedingly isolated from dependable electrical grids and refrigerated storage and transport vehicles.

Usually, nontraditional crops also are grown using many chemicals—fertilizers, herbicides, and pesticides—that ward off diseases, pests, and promote growth with more precise timing. Most of these chemicals are available throughout the region. However, the foreign exchange crises that recently plagued Guatemala and Honduras caused the price of these substances to rise faster than final crop prices were rising in local currency. The rural poor, especially when they are far from the main roads, usually cannot afford even minimal amounts of chemicals.

More cost-effective practices—such as integrated pest-management schemes (using fewer pesticides) and nonchemical fertilizing methods—are relatively underutilized in most parts of Central America, though their potential savings could be enormous.[8] Among the underused methods are several techniques that build up the biomass (plant and animal matter) in eroded soil. They include creating rock barriers and planting grasses and trees to improve the water absorption; terracing and contour plowing to stabilize soils; and, especially, growing nitrogen-fixing plant varieties (velvet beans, for example) that can add tons of biomass as well as nitrogen to the soil. These techniques enhance the soil without using chemicals and work well combined with traditional food crops—for instance, intercropping corn, velvet beans, and small experimental quantities of nontraditional vegetable crops. Rural farmers can easily understand these methods, which have been strongly supported by organizations such as World Neighbors, a group that encourages site-specific experimentation with low-input agriculture in Honduras, Guatemala, and Nicaragua.

Unfortunately, the same ignorance that leaves these highly practical techniques untried also leads to abuse of pesticides. As a result, incorrect applications cause local environmental contamination and health hazards and force exporters or customs officials in importing countries to reject produce. Not surprisingly, the technology involved in nontraditional agricultural production is not matched by efforts to improve the education of poor farmers. Private sector and nongovernmental organization activity to increase the access of the poor to appropriate crop-production technologies is only thinly evident in each country.

Marketing Problems

Once a nontraditional crop is harvested, farmers face a series of obstacles in transporting and exporting their produce. First, packaging requirements for fresh or chilled nontraditional produce can be quite specific to the crop involved (such as size-graded containers or packages that allow periodic spraying with water in transit). The industry is so new that there is little choice among packaging suppliers. In addition, it is far from competitive or highly integrated with the export marketers. As a result, small farmers face unfair pricing practices.

Second, Central America's antiquated telephone systems compound these market imperfections. Small-scale producers cannot easily seek out alternatives because of their isolation from business communications networks.

The third and by far most significant barrier to nontraditional agriculture is the weak transportation network. An inability to get goods to the market in a timely manner is the death knell for a fresh-food farmer's business. Throughout Central America, roads that can bear truck traffic are poor or nonexistent. Refrigerated truck services are expensive (when they are available). External transportation links are also underdeveloped, with few local airlines operating freight planes. Foreign refrigerated air shipping services do not pass through the region at convenient times, being geared more for transport away from the United States than into it. Finally, existing Central American national airlines have successfully pressed for regulations that make it difficult for cargo planes returning empty from points in the south to obtain landing permits, although their rates would certainly be low for shipments north to the United States.

ENVIRONMENTAL IMPACTS

The environmental impacts of agricultural production come in two major forms: *direct effects*, which depend upon the specific crop and growing techniques; and even more substantial *indirect effects*, when rural poverty triggers short-sighted production choices aimed purely at survival.

Direct Production Concerns

Much has been made of the problems associated with pesticide use to grow both traditional and nontraditional agricultural products for export.[9] The rate of pesticide use and abuse is high in Central America. (See Appendix, Figure 17.) Producers who cannot afford the chemicals are often incapable of competing in the international marketplace. On the environmental side, strong evidence exists that pesticides applied on nontraditional crops are excessive and likely to cause resistance in the pest populations. Moreover, because of pesticide applications later in the growing cycle than recommended, many harvests retain unacceptable pesticide residues, which result in numerous detentions at the borders of importing countries.

The promotion of nontraditional exports is not the source of pesticide abuse. First, the pattern of pesticide use antedates the interest in nontraditional agriculture. In fact, many traditional crops—especially cotton, bananas, and coffee—have been grown in ways that have contaminated soils with high levels of chemical residues.[10] Indeed, nontraditional tree crops actually can rejuvenate degraded lands over time, by putting nutrients back in the soil.

Second, where producers continue to abuse their land, the behavior has been found to be better correlated with low education and low awareness rather than with the type of crop.[11]

Third, where chemical abuses continue with nontraditional crops, the production structure and relationships with purchasers explain the problem more than do the specific requirements of the crop being cultivated. In particular, individual growers (small or large) have worse records than do those who are in cooperatives or associated with export contracting. The implication of this last pattern is that, as exporters' concerns about pesticides increase, the least-educated, least-organized farmers are the ones who lose contracts, thereby reinforcing the unequal gains among nontraditional producers.[12]

Finally, Central American pesticide laws in general are not lax (with the exception of Honduras). Of course, in many countries, enforcement is difficult. Substantial amounts of chemicals are illegally repackaged in poorly identified containers before being distributed to producers.

In such cases the suppliers, not the growers, should be blamed for the misapplications.

Another concern regarding the environmental impact of nontraditional production is that it will cause over-intensive use of land. This fear is largely unfounded. Because of crop rotation and higher profits, farmers should find fewer, not more, reasons to overuse their land or extend production into marginal areas or forests. On the grounds of preventing soil erosion and deforestation, nontraditional agriculture should have a net environmental benefit. This is especially true when cattle ranching (often land-expensive) is replaced by nontraditional tree crops, which is now occurring in overgrazed areas of Costa Rica. Indeed, nontraditionals can be an economical way to reclaim cattle pastures. Furthermore, the soil needs of the new crops require farmers to replenish the soil nutrients—they cannot be grown by slash-and-burn techniques that diminish land quality after short periods of cultivation.

On the other hand, the irrigation and chemical needs of many nontraditional crops can lead to runoff of pollution into waterways. This is a less significant concern in the many water-abundant regions in Guatemala and Costa Rica, where the toxicity of chemicals is usually diluted to nonhazardous levels, but it cannot be so easily ignored elsewhere.

The largest environmental pitfall of nontraditional crops is the potential for the rural poor to still cultivate such crops using damaging techniques, even though they have little prospect for securing export contracts. Unless these poor farmers receive the information they need to grow the crops in an environmentally sound manner, the produce they sell locally will most certainly be highly contaminated.

In principle, the private sector has an interest in assisting with the dissemination of production information to the poor who will be the growers of their country's exports. Supply contracts with poor farmers may overcome the tendency of such growers to cultivate contaminated produce. The danger is that the private sector may instead concentrate export efforts among the largest producers. This may be bad for the environment if it leads to forms of land-ownership (such as share-cropping) that do not involve the producers in direct concern for ecological stewardship of the land. (For a more detailed discussion of land tenure and the environment, see Strasma and Celis, Chapter 5.)

Indirect Impact of Poverty

When farmers lack cash income or the landless lack work opportunities, they tend to adopt a variety of survival behaviors that are devastating to the environment.[13] To increase income poor people will farm on very marginal lands, such as on steep slopes, which contributes to soil erosion and the runoff of silt into waterways. They also farmland that may be more suitable as fallow swampland, to the detriment of wildlife and fisheries. Forests are cut to sell timber, to obtain fuelwood, or to increase pastures or croplands. Inattention to soil nutrients and shortcuts on grading the land can lead to severe soil erosion as well as to poor crop quality.

If the poor are desperate enough, they will migrate into virgin forests or protected parklands, where they will use damaging slash-and-burn methods to clear the land. Many will give up farming altogether and join the hordes that descend upon Central America's burgeoning cities, causing further environmental damage in slums receiving little attention from city services.

Consequently, as long as profitable nontraditional production is out of the reach of the poor, or even exacerbates inequities in rural areas, then the environment will suffer. The cultivation of nontraditional crops must be made profitable for poor farmers as well as for rich ones if the indirect environmental effects of poverty are to be effectively combatted. If, instead, an unbalanced focus on exports fails to address the problem of production (and income-generation) by poor people, they will be forced to increase consumption of their natural resources.

The worst-case scenario would result if nontraditional export agriculture distorts land prices and thereby reduces the availability of land for the poor, while government programs are diverted away from poverty-oriented development and, instead, benefit large-scale nontraditional farmers. The effect of such conditions would be that the increasingly desperate rural poor would cause severe environmental degradation.

POLICY FAILINGS IN THE PROMOTION OF NONTRADITIONAL AGRICULTURE

A nontraditional agricultural export strategy that is also pro-environmental and pro-poor will require the reorientation of a number of public policies in both Central America and the United States to remove the obstacles that poor farmers face in adopting and successfully producing nontraditional crops.

Central American Policies

In its desire to boost exports, Central America has sought public policies that would create a better business environment and that would provide exporters with greater incentives. In many respects, however, these "reforms" have produced more problems for the poor than they have solved.

EXCHANGE RATES. Under concerted pressure from the International Monetary Fund, the World Bank, and bilateral aid donors, virtually all of the region's governments have tried to foster a pro-export climate by devaluing their currencies. Adjustments of exchange rates have been incomplete and accomplished at great political cost. In the cases of Guatemala and Honduras, the rate adjustment came in a large, abrupt collapse, causing import prices to jump. The resulting change in the relative prices of agricultural inputs was especially difficult for small farmers to handle. The short-term effect of these price alterations on cash flow represented yet another obstacle to poorer farmers adopting nontraditional crops.

TAX POLICY. Despite the fiscal austerity implemented in the 1980s, a number of tax measures were inaugurated to assist exporters. In Costa Rica, for example, the government established a tax rebate program (Certificados de Abonos Tributarios, or Tax Payment Certificates) to promote export sales. The Costa Rican tax breaks for the export marketers are mostly collected by a very small number of large companies. More than half of the rebates have gone to less than 5 percent of the companies, while 78 percent of the companies have received only 15 percent of the rebates.[14] In Guatemala laws and export taxes were changed to eliminate what had been a series of disincentives to exporters. Though laudable, these actions have reduced the availability of government resources and have consequently aggravated the current government deficit. Accordingly, government expenditures benefiting the rural poor have suffered.

AGRICULTURAL RESEARCH AND EXTENSION. Government activities in agricultural research and extension are notoriously underfunded and overcentralized. Typical of all Central America, most of the Guatemalan Ministry of Agriculture's budget is spent inside the district surrounding the capital and more than half of the extension agents work in the capital. Fiscal pressures have accentuated this problem and, thus, reinforce an agricultural development policy biased toward large growers.

PESTICIDE TESTING. The promotion of nontraditional exports requires the use of pesticides to yield quality produce acceptable in foreign markets. However, local testing facilities are inadequate for the task of helping producers refine their pesticide use. Few residue testing laboratories exist and most lack the up-to-date equipment necessary to warn farmers of pesticide residues that are unacceptable in foreign markets. Also, these laboratories are not able to conduct the kind of wide-ranging field sampling that is needed to identify the location of and reason for the residue problems. Furthermore, all countries in Central America lack a certification system for pesticide application workers. Consequently, chemicals are applied by people with very little knowledge of the dangers to farmers or of the residues that will persist on the harvested produce.

FOOD SAFETY STANDARDS. Compounding the pesticide problem, domestic food safety standards remain lower than U.S. import standards, making it possible (though not very profitable) to dump products on local markets when they cannot meet export requirements. This two-tiered system slows the rate of adjustment to external health and safety standards, thereby damaging Central America's environment and its populations' health.

PESTICIDE USE. In the Guatemalan highlands, where literacy is not widespread, pesticide instructions are often misunderstood. Consequently, the highland poor are gradually being squeezed out of the nontraditional business by richer, better-educated producers who can guarantee exporters a higher rate of acceptance of the goods into the U.S. market, without the exporter having to use expensive product screening to be certain about residue levels.

PUBLIC AGENCY FINANCIAL ACCOUNTABILITY. Government expenditures are poorly tracked in Central America (with the exception of Costa Rica). This lack of public financial accountability hides corruption and makes it difficult to assess the overall effects of government activities in relation to rural development strategies. In general the "have-nots" also do not know who is benefiting from government spending at their expense. As long as this persists, the poor can play but a small role in fostering public policies with broad-based benefits to rural populations.

U.S. Trade and Aid Policies

Begun in 1984, the U.S. Caribbean Basin Initiative (CBI) expands the duty-free treatment of products imported from Central America, thereby overcoming the anti-agriculture bias and the escalating tariff structure that still face other developing countries. The CBI's tariff reductions give Central American exporters of nontraditional produce a preferential advantage over potential competitors in Mexico, South America, Asia, and Africa (see Annex to this chapter). Although the overall results of the CBI preferences have been less impressive than once hoped,[15] the trade advantages for nontraditional products are significant (for example, eliminating 17.5 to 35 percent tariffs on some fruits and vegetables produced in Central America).

Nonetheless, a number of U.S. trade policies as well as aid policies continue to work against Central American exporters, especially the poorest farmers. The U.S. policy failings most relevant to nontraditional agriculture include marketing orders, government-sponsored advertising campaigns, sanitary regulations, aid restrictions, market information activities focused on Central America's big producers, poorly targeted rural credit activities, and inadequate land-tenure policies, all of which are detailed in the following pages.

MARKETING ORDERS. U.S. trade law includes a number of product-specific quality and appearance import requirements, the most significant ones for Central Americans being agricultural marketing orders (see Table 3). Under the Agricultural Marketing Agreement Act of 1937, mini-

TABLE 3. U.S. MARKETING ORDERS RESTRICTING FOOD IMPORTS FROM CENTRAL AMERICA

17 Restricted Products	Eligible, But Not Restricted[a]
Avocados	Apples
Dates (not for processing)	Cucumbers
Filberts (hazelnuts)	Egg Plant
Grapefruit	Green Peppers
Grapes (for table use)	Mangoes
Kiwi Fruit	Pistachios[b]
Limes[b]	
Nectarines	
Olives (not Spanish-style)	
Onions	
Oranges	
Plums	
Potatoes	
Prunes	
Raisins	
Tomatoes	
Walnuts	

[a]Imports may be restricted by federal marketing order standards only if the U.S. producers first impose identical requirements for minimum grade, size, quality, and maturity on their own shipments within the United States.
[b]U.S. producers of limes also benefit from federal research and promotional "marketing" campaigns.
Source: Agricultural Marketing Agreement Act of 1937, as amended.

mum requirements for grade, size, quality, and maturity can be imposed on imports, if U.S. producers impose the same standards on their own shipments within the United States. Thus, if a product is listed in the law and U.S. producers can agree on a uniform set of standards (for part or all of the year), then the U.S. Department of Agriculture will impose the same restrictions on competitors' imports. With the addition of five more products in the 1990 Farm Bill (P.L. 101-624: The Food, Agriculture, Conservation, and Trade Act of 1990), 23 agricultural products are currently eligible for such marketing orders. U.S. producers have chosen not to restrict themselves (nor, therefore, imports) in six of those product categories, but the remaining 17 face such domestic and import shipment restrictions.

These restrictions usually amount to an effort to reduce the number of undersized produce items in bulk shipments, which is justified on the grounds that consumers demand such quality control. In fact, the minimum-size requirements are sometimes waived when special packaging is introduced. The overall economic effect of these orders is to place an expensive packaging burden on producers, thereby minimizing the cost advantages of foreign producers with cheaper labor. Additionally, the standards favor plant varieties more easily grown in the United States. One of the environmental effects of marketing orders with cosmetic standards is that producers (foreign and domestic) use more chemicals in production to help ensure that a higher percentage of their yield meets the standard (since the marketing orders make the shipment of their substandard produce illegal in the U.S. market).

U.S. GOVERNMENT PROMOTIONAL CAMPAIGNS. Promotional advertising campaigns are conducted by the U.S. Department of Agriculture for 12 agricultural product categories, financed by fees on U.S. farmers. These federal research and promotional efforts primarily promote U.S. consumption, but the emphasis is on consumption of *U.S.* food products. This double-edged sword is relevant to Central Americans producing limes and watermelons, as the other 10 products are not grown in the region.

SANITARY REGULATIONS. U.S. sanitary regulations seek to minimize risks to animal, plant, and human health in the United States. Most of these restrictions are in the form of absolute import prohibitions or time-specific quarantines implemented by customs agents. Regulations concerning pesticide residue limits on food are of the greatest importance to nontraditional crop exporters. In recent years numerous Central American food products have been rejected at the border because samples contained harmful levels of pesticide residues. In many cases the pesticides involved have been added to lists of chemicals restricted or banned by the U.S. Environmental Protection Agency (EPA) and the Food and Drug Administration (FDA).

Central American exporters face three problems with U.S. food safety regulations. First, the standard-setting authority is very decentralized. In addition to regulations emanating from the EPA, the FDA, and the U.S. Department of Agriculture, each of the 50 U.S. states has the authority to establish regulations within its own borders. Although the EPA and the FDA coordinate their activities to some extent, the state regulations need not conform to those of the federal government, and in some cases they are more restrictive.

Second, federal chemical residue regulations change rapidly. The typical Central American farmer must make innumerable production decisions well in advance of planting. In the 1980s U.S. regulations frequently changed between the time pesticides were applied and when the product went through customs. Certainly, the United States is justified in quickly implementing important health and safety regulations, but the situation presents an added risk for the producers and investors of nontraditional exports.

Third, the economic risks associated with pesticide residue regulations are compounded by an inadequate process for notifying concerned parties overseas. Most of the blame for this problem can be placed on Central America's weak agricultural extension systems. However, to some extent, the notification process among countries is insufficient. The problem is evident in the actions of Chemonics, a U.S. private consulting group, which has had to establish an information flow on pesticide regulation to support its export promotion programs in the region that are funded by the U.S. Agency for International Development (USAID). Numerous U.S. and Central American private-sector groups identify pesticide regulation issues as their most time-consuming problem as they try to develop nontraditional production and exports. Part of the difficulty stems from the variety of trade names that commercial chemical firms apply to generic chemicals. Consequently, the foreign grower may not be aware of using a restricted or banned product even when being conscientious about checking the notifications.

TRADE-RELATED AID RESTRICTIONS. Two major legislated constraints on U.S. aid policy hinder the potential of USAID to assist in the production of nontraditional agricultural exports. The first of which is a clause in U.S. foreign aid law prohibits that assistance be given to activities that would directly compete with U.S. exports. For agricultural products this restriction is primarily a problem for basic grains, soybeans, and cotton, since the United States does not export most nontraditional crops. However, any agency conflicts over interpretation of this law have been resolved in favor of U.S. Department of Agriculture officials concerned with domestic interests, not USAID officials.[16] Restrictive interpretations of that law will present a greater problem in the future when Central American producers expand their frozen food business, thereby overcoming the seasonal differences that currently reduce their competition with U.S. producers.

The second legislative constraint, and one that is a more immediate drawback, is the outright ban on aid to any citrus industry. Citrus is already being produced in parts of Central America. Yet, large swaths of the region's potential citrus land remain planted in other, less-profitable crops, often without regard to the poor who could be helped through citrus production.

MARKET INFORMATION ACTIVITIES. USAID has been successful in fostering the private-sector contacts needed to further international commerce in nontraditional products. Unfortunately, the exchange of information has concentrated on helping big business associations and their members; few facts have reached small farmers. The USAID-funded PROEXAG project, in particular, has been highly successful in establishing information flows across borders to the Central American business community. Although preliminary efforts of the project centered on large groups of grower associations, success has not been limited to the rich merchant class. The question now is whether or not the information channels that PROEXAG has established can benefit larger numbers of rural farmers than they have in recent years.

RURAL CREDIT. The record on facilitating credit and reducing costs is most unsatisfactory. USAID has been hampered by requirements that its lending be delivered through Central American government agencies, which have a bad record for channeling money to the poor. USAID has sought to reduce interest rates in rural areas by subsidizing private- and public-sector financial institutions. Despite these efforts many Central American businessmen acknowledge that the greatest beneficiaries of agricultural lending have been the bankers, not the poor farmers.

LAND TENURE. Limited access to land remains a major obstacle to the poor. Once the first concern of USAID in the region, land reform is no longer politically feasible. Instead, USAID is currently investigating programs to make credit more accessible to the landless and small property owners wishing to purchase land. The reasoning is that, without a radical change in politics, land tenure will not be altered to benefit the poor. Therefore, alternative means for supporting equitable land ownership must be found, especially as the production of nontraditional crops alters relative local property prices. As John Strasma and Rafael Celis point out in Chapter 5 of this volume, reform of land tax systems is a necessary complement to policies designed to facilitate land ownership by the poor.

However, some officials in USAID favor the "share-cropping approach," that is, leaving large landholdings titled to the wealthy, while providing a short-term production opportunity to those willing to rent the land. The poor would benefit most from growing nontraditional crops on leased land if they also were provided with significant technical assistance. Yet, because rental markets in the region are often exploitative, tenant farmers could be severely "gouged" under such a system—unless it was regulated by the state or confronted by strong, collective organizations of poor farmers.

POLICY RECOMMENDATIONS

The following recommendations for action by Central America and external actors are based on the premise that nontraditional agricultural exports could become important to Central American balance of payments, poverty alleviation, and environmental conservation. These policy changes (summarized *in order of priority* in Tables 4 and 5) may not be inexpensive, quickly accomplished, or even politically palatable. Yet policymakers should recognize that, without policy change, nontraditional agricultural production will tend to exaggerate environmental damage as well as income inequities between the rich and the poor.

TABLE 4. CENTRAL AMERICA'S POLICY STEPS TO ENCOURAGE ADOPTION OF NONTRADITIONAL AGRICULTURAL EXPORTS BY THE POOR

Immediate Actions

	Objectives
1. Create new credit programs directed to the needs and characteristics of small producers.	1. Rectify the current social imbalance of access to credit.
2. Decentralize and strengthen agricultural extension services, incorporating *campesino-to-campesino* teaching methodologies.	2. Strengthen understanding within isolated communities of the possibilities for diversification into nontraditional crops.
3. Regulate business practices of export companies to prevent unfair price discrimination or other oligopolistic practices.	3. Let a true free market develop, in which small producers are assured of fair deals from middlemen.
4. Open government finances to public inspection, especially in the area of agricultural spending.	4. Inform rural constituencies of the potential positive role government programs can play, if demanded.
5. Revise export tax incentives to eliminate costly, trade-distorting incentives for large companies.	5. Establish equitable incentives that help put cash in the hands of poor farmers willing to diversify.

Longer-Term Actions

	Objectives
1. Improve rural feeder roads, trucking fleets, electrical grids, and telecommunications.	1. Eliminate production/marketing bottlenecks resulting from under-investment in rural infrastructures.
2. Reform ministries of agriculture.	2. Root out corruption that deprives rural areas of government services.
3. Promote land reform and secure land tenure.	3. Ensure equitable access of the rural poor to the land they need to produce crops and generate income.
4. Strengthen the access of poor and isolated people to educational services.	4. Increase the ability of the poor to take advantage of opportunities for better work and living standards.
5. Disseminate population planning techniques and supplies.	5. Reduce population pressure on region's diminishing resources.

TABLE 5. ACTIONS BY THE UNITED STATES AND OTHER EXTERNAL ACTORS TO SUPPORT A PRO-POOR NONTRADITIONAL AGRICULTURAL EXPORT STRATEGY

Immediate Actions	Objectives
1. Provide financial assistance to facilitate credit reform and strengthen agricultural extension.	1. Establish more services for poor, small farmers.
2. Provide technical assistance through public administration reform.	2. Eliminate corruption that deprives rural areas of government services.
3. Cease U.S. marketing orders on fruits, vegetables, and nuts.	3. Establish access to the U.S. market unhindered by superficial standards.
4. Cease ban on U.S. foreign aid to citrus growers.	4. Support region's comparative advantage in the citrus trade.
5. Improve the flow (quantity and timeliness) of information on changes in U.S. pesticide regulations.	5. Reduce harmful pesticide practices and minimize unnecessary import detentions and rejections.
6. End restrictions on U.S. foreign aid to developing production that may compete with domestic producers.	6. Support efficient, equitable, and environmentally sound production wherever possible.
7. Conclude GATT trade negotiations to liberalize trade.	7. Quickly implement reductions in tariffs and nontariff barriers against tropical products as well as labor-intensive manufacturing goods.

TABLE 5. (continued)

Longer-Term Actions	Objectives
1. Provide grants for improvements in rural infrastructure (especially roads and electrical grids).	1. Eliminate production/marketing bottlenecks resulting from under-investment in rural infrastructure.
2. Provide technical advice on the reform of agricultural ministries and subagencies.	2. Eliminate corruption that deprives rural areas of government services.
3. Reduce subsidies to domestic farmers that distort world markets.	3. Establish reasonable world-price incentives for developing country farmers.
4. Expand research on and dissemination of integrated pest-management technologies.	4. Cut farm costs, reduce pesticide abuse, and control pest threats thereby making nontraditional agriculture possible for the poor.
5. Support family planning and human-resource training programs.	5. Increase the ability of poor people to take advantage of opportunities for better work and living standards, and reduce the population pressure on Central America's resource.
6. Target research on nontraditional agricultural production problems, especially in Central American climates.	6. Address the production problems faced by a large number of developing-country farmers rather than those of a small number of modern farms in industrial countries.
7. Encourage private research and the development of substitutes for banned chemicals.	7. Develop chemicals that are safe and useful in developing countries.
8. Harmonize worldwide consumer safety standards as they relate to tradeable goods.	8. Improve health in developing countries while minimizing trade conflicts that endanger income opportunities for small farmers.

Central American Action

If Central Americans are committed to implementing a more equitable agrarian development strategy, nontraditional agricultural exports can aid in reducing poverty without destroying the environment as much as the current types of production do. The key actions needed in the region to assist the poor in producing and exporting nontraditional crops are credit reform, improved agricultural extension, improved rural infrastructure, and reformed ministries of agriculture. Additional pro-poor, pro-environment policy changes include regulating export business practices, revising export tax incentives, opening public finances for inspection, regulating land tenure, and improving the poor's access to education and family planning services.

COUNTRY-SPECIFIC POLICY CONCERNS. Costa Rica is fortunate because most of these policy recommendations are not only palatable but also are already either partially in place or high on the agenda of national leaders. Perhaps, then, the nation's most valuable next step is to seek a balance in pursuing nontraditional production. Such agricultural exports should remain no more than a tool for its leaders' broader development goals. The potential for expanding exports is strong but not unbounded. Consequently, Costa Rica would be wise to channel as much of its present success as possible into developing the rest of its economy. The government should moderate its export promotion tax breaks and redirect its concerns to long-standing equity problems in rural areas. In so doing, special care should be taken that the privatization of governmental activities (perhaps laudable because of its efficiency) does not lead to the abandonment of important social goals for the countryside.

Guatemala's situation is one of both success and severe limitations. The undisputed achievements of a handful of producers shipping fresh vegetables out of Guatemala City's airport should become less of an exception and more the rule. Nontraditional agriculture presently remains somewhat marginal to development—even to export earnings. The country's leaders need to seek ways to broaden the base of this strategy, lest the striking income inequities grow. To do this will require a serious look at the operations of the Ministry of Agriculture, especially regarding rural extension and credit. In addition, the infrastructural problems with the telephone system, electricity, and highways—although not as severe as in Honduras—are still glaring impediments to most potential nontraditional crop producers. To embark on such changes, the nation's leaders will have to reverse their historic apprehensions about the highland Indians (race and class warfare—smoldering for decades—has been fueled by arbitrary police actions and other forms of discriminatory public and private activity). Development will come to a halt, poverty will continue to mount, and ecological disaster will follow if old fears dictate government policies in the 1990s. The prosperity of Guatemala's rich can no longer be separated from the fate of the western highlands.

In many ways Honduras has barely begun the process of exporting nontraditional crops. So many of the prerequisites for production and shipment are lacking that the exporters have had great difficulty establishing supply linkages. Some regions are so isolated that their only medium-term export prospects are sales across the border to other impoverished and isolated people in El Salvador or Nicaragua. Even farmers along the country's main highway suffer from major transportation delays because of the road's poor condition and the aging truck fleet. Government agricultural services cannot precede roadway building. Nontraditional exports from the highlands are merely a hope for the future. Thus tax incentives to highland nontraditional crop exporters at this stage would prove fruitless.

Lowland exports of tropical fruit and fish products have better near-term prospects. Consequently, improved transportation to the coast would help the poor find work in lowland ports. This would aid in alleviating poverty and in lessening environmental degradation, both of which would complement the longer-term actions needed to promote nontraditional agriculture.

Industrial-Country Action

Although the preceding major policy recommendations for Central American nations are essential, the United States and other industrial countries can improve their own policies to enhance activities in Central America, thereby helping to improve the opportunities for prosperity, equity, and environmental conservation in the region (Table 5).

U.S. TRADE. Although generally favorable toward Central American trade, U.S. import policies could be more positive. Marketing orders should be ceased entirely. Health and sanitary import standards can be enhanced by moving toward uniform, federally established standards using a more rapid and predictable process of notifying Central American growers about chemical restrictions. Additionally, the clauses in foreign-aid legislation prohibiting assistance to competitors—such as foreign citrus producers—should be eliminated, or at least targeted at only "high-tech" manufacturing.

INTERNATIONAL TRADE COOPERATION. A successful and rapid conclusion of the Uruguay Round of multilateral trade negotiations through the General Agreement on Tariffs and Trade is the best way to ensure that global trade liberalization continues. To complement trade liberalization, U.S. government expenditures on domestic farm programs should be converted into income supports for farmers that are not tied to production levels. After the Round, governments should continue to press for greater global harmonization of consumer safety standards for imports. Strong and consistent food safety standards are vital to maintaining consumer confidence. Thus, the insistence of industrial countries on stringent import standards for health reasons makes sense for both the buyers and the sellers. Insufficient attention to safety issues will cause disruptive and abrupt trade bans. Predictable market access is critical to Central America's rural development.

U.S. ASSISTANCE. Restrictions regarding lending by the Agency for International Development directly to beneficiaries should be eased until credit reforms are completed. Additionally, USAID should assist with public administrative reforms in general. The agency should give more attention to the possible uses of integrated pest-management techniques as well as to appropriate agricultural research for the region's special problems. Natural resource management activities should focus as much on human resource development as on conserving the forests. Population planning and education programs are closely related to natural resource conservation.

PRINCIPLES FOR ADVOCACY

Outright and absolute environmental protection is not feasible without providing impoverished people with survival alternatives. Above all else, Central Americans require production opportunities. Yet, production in the region is increasingly destroying the very natural systems on which it depends. Thus, environmentalists and development experts now share a goal of finding a path to sustainable development. Any policies intended to foster sustainability must be evaluated according to their effects on efficiency, equity, and natural resource conservation. To pursue any one of these three objectives but neglect the others will prove destructive to the environment, the people, and the region.

Nontraditional agricultural export strategies have been criticized as being overly devoted to efficiency, to the neglect of equity and environmentalism. Even if true in the past, it need not remain so. The challenge is to alter public and private practices to overcome the obstacles that presently prevent nontraditional agriculture from being equitable and environmentally sound. Ultimately, success in environmental terms will be achieved when nontraditional agricultural production and exports truly help alleviate poverty.

Notes

[1] See James W. Fox, "Is the Caribbean Basin Initiative Working?" (AID/LAC/DP paper, October 31, 1989) for data showing the resounding success of nontraditional exports—both manufactured and agricultural.

[2] The size of manufacturing exports from Central America far exceeds nontraditional agriculture, but the growth rate of the latter is very high. This paper does not address the potential of manufacturing export growth to development in Central America, but the author has treated the subject elsewhere. See Stuart K. Tucker, "The Potential of Trade Expansion as a Generator of Added Employment in the Caribbean Basin," in *Migration Impacts of Trade and Foreign Investment*, Sergio Diaz-Briquets and Sidney Weintraub (eds.), (Boulder, CO: Westview Press, 1991).

[3] This theory is well expressed in *Trade Development*, USAID Policy Paper (Washington, DC: USAID, July 1986).

[4] Measured in terms of yield per hectare.

[5] The PROEXAG project (funded by USAID and run by Chemonics) has worked extensively with national export business associations to develop information on the wide variety of potential exports from Costa Rica, El Salvador, Guatemala, and Honduras.

[6] James W. Fox, "Feedback Loops and Economies of Scale: Achieving Export-Led Growth in the Caribbean Basin" USAID Bureau for Latin America and Caribbean Staff Working Paper No. 2 (Washington, DC: USAID, August 1990).

[7] The capital and land requirements discussed here are unpublished estimates compiled by USAID/Honduras and various export promotion business groups in Guatemala and Honduras and conveyed to the author during interviews in 1990.

[8] Lewis A. Fischer, "Assessment of Financial Aspects of Pest Control in Agriculture," *Journal of Financial Management and Analysis*, Vol. 2, No. 1 (January-June 1989), pp. 12-17.

[9] See Douglas L. Murray and Polly Hoppin, "Pesticides and Nontraditional Agriculture: A Coming Crisis for U.S. Development Policy in Latin America?" Texas Papers on Latin America, pre-publication working papers (Austin: University of Texas at Austin, 1990).

[10] See Robert G. Williams, *Export Agriculture and the Crisis in Central America* (Chapel Hill, NC: University of North Carolina Press, 1986) for discussion of the problems associated with traditional cash crops.

[11] Polly Hoppin, "Pesticide Use in Four Nontraditional Crops in Guatemala: Implications for Residues," Consortium for International Crop Protection (College Park, MD: University of Maryland, June 16, 1989), mimeograph.

[12] Ibid.

[13] H. Jeffrey Leonard (ed.), *Environment and the Poor: Development Strategies for Common Agenda*, U.S.-Third World Policy Perspectives No. 11 (New Brunswick, NJ: Transactions Publishers in cooperation with the Overseas Development Council, 1989); and Jeffrey H. Leonard, *Natural Resources and Economic Development in Central America* (Washington, DC: International Institute for Environment and Development, 1987).

[14] Central Bank of Costa Rica, data for March 1988 to September 1989.

[15] For an assessment of the nonagricultural aspects of the CBI program, especially its shortcomings, see the following works by Stuart K. Tucker: Statement on the Impact and Effectiveness of the Caribbean Basin Initiative Before the Subcommittee on Trade of the U.S. House Committee on Ways and Means, February 25, 1986; and "Trade Unshackled: Assessing the Value of the Caribbean Basin Initiative," in *Central American Recovery and Development: Task Force Report to the International Commission for Central American Recovery and Development*, William Ascher and Ann Hubbard (eds.) (Durham, NC: Duke University Press, 1989), pp. 357-392.

[16] This problem is illustrated by the blockage of an aid package intended to help Bolivian soybean producers. See Allan I. Mendelowitz, "Restrictions on U.S. Aid to Bolivia for Crop Development Competing with U.S. Agricultural Exports and Their Relationship to U.S. Anti-Drug Efforts," Testimony Before the Committee on Agriculture, Subcommittee on Department Operations, Research, and Foreign Agriculture, and Subcommittee on Wheat, Soybeans, and Feed Grains, House of Representatives (Washington, DC: United States General Accounting Office, June 27, 1990).

ANNEX 1. CENTRAL AMERICA'S NONTRADITIONAL AGRICULTURAL EXPORTS ENTER DUTY-FREE, WHILE OTHER COUNTRIES FACE SOME BARRIERS

Harmonized Tariff Schedule (HTS)	Selected Items	Under U.S. CBI	Under MFN	Under GSP	Graduated from GSP
0603	Cut flowers				
	Fresh miniature carnations	Free	4.0%	Free	
	Fresh roses	Free	8.0%	Free	
	Fresh chrysanthemums, standard carnations, anthuriums, and orchids	Free	8.0%	Free	
	Other fresh cut flowers	Free	8.0%	Free	
	Nonfresh cut flowers	Free	5.0%	Free	Colombia
0702	Tomatoes, fresh or chilled				
	3/1-7/14 or 9/1-11/14	Free	$0.046/kg	$0.046/kg	
	7/15-8/31	Free	$0.033/kg	$0.033/kg	
	11/15-2/29	Free	$0.033/kg	Free	
0703	Onions, fresh or chilled				
	Onion sets	Free	$0.013/kg	Free	
	Garlic	Free	$0.017/kg	Free	Mexico
0704	Cabbage, etc., fresh or chilled				
	Cauliflower and headed broccoli				
	6/5-10/15	Free	5.5%	Free	
	Other times:				
	Not reduced in size	Free	12.5%	Free	Mexico
	Cut or sliced	Free	17.5%	Free	Mexico
	Brussels sprouts	Free	25.0%	Free	Mexico
	But until 1/1/93	Free	12.5%	Free	Mexico
	Sprouting broccoli	Free	25.0%	25.0%	Mexico
0705	Lettuce and chicory, fresh or chilled				
	Head lettuce 6/1-10/31	Free	$0.0088/kg	Free	

ANNEX 1. CENTRAL AMERICA'S NONTRADITIONAL AGRICULTURAL EXPORTS ENTER DUTY-FREE, WHILE OTHER COUNTRIES FACE SOME BARRIERS (continued)

HTS	Selected Items	U.S. CBI	MFN	GSP	Graduated GSP
0705 (continued)					
	Head lettuce	Free	$0.044/kg	Free	Mexico
	Other lettuce				
	Other times				
	6/1-10/31	Free	$0.0088/kg	Free	Mexico
	Other times	Free	$0.044/kg	Free	Mexico
0707	Cucumbers, fresh or chilled				
	12/1-2/29	Free	$0.049/kg	Free	Mexico
	3/1-4/30	Free	$0.066/kg	Free	Mexico
	5/1-6/30	Free	$0.066/kg	Free	
	7/1-8/31	Free	$0.033/kg	Free	
0708	Leguminous vegetables, fresh or chilled				
	Peas				
	7/1-9/30	Free	$0.011/kg	Free	
	Peas				
	Other times	Free	$0.044/kg	Free	Mexico
0709	Other vegetables, fresh or chilled				
	Asparagus				
	9/15-11/15, (by air, and not reduced)	Free	5.0%	5.0%	
	Other times	Free	25.0%	25.0%	25.0%
	Peppers	Free	$0.055/kg	Free	Mexico
	Spinach	Free	25.0%	25.0%	
	Chayote	Free	12.5%	Free	
	Okra	Free	25.0%	Free	
	Squash	Free	$0.024/kg	Free	
	Sweet corn	Free	25.0%	Free	Mexico
0710	Frozen vegetables				
	Leguminous vegetables	Free	25.0%	25.0%	Mexico

ANNEX 1. CENTRAL AMERICA'S NONTRADITIONAL AGRICULTURAL EXPORTS ENTER DUTY-FREE, WHILE OTHER COUNTRIES FACE SOME BARRIERS (continued)

HTS	Selected Items	U.S. CBI	MFN	GSP	Graduated GSP
0710 (continued)	Peas				
	7/1-9/30	Free	$0.022/kg	Free	
	Other times	Free	$0.044/kg	Free	
	Spinach	Free	17.5%	17.5%	
	Sweet corn	Free	17.5%	17.5%	
	Tomatoes				
	3/1-7/14 or 9/1-11/14	Free	$0.046/kg	$0.046/kg	
	7/15-8/31	Free	$0.033/kg	$0.033/kg	
	11/15-2/29	Free	$0.33/kg	Free	
	Other, not reduced in size				
	Brussels sprouts	Free	25.0%	Free	
	But until 1/1/93	Free	12.5%	Free	
	Other	Free	25.0%	Free	
	Other, reduced in size				
	Asparagus	Free	17.5%	17.5%	
	Broccoli	Free	17.5%	17.5%	
	Brussels sprouts	Free	17.5%	17.5%	
	Cauliflower	Free	17.5%	17.5%	
	Okra	Free	17.5%	17.5%	
	Other	Free	17.5%	17.5%	
0711	Vegetables, provisionally preserved				
	Onions	Free	8.0%	Free	
	Cucumbers	Free	12.0%	Free	
0712	Dried vegetables				
	Onions	Free	35.0%	35.0%	
	Garlic	Free	35.0%	35.0%	
	Parsley	Free	6.0%	Free	
	Tomatoes	Free	13.0%	13.0%	

ANNEX 1. CENTRAL AMERICA'S NONTRADITIONAL AGRICULTURAL EXPORTS ENTER DUTY-FREE, WHILE OTHER COUNTRIES FACE SOME BARRIERS (continued)

HTS	Selected Items	U.S. CBI	MFN	GSP	Graduated GSP
0801	Coconuts, brazil nuts, cashew nuts				
	Coconuts	Free	Free	Free	
	Cashew nuts	Free	Free	Free	
0802	Other nuts				
	Macadamia nuts				
	In shell	Free	$0.029/kg	Free	
	Shelled	Free	$0.11/kg	$0.11/kg	
0803	Bananas or plantains				
	Bananas	Free	Free	Free	
	Plantains, fresh	Free	Free	Free	
	Plantains, dried	Free	3.0%	Free	
0804	Dates, figs, pineapples, avocados, mangoes, etc.				
	Pineapples				
	Not reduced, bulk	Free	$0.0064/kg	$0.0064/kg	
	Not reduced, crate	Free	$0.0131/kg	$0.0131/kg	
	Reduced	Free	$0.0055/kg	$0.0055/kg	
	Avocados	Free	$0.132/kg	$0.132/kg	
	Mangoes				
	Fresh, 9/1-5/31	Free	$0.0827/kg	Free	
	Fresh, other items	Free	$0.0827/kg	$0.0827/kg	
	Dried	Free	$0.033/kg	Free	Mexico
0805	Citrus fruit, fresh or dried				
	Oranges	Free	$0.022/kg	$0.022/kg	
	Mandarins	Free	$0.022/kg	$0.022/kg	
	Lemons	Free	$0.0275/kg	$0.0275/kg	
	Limes	Free	$0.022/kg	$0.022/kg	

ANNEX 1. CENTRAL AMERICA'S NONTRADITIONAL AGRICULTURAL EXPORTS ENTER DUTY-FREE, WHILE OTHER COUNTRIES FACE SOME BARRIERS (continued)

HTS	Selected Items	U.S. CBI	MFN	GSP	Graduated GSP
0805 (continued)	Grapefruit				
	8/1-9/30	Free	$0.022/kg	$0.022/kg	
	10/1-10/31	Free	$0.018/kg	$0.018/kg	
	Other times	Free	$0.029/kg	$0.029/kg	
	Other	Free	0.9%	Free	
0806	Grapes, fresh				
	2/15-3/31	Free	$1.41/m³	$1.41/m³	
	4/1-6/30	Free	Free	Free	
	Other times	Free	$2.12/m³	$2.12/m³	
0807	Melons and papayas				
	Cantaloupes				
	8/1-9/15	Free	20.0%	20.0%	
	Other times	Free	35.0%	Free	
	Watermelons				
	To 1991: 6/1-5/15	Free	Free	Free	Mexico
	12/1-3/31	Free	20.0%	Free	
	Other times	Free	20.0%	20.0%	
	Papayas	Free	8.5%	8.5%	
0808	Apples, pears, and quinces, fresh				
	Apples	Free	Free	Free	
	Pears and quinces				
	4/1-6/30	Free	Free	Free	
	Other times	Free	$0.011/kg	$0.011/kg	
0809	Apricots, cherries, peaches, plums, and sloes, fresh				
	Peaches				
	6/1-11/30	Free	$0.004/kg	$0.004/kg	
	Other times	Free	Free	Free	

ANNEX 1. CENTRAL AMERICA'S NONTRADITIONAL AGRICULTURAL EXPORTS ENTER DUTY-FREE, WHILE OTHER COUNTRIES FACE SOME BARRIERS (continued)

HTS	Selected Items	U.S. CBI	MFN	GSP	Graduated GSP
0809 (continued)	Plums				
	1/1-5/3	Free	Free		
	Other times	Free	$0.011/kg	$0.011/kg	
0810	Other fruit, fresh				
	Strawberries				
	6/15-9/15	Free	$0.004/kg	$0.004/kg	
	Other times	Free	$0.017/kg	$0.017/kg	
	Raspberries, blackberries, mulberries, loganberries				
	9/1-6/30	Free	$0.007/kg	$0.007/kg	
	Other times	Free	Free	Free	
	Cranberries, blueberries	Free	Free	Free	
	Kiwi fruit	Free	Free	Free	
0811	Fruit and nuts, frozen				
	Strawberries	Free	14.0%	Free	
	Raspberries, blackberries, loganberries	Free	7.0%	Free	Mexico
0904	Pepper				
	Black				
	Crushed or ground	Free	Free	Free	
	Capsicum (hot)	Free	Free	Free	
	Paprika	Free	$0.03/kg	Free	
	Anaheim and ancho	Free	$0.11/kg	$0.11/kg	
	Other not ground	Free	$0.055/kg	Free	
	Other ground	Free	$0.0112/kg	Free	
	Pimenta	Free	Free	Free	

Source: Extracted directly from the U.S. Harmonized Tariff Schedule, 1990.

Chapter Five

Land Taxation, the Poor, and Sustainable Development

John D. Strasma and Rafael Celis

INTRODUCTION

Land policies are at the very heart of the problems of poverty, deforestation, and agricultural productivity in Central America. Despite land reforms in several countries, much arable land remains in holdings that are too large or too small for efficient production. Present policies create perverse incentives that cause much land to be over- or underutilized. Some of those policies, though well intended, actually discourage investment and induce low productivity, deforestation, squatting, and violence.

One implicit policy with damaging repercussions has been *not* having an effective land tax. Because land taxes are low, city dwellers can easily afford to own land as a speculative investment, inflation hedge, or for weekend relaxing. And because these nonfarmers bid up the price of land, the landless worker or small farmer can't afford to buy it. Without the revenue generated by effective land taxes, local governments are impoverished, unable to provide needed roads, schools, and other services to any residents, including the poor.

Land taxes are one of the most effective potential policy measures now available in Central America to reduce both poverty and the destruction of natural resources in a manner compatible with sustainable development. Land-tax reform, already under way in Costa Rica, is a feasible solution elsewhere. If land values are established with community input, and if revenues are earmarked to local governments, infrastructure, and schools, a land tax could promote decentralization and participatory democracy, while increasing production and reducing poverty. In this chapter we analyze the present taxation of agricultural lands in Central America, finding it both inadequate and counterproductive.

Land taxes alone would not solve all problems. More direct land redistribution programs are also needed. Major land reforms were implemented in El Salvador and Nicaragua during the 1980s, as were modest experiments in Guatemala. Significant redistribution efforts in Costa Rica, Honduras, and Panama took place in the 1960s and 1970s. All were successful, in part, although the executing agencies were short on resources. The programs did not adequately define the rights and responsibilities of the beneficiaries, and none of these reforms reached the majority of the rural poor.

The next stage of land reforms—a land taxation process friendly to both the rural poor and the environment—is overdue. It is time for governments to treat the landless as potential small farmers in market economies, rather than as permanent political clients dependent on underfunded, paternalistic government agencies.

The first major step needed throughout Central America is a cadastral survey, or an inventory of land, to 1) more clearly define rights to land and 2) demarcate holdings—state lands (protected and not) and private holdings (be they large or small, cooperatively or individually held). Governments must define the land available for squatting and the trees that may and may not be cut.

This chapter also examines the potential relationship between agrarian reforms and pressure on fragile lands. Those with the power to use the land tend to do so with only short-term profits in mind. Existing laws, regulations, and policies largely encourage this shortsightedness; laws that do take a longer view are seldom implemented.

An alternative strategy is needed, one in favor of both the poor and natural resources. A modern land survey and tax are key parts of this strategy. To implement them, we suggest a list of the decisions and steps required. If these are completed, land surveys and land taxation would become effective instruments for initiating sustainable development in Central America.

POVERTY, POPULATION, AND FRAGILE LANDS

Central America's food productivity is not keeping pace with its population growth of nearly 3 percent a year. Highly productive lands in Central America are fully occupied, so people move into marginal areas or overcultivate arable lands. Vast stretches of dry and humid tropical forest in Guatemala, for example, are rapidly being settled by landless families from overpopulated farming regions. In Panama and El Salvador, once-productive coffee lands have become low-yield areas because soil conservation is not practiced.[1]

At the same time, a few hundred cattle graze on some large estates in flat valleys with good soils suitable for intensive cropping. Absentee ownership explains some of these cases, while other owners have neither the knowledge nor the capital to switch to crop farming. Yet as a result of tradition, peer pressure, or inertia, land is not sold even when it is not used productively. As long as land taxes are low, this pattern can continue for years.

On the nearby hillsides, hundreds of poor tenant farmers struggle to raise crops. To survive, they cut down the remaining trees and plant a few more rows of maize. Springs dry up, trees die, and soon the farmers find it harder than ever to find firewood. Wild animals vanish, removing a source of protein and cash income. This all contributes to a vicious cycle of poverty and environmental degradation, especially notable in El Salvador, southeastern Guatemala, and in the Tatumla, Sabacuante, and Río Grande watersheds of Honduras.

Field studies done for this chapter in the Jutiapa area of Guatemala found that most land is owned by small landlords who traditionally rent to even poorer tenants on a year-to-year basis. Neither has any incentive to use soil conservation practices, and they don't. Tenants do not have tenure security that would encourage them to make such investments in the land. And, though "living fences" are good sources of forage and firewood, landowners do not plant trees because, they say, the tenants "steal" them. Such a standoff is counterproductive for all concerned.

Land policies in Guatemala and elsewhere in Central America are often inappropriate relics of times when populations were smaller. Although land reforms and resettlement programs provided some relief, they have largely exhausted their potential under present political and economic climates. More appropriate policies, such as a land tax, could encourage landlords to sell some parcels outright, on credit, to their present tenants. The buyers would then pay taxes, but as owners they would also have a reason to plant trees, grow improved varieties, and care about the land they would leave to their children.

OVERVIEW OF LAND AND TAX POLICIES IN CENTRAL AMERICA

No single policy has caused all these problems; no one policy change can cure them. Deficient registries of public lands, counterproductive policies with respect to squatting, and inadequate rural credit all play roles. However, a major responsibility lies in the inadequacy of land taxation.

Throughout Central America, land taxes are too low. Rates in Wisconsin, for instance, average about 2 percent of the market value of land and buildings every year[2]; in Central America, they are much lower. Partly because real-estate taxes are low, land is expensive and beyond the reach of the landless. Moreover, local governments forgo an ideal revenue source.

Taxation in Central America

Tax burdens overall, like land taxes specifically, are relatively light in Central America, especially for the very rich. Total taxes are under 20 percent of gross domestic product (GDP) in Central America, compared to around 30 percent of GDP in industrialized nations.[3] Indirect taxes on sales, value added, or transactions are much more important than direct taxes on income and wealth. They are also highly regressive. Although indirect taxes often exempt subsistence foods, they usually hit soap, matches, work clothes, fuel, and similar basics. Yet they seldom reach the major expenses of the rich.[4]

Table 1 shows estimated tax burdens and tax structures for Central American countries in 1989. The highest total tax level was that of Costa Rica, at $235 per capita, or 14 percent of GDP. Nicaraguans paid $124 per capita in taxes, but because incomes were lower, the relative burden was higher, at almost 18 percent of GDP. The lowest tax burdens in the area were in El Salvador and Guatemala; at $83 and $68 per capita, respectively, both countries' overall tax levels were equivalent to less than 8 percent of GDP.

Credible data for the total tax burden of Central American farmers do not exist. Production, trade, and net incomes are more heavily taxed throughout the region than are property or capital. Most of the taxes are paid by commercial farmers who buy fertilizer and pesticides, and who produce for export or for the national market. Those who own land but do not produce a great deal with it pay very little. One tax falls mainly on some of the wealthy farmers: the export tax on coffee and other traditional exports such as cotton, cocoa, and sugar.[5] These taxes, as well as discriminatory exchange rates, fall heavily on producers and not at all on those whose lands are unproductive.

The Region's Land-Tax Experiments

Land taxes are not a novel idea in Central America, but they have fallen into disuse through neglect.[6] *Costa Rica's* tax on urban and rural real estate produced some 20 percent of total government revenues until 1960.[7] Assessed values were not indexed for inflation, so despite rate increases, land taxes generated only 1 percent of revenues by 1989.[8] The

TABLE 1. CENTRAL GOVERNMENT TAX LEVELS, 1989

Country	GDP Per Capita (dollars)	Taxes Per Capita (dollars)	Taxes Per GDP (percent)
Costa Rica	1,659	235	14.2
El Salvador	1,074	83	7.7
Guatemala	888	68	7.7
Honduras	913	121	13.2
Nicaragua	694	124	17.8
Panama	1,890	172	9.1

Source: Data calculated from *Economic and Social Progress in Latin America* (Washington, DC: Inter-American Development Bank, 1991), Statistical Appendix.

tax is progressive, from 0.36 percent of assessed value over about $1,600 to 1.41 percent on properties assessed at more than $30,000.

El Salvador's land tax in the 1970s was 1 percent a year on values that were declared by landowners. (To the dismay of many owners, the values they declared in 1976 and 1977 were the main basis for compensation payments in the land reforms of 1980.[9]) In 1986, under President José Napoléon Duarte, this tax was replaced by a tax on net wealth, including business capital as well as real estate. Real-estate values in the new tax are still those declared by owners; in any case, the market has been depressed by the civil war. A modern unit value land-tax system (described later in this chapter) could be a solid revenue source as peace returns to El Salvador.

Guatemala's land tax has a base rate of 0.3 percent a year. However, implementation is poor and tax values are so far below market values that the actual tax is less than $0.25 per acre per year.[10] The tax contributes little revenue and has no perceptible impact on the decisions made by landowners. Guatemala also has a punitive tax rate (more than 5 percent) that is supposed to be applied to "idle" land. However, there is no credible evidence that it has ever been used except as a way to harm political enemies or to bargain over the price of land that the government sought to acquire.[11]

Honduras has a land tax, with revenues earmarked for use by the municipalities. Assessments lag far behind market prices, as they are not indexed for inflation or economic growth. The rate is so low (0.1 percent per year) that it is one of the smallest sources of municipal revenues.[12] Recently, a national cadastral office successfully revalued real estate in several municipalities. The rate remains extremely low, but the increased tax base paid for the reassessment in the first year.[13]

Honduras is also reforming the basic municipal statutes to facilitate decentralization of the public sector. One draft bill raises the land-tax rate to 1.0 percent a year on market values.[14] Revenue would go to the local government, after deducting the expenses of the cadastral survey. Two percent would be better; with that rate and accurate values, local governments could provide badly needed infrastructure, services to residents, and protection of natural resources. At a 1 percent rate, local governments might still need some subsidies from the central government, itself financially strapped.

In *Nicaragua* inflation rendered assessed values meaningless by 1990. Moreover, just before yielding to the Chamorro administration, the Sandinista regime transferred many state-seized mansions and other prime real estate to some of its own leaders, as well as farms and urban housing projects to its followers and some of the poor. Conflicts over the ownership of such properties impede rational discussion of other land policies, including taxes.

Panama also has a land tax. However, taxable values are far below market values, and no serious efforts have been made to modernize the tax.

Table 2 compares the revenue importance of taxes on property—including land, buildings, inheritances, and motor vehicles—to other types of taxes in Central America. Urban real-estate taxes probably generate more than half of total property taxes. No figures are available for rural land taxes alone, but they are clearly insignificant as a share of total national tax revenues.

The region's tax structure, as portrayed in Table 2, merits a few further clarifications. First, for El Salvador and Panama taxes on property include a tax on net wealth. Since real estate is the biggest component of net wealth and a tax on wealth is the easiest to enforce, this has all the virtues of a real-estate tax plus the advantage of equity vis-à-vis wealthy people holding other types of capital assets. Adequate assessment would require all the techniques of modern real-estate taxation.

Traditional exports like coffee, sugar, and cotton are taxed heavily. But Table 2 does not reflect all discriminatory policies that affect farmers. For instance, farmers often suffer under multiple exchange rates. The coffee exporter gets fewer pesos or colones per dollar earned than he would if there were a uniform exchange rate. Farmers who sell in the domestic market can be adversely affected by price ceilings on basic grains or by cheap, imported grains and dried milk "dumped" by European countries and the United States. Both policies lower prices, discourage production, and reduce farmers' incomes.

Land-tax revenues are also low because of special exemptions. For example, under Costa Rica's National Reforestation Law, lands replanted

TABLE 2. TAX STRUCTURES IN CENTRAL AMERICA, 1989 (percent)

Country	Total Tax Revenue as Share of GDP[a]	Property Taxes[b]	Net Income Taxes[c]	Sales and Production	Import and Export Taxes
Costa Rica	14.2	1.1	16.1	50.0	31.2
El Salvador	7.7	4.3	23.0	19.6	18.7
Guatemala	7.7	2.2	22.1	42.4	24.9
Honduras	13.2	1.1	29.0	35.5	36.7
Nicaragua	17.8	1.3	23.1	59.8	11.8
Panama	9.1	7.7	35.8	21.8	15.7

[a]Does not include certain stamp and miscellaneous taxes, so the totals are less than 100 percent.
[b]Taxes on real estate, motor vehicles, and inheritances.
[c]Taxes on income and profits, plus social security taxes.

Source: Data calculated from *Economic and Social Progress in Latin America* (Washington, DC: Inter-American Development Bank, 1991), Statistical Appendix.

with timber-yielding trees or fruit trees are exempted from the property tax as an incentive. Individuals and corporations in Costa Rica also are exempted from the income tax on profits from the sale of products derived from such plantations.[15]

Finally, the tax revenues shown in Table 2 do not capture local contributions of labor, money, or material to maintain roads, schools, and services. For example, some land redistribution beneficiaries in Costa Rica taxed themselves to keep an access road in minimum repair, because neither the Ministry of Public Works nor the municipal government would do so.[16] Local residents routinely organize raffles or other benefit events to support rural schools and community services.

NONREVENUE ADVANTAGES OF LAND TAXES

An annual tax on rural land intrigues economists. It is a fixed expense that raises the cost of holding property idle for speculation. Any significant tax is relatively onerous to an owner who earns little income from his land. If he invests and works to increase its productivity and income, the land tax does not increase, so the burden becomes relatively lighter.

Modern tax assessment requires a cadastral survey that estimates the potential yield of a hectare of each soil type. The resulting tax should encourage owners to rent or sell land from which they derive little income. The increased supply of land will naturally depress land prices or make sellers offer better terms. As a result, the relatively poor will find it easier to buy or rent land with which they can raise their income by much more than the yearly tax.

The land tax also is preferable to a tax on agricultural production or exports, from the government's point of view. Most tax incentives cut revenues. Land taxes can generate substantial revenues—yet they do not penalize the most productive, as do taxes on agricultural commodities or exports.

A significant land tax also makes tax incentives more effective. All Central American countries offer exemptions from the land tax for approved investments. But the tax is so low to begin with that the exemption makes little difference to the investor's rate of return. A higher tax makes an exemption much more attractive.

A well-designed tax could also help resolve the Nicaraguan land disputes:

■ Taxes paid by whoever wins ownership could help compensate the dispossessed.

■ A high tax would drive down market values and, hence, the amount of compensation that is needed.

■ A land tax that is progressive, according to total holdings, could make some former owners less insistent that all of their land be returned.

■ A heavy tax on market value, progressive for total holdings and retroactive to the beginning of the Chamorro administration, might induce some Sandinista leaders to return some of the real estate they seized for themselves.[17]

■ A nominal flat fee, for instance, of $5 a year for all holdings worth less than $1,000 would simplify administration. It would confirm the rights of the poor, while assuring them that they would not be taxed heavily on tiny parcels or urban shacks that are often their only real security.

Why Are Land Taxes Not More Widely Used?

Given these advantages, why doesn't Central America have heavy land taxes? There are four reasons:

1) Until recently, assessment was costly and took years.

2) Landowners, with the World Bank and International Monetary Fund (IMF) as allies, hope to repeal export taxes without having to accept land taxes.

3) Developing-country governments covered deficits by borrowing, mostly from abroad.

4) Leaders preferred to centralize their power, by allocating annual grants to local governments instead of permitting them to assess their own taxes.[18]

This situation changed drastically in the last decade. Voluntary net new lending to Central America by commercial banks dried up. To secure external funds, developing countries now must embrace official lenders' structural adjustment programs, which require more taxes and reduced deficits.

For instance, during the 1980s the World Bank and some other aid agencies urged various countries to adopt land-tax reform as a trade-off for lower export taxes and lower taxes on farm income. There are no success stories yet. In Argentina the government promised just such a reform and the World Bank funded a cadastral survey. The legislature refused to create a new federal land tax, partly because the trade-off fell apart. Instead, the federal government, desperate for revenues, wanted to continue taxing agricultural exports directly or via unrealistic exchange rates. Because that would have raised taxes on farmers without comparable sacrifice by others, it did not pass at that time.

With Dutch funding and technical assistance, Costa Rica began a national reassessment in 1990. It plans to reassess all urban and rural property in the capital city and adjacent areas, at market values, by 1995.[19] The Honduran National Cadastral Survey Office reassessed land values in several municipalities a few years ago but has no funds or staff to extend this work.

PROBLEMS AND ACCOMPLISHMENTS OF LAND REFORMS IN CENTRAL AMERICA

Every Central American nation has tried some kind of land redistribution program. Costa Rica, Guatemala, Honduras, and Panama created government agencies to buy land for impoverished laborers and poor subsistence farmers, often after they had seized private farms.[20] El Salvador and Nicaragua expropriated many large farms and redistributed them to their workers through land reforms. Separately, tenants in El Salvador were allowed to buy the small parcels they had rented in March 1980, at tax values and with long payment terms, whether or not landlords wanted to sell.

In all these programs the stated goals included increased productivity, employment, and democracy through processes that allowed the landless laborer to escape poverty through access to formerly underutilized land. Essentially, each effort signed up 5 to 20 percent of the rural families either as "provisional" title holders or as members of collective production enterprises. In every country, most of the "beneficiaries" were better off than before. However, because their rights and obligations were poorly defined, many felt insecure and subject to arbitrary cancellation and eviction by the agency staff at any time. In most cases the beneficiaries were supposed to repay the government for the land received, but collection efforts have been weak and the programs have had to be highly subsidized. In all cases the government wanted to reduce conflict over land, but it also sought political loyalty and support from beneficiaries.

What are the major lessons that can be drawn from Central American land reforms and land programs?[21] First, no one seriously disputes that they were needed: idle land and idle workers were highly visible, and market processes were not stimulating their productive use. Second, none of the experiments solved all of the national needs to increase production, reduce rural poverty, or give all the landless access to land. Third, all were "top-down" efforts, centralized, overstaffed, and underfunded, with a strong dose of paternalism by planners and staff.

The reforms in El Salvador and Nicaragua illustrate some of the problems and accomplishments of land reform. The programs benefited around 20 percent of the rural labor force, but a substantial number of landless people remain. One reason is that reforms generally transferred the expropriated farms to the resident laborers. *Minifundistas* (those with too little land to support themselves), migrant workers, and many others were left out.

State Farms Versus Individual Parcels

In Nicaragua the land reform agency initially insisted that expropriated farms be operated by the state, to maintain production of export cash crops such as coffee and cotton.[22] In El Salvador there were two separate land reforms in 1980. All farms of more than 500 hectares were expropriated by the Salvadoran Institute of Agrarian Transformation (ISTA) in March 1980. The workers were told that the land belonged to them, but in fact ISTA insisted that each farm remain a production unit. Plans and decisions were made by a committee elected by the workers, but veto power was exercised by an ISTA functionary who did not even live on the farm. Many beneficiaries felt they had merely changed employers.

On most of the expropriated farms, output per hectare remained near the national average levels. This was short of the potential, given the above-average quality of much of the land formerly owned by large holders. The government insisted that large units were needed for scale economies and for political reasons.[23] Unfortunately, the war, theft, inefficiency, and incompetence by some cooperative managers and state functionaries made many farms unprofitable. Doubting that the land would ever really be theirs, members of the profitable cooperatives mostly voted to take the profits in improved housing and benefits, rather than paying off the land debt.[24]

In the second part of the Salvadoran reform of 1980, tenants tilling small plots were allowed to buy them, at the value declared by the owner for property tax purposes three years earlier. The agency in charge of that part of the reform, the National Financial Agency for Agrarian Transformation (FINATA) was less dogmatic about imposing collectivism. Having made their own decisions as renters, few of the ex-tenants were willing to pool land and submit to collective farming. By 1990 some 38,000 new owners had received individual titles and had paid all or most of the purchase price. Most of their plots are on steep slopes, and one now sees some land-conserving investment in terraces, erosion control, and tree crops.[25] When they were tenants on year-to-year leases, these same families had no incentive to make these investments. Now they do.

A third Salvadoran land reform began in 1992 with implementation of the U.N.-sponsored Peace Agreements. All remaining land in holdings over 245 hectares is being expropriated, and other private land is being purchased to settle the demobilized guerrillas and soldiers on terms similar to those of the 1980 land reforms.

Other Issues in Land Redistribution Programs

The Honduran, Guatemalan, and Costa Rican land distribution programs resembled Nicaragua's and El Salvador's expropriation of larger farms. In Costa Rica and Honduras the government usually intervened after workers had occupied a farm; there and in Guatemala the land was supposed to be sold to the workers at low prices and on long payment terms. In practice, those participating in the programs in all five countries have had to struggle twice: first to gain possession of the land, and then to secure actual full ownership of it, free of state tutelage.

CLIMBING THE "TENURE LADDER." Many state functionaries do not see the landless as future small farmers who could learn to make important decisions for themselves. Few urban politicians grasp the concept of the "tenure ladder" so familiar in the successful growth of U.S. agriculture. That is, a young man starts as a laborer for his father, then works for a neighbor, and then rents some land. If successful, he saves and in time buys property of his own. If unsuccessful, he continues as a laborer or tenant, or moves to town.

Central American land programs expect all participants to remain on their assigned plots, going directly from being landless laborers to being operators, individually or in groups. The unsuccessful are not encouraged to leave, even though other landless are ready and eager to enter in their places. Cynics might suspect that as long as some workers are clearly not ready to run farms of their own, the agency staff envision permanent employment for themselves as supervisors or advisors.

USE RIGHTS OF LAND, BUT NOT OWNERSHIP. In all five Central American countries many politicians did not want to actually transfer land to the landless. They viewed the landless as political supporters, to whom they would prefer to give the *use* of the property but to whom they would deny legal *ownership*. Nor were the politicians willing to allow beneficiaries the right to transfer the land to someone else without permission, as an owner could. Therefore, even though most of the reform laws and land redistribution programs stated that the land would be sold to beneficiaries, the agencies were consistently slow to set prices for the land and made no serious effort to collect payments. Many participants insisted on making payments and then found that the title they received was little more than the right to continue using that parcel as long as they did so personally. Land *does* change hands frequently among small farmers in Central America, despite regulations and laws to the contrary in all of the land programs. Some farmers suffer accidents or have family problems and must stop working their land. Others simply decide they want to work elsewhere. Yet, until recently, all of the programs forbade beneficiaries from reselling the land they had received without agency permission. Such permission was seldom granted. When it was forthcoming, agency staff wanted to choose the next family to use the plot, even if a third family offered to pay more. The *campesinos* quickly learned not to ask, but just to sell their "rights" to someone else, illegally, behind the back of the land agency.

Paternalistic politicians claim that the freedom to sell will lead to a reconcentration of land into large farms; however, there is no evidence that this is the case.[26] If the poor have easy access to the land market, the buyers will be other *campesinos*. Large ranchers do not want to pay "retail" prices to buy small parcels.[27]

RECENT TRENDS TOWARD TITLING. In the last three years, under pressure from the beneficiaries and external aid agencies, most of the land programs have grudgingly allowed some beneficiaries to "graduate" to independence. Under President Alfredo Cristiani some Salvadoran cooperatives have finally received titles and independence and are paying for the land. In Costa Rica, Honduras, and El Salvador titles have been issued to many squatters and other beneficiaries, though the number of titles actually issued tends to lag far behind announced goals. To keep the pressure on, the U.S. Agency for International Development (USAID) in Costa Rica now reimburses survey and registry expenses of that government's Institute for Agrarian Development (IDA) only for titles actually issued to beneficiaries. A similar approach was used successfully in El Salvador.

Although the trend is toward guaranteeing beneficiaries' clear, unambiguous ownership status like that of any other property owner, paternalism lingers. For instance, under the pretext of "preventing *minifundia*" (i.e., farms too small to employ a family), Honduran law forbids the issuing of titles to squatters who occupy fewer than 1 hectare of public land. In some densely populated areas, this excludes most squatters, even if they grow vegetables or other labor-intensive crops very efficiently.[28] Again, without legal security, the squatters may hesitate to invest in soil conservation. In effect, the society tells them they are second-class citizens, not worthy to be landowners.

Paternalism also lingers in Costa Rica, where beneficiaries of land programs who sell their parcels may only do so with permission from the board of directors of IDA, the land agency in San José. Getting permission requires time, travel, and a lawyer. If a beneficiary cannot farm his parcel and wants to sell to another small farmer who will farm it, this should be facilitated, not made more difficult. Approval should be available locally and granted automatically, at least if the buyer is another *campesino*.

LAND MARKETS AND LAND BANKS AS A PROPOSED SOLUTION FOR THE LANDLESS

Land reform is an episode in a nation's history. It is complete when two things happen: 1) the small farmer beneficiaries finally obtain clear, secure rights to their plots, free of government supervision; and 2) the state announces that it will not be expropriating any more large holdings for redistribution. Some countries—Japan, Taiwan, and Egypt—completed the cycle in a few years. Bolivia, Costa Rica, Honduras, Nicaragua, and El Salvador took a decade or more. The People's Republic of China took 30 years, and Russia and Mexico have just started to wrap up their 70-year-old reforms.

In every Central American country, when the land reform or land redistribution program ends, there are still large numbers of rural poor who want property on which to support themselves. Donor agencies sometimes suggest that the poor could buy land, instead of seizing a piece of the scarce remaining public forests. That can only work, however, if property prices are reasonable in relation to the income that can be earned by farming a purchased parcel, and if there is some efficient, low-cost mechanism by which buyers and sellers can finance the sale.

When land ownership confers privileges, such as cheap credit or the ability to evade taxes on other sources of income, the wealthy bid up property prices beyond what the landless can afford to pay with their earnings from farming.[29] A heavy land tax would make it expensive to hold property unproductively, so some present owners would become eager to sell, thus lowering the price of land.

In effect, the landless poor would buy land on installments, paying a reasonable price to the seller and thereafter a tax to the state. However, even if land prices fall enough to allow a buyer to pay for the land from farm earnings, some kind of financial mechanism for land purchase is needed.

For instance, sellers can agree to finance the buyers by accepting payments over years (as with land contracts in the United States). Or a new or existing bank can offer long-term mortgage loans to the poor, for the specific purpose of buying a small parcel of land to farm. Given the shortage of long-term savings in Central America, such a *campesino* land mortgage bank would probably need external funds to start. Donor agencies, however, are well aware that, under existing farm credit programs in Central America, neither the rich nor the poor have good repayment records.

Thus, to enable the small farmers of Central America to buy land in the market, any such mortgage loan program must break with the past. If loans are not collected on time, with interest rates that keep up with inflation, initial capital will be quickly dissipated, and there will be no funds with which to finance other poor and landless persons wanting to buy parcels to farm.[30]

SQUATTERS AND TREES

The world press often presents a picture in which fragile tropical forest lands are being devastated by poverty-stricken squatters who move in, slash and burn the forest, and eke out an existence by raising traditional corn, frijoles, and root crops. The squatters are portrayed as desperate, with no alternative way to find land to farm. This is sometimes the case, but often it is not that simple.

Even after an area is declared "protected," it remains vulnerable. It was recently reported that there are only six government guards in Costa Rica to safeguard seven different protected areas.[31] And during a time of government retrenchment, it is unlikely that more guards will be hired. Moreover, few of the areas are clearly fenced and posted. Thus, in the unlikely case that squatters are caught, they (and the lumber companies or cattlemen behind them) could readily argue that they were unaware of the land's protected status.

A few squatters are "professionals," who form groups to seize land and use their political skills to pressure the government to buy it for them. Some then actually farm their assigned parcels, while others sell their rights. In other instances lumber companies have reportedly encouraged the poor to invade fragile, old-growth tropical hardwood forests. Despite laws and decrees that forbid the cutting of these trees, drivers on Central American roads often encounter trucks with the huge trunks being hauled to sawmills. Ranchers also encourage squatters to cut forests so more grazing land will be created. Banana companies and commercial farmers encourage squatting and clearing to buy the cleared land cheaply for export crops.

In some cases, laws and credit policies actually encourage commercial farmers seeking more land for new export crops to clear old-growth forests. For example, Costa Rican law allows the granting of titles to public land only after it has been cleared, even if that is forbidden by other laws.[32] The government actually contributes to the problem of deforestation—each time it establishes a new protected area, it pays existing settlers about twice as much per hectare for cleared land as it does for forested areas. Moreover, the government announces new "protected" areas before it marks the boundaries or determines who already resides there. Squatters rush in and remove the very trees that the government seeks to protect, in order to sell "their" land for the highest possible price.[33]

Central American agrarian law also favors deforestation by squatters and others. Forest lands, for example, are regarded as unimproved and underutilized. Agrarian law defines the clearing of forests as an improvement because it prepares the land for raising crops or grazing cattle, which would be "productive."

Another unintended perversity of Central American agrarian law is illustrated by a Costa Rican law that requires victims to pay for the destruction of their own forests in certain circumstances. If squatters escape notice for 90 days (or persuade agrarian judges that they have done so), then they must be paid for the labor of cutting down trees, even if it was done without permission and against the wishes of the forest's lawful owner.

If squatters escape notice for a full year, Costa Rican lawyers advise clients that it is almost impossible to evict them.[34] Groups of squatters can petition the IDA to buy the land they have invaded, on their behalf. Once the property has been seized by squatters, the owner is under considerable pressure to sell cheaply, because no one but IDA will even consider buying the land. Thus absentee owners may pay a very high price for failing to guard their holdings.[35]

AGRICULTURAL CREDIT: A MARKET OR A WELFARE SYSTEM?

Agricultural credit policies have also contributed to both deforestation and poverty in Central America.[36] Until recently, large landowners could easily obtain large loans to finance expansion of cattle raising to export beef, while small farmers had serious problems obtaining credit. More recently, financing has been relatively abundant for those planning to go into nontraditional export crops. But, as Stuart Tucker points out in Chapter 4, poor, small farmers also typically are at a disadvantage in access to credit for these new ventures.

Attitudes and Traditions of Lenders and Borrowers

Debts related to farms and farming, unfortunately, are not taken very seriously in Central America. Both the law and populist politicians presume that borrowers are worthy souls; if they do not repay, surely it is because they are unable to do so, and their loans should be refinanced, not foreclosed. Besides, banks find it expensive to serve small borrowers; if a landless family does find land it can buy or rent, it will still have trouble securing a source of production credit at a reasonable cost. The state agricultural development banks serve a few small farmers, because that is their mandate, but poor loan recoveries and high costs cause them to be chronically short of loanable funds.

It should be noted that large borrowers are typically no better as clients. Farmers with substantial holdings are seldom more creditworthy than are the small farmers; they often use the legislative process and personal influence to avoid repaying bank loans.[37]

Land Transfers on Credit Are Impeded

Central American countries' credit regulations also hamper the *campesino* who wants to sell a parcel to another small farmer. Even after *campesinos* have full title, which makes it legal to sell their parcels without permission, it is usually illegal to obtain a mortgage on land that was ever held by the land agency.

The theory behind this rule is apparently that if the poor could mortgage their land, they might borrow, and if they did borrow, they might be unable to repay, and so they would lose their land. Therefore, the poor should not be allowed to mortgage their land even if that is the only way they can secure credit at all.

Yet by definition, a poor person is unlikely to be able to pay cash for a piece of farmland. If buyers are not allowed to mortgage land to the sellers, they will not be able to purchase the land at all. Without mortgages, sellers have no effective way to collect unpaid balances. Thus, the anti-mortgage rule means that *campesinos* who want to sell their parcels cannot sell to other *campesinos*. Instead, they must sell to the rich, who can pay in cash.

Rental of Small Parcels

In most countries, people too poor to buy land do rent it, sometimes from the wealthy, but sometimes from other poor families. Central

American land distribution programs forbid beneficiaries to rent their assigned parcels, because rental has been defined ideologically as "exploitation." Yet there are accidents, illness, and other emergency situations in which farmers are unable to till their land. Why should they not be allowed to rent it to others, especially if the land is the original farmer's only possible source of income? Though illegal, rental is frequent. Nevertheless, both parties run considerable risk of detection and punishment by expulsion of both without compensation.

Rental is a well-established form of tenure in Central America and elsewhere. It is often a first step toward land ownership by a young farmer. Land taxes pressure large owners to rent or sell underutilized lands; ideological bans on rentals prevent one of these options and should be repealed, as Honduras did in early 1992.

Environmentally Friendly Leases

The traditional precarious rentals, in which tenants are moved to a new parcel every year, discourage conservation. We found ample evidence of this in Guatemala, as already mentioned. Instead, leases should specify longer-term rentals, perhaps with renewal automatic except in specified situations.[38] Owners and tenants should be encouraged to share soil conservation investment costs, with incentives to farm in a sustainable manner.

Rent legislation can be problematic when there is great population pressure on farmland. Salvadoran tenants were enabled to buy whatever parcel they rented in 1980, at its tax value, whether the owner wished to sell or not. Field research showed that this led to tree planting and terracing—investments no year-to-year tenant would have undertaken.[39] However, owners became unwilling to rent other land to other tenants, lest a new law be passed and they lose more property.

TREES, TENURE, AND TAXES: A SUGGESTED STRATEGY

The land situation described in the preceding pages needs reform urgently. Some potential cropland is grossly underutilized, while hillside parcels are eroded and abused because tenure laws, customs, and regulations do not allow poor farmers access to better lands. Squatters are tolerated, discouraging long-term investment by owners, and squatters have incentives to cut trees—especially the old-growth tropical hardwoods in recently announced protected areas. There are tax and credit incentives to plant trees, but only in plantations. Yet it is the mixed tropical forest with its many old-growth hardwoods that offers most of the environmental benefits and biological diversity the world needs. Little has come from piece-meal efforts to date; an overall strategy is needed.

Cadastral Survey

The essential first step of a strategy to address these problems would be a cadastral survey or inventory of all rural land. Maps or air photos would be clearly marked to show where the boundaries of property units are, and markers on the ground would make them evident to all comers. Conflicting claims of land rights would be identified, and a land court or other mechanism created or improved to resolve them justly and expeditiously.[40] The participants in state land programs would have clearly defined terms on which they could buy full, negotiable, legal title to the land they till.

Focus on Employment

Employment must have a central role in a development strategy that both protects tropical forests and is pro-poor. Unemployed, landless laborers need to see a future for themselves in the protection rather than the destruction of forests. Part of the revenues from an effective land tax could be used to hire the poor as forest guards instead of letting them continue to eke out a living as poachers and land invaders. In short, policies need to make protecting trees more attractive than stealing them. One promising strategy is to arrange state forestry management on the basis of long-term maximization of employment. For instance, certain pines in Honduras should not be harvested more frequently than every 20 years because this cycle permits the extraction of resin, cones, and firewood, in addition to lumber. On such a rotation, jobs are maximized in the long run at the sawmills and in the forests. Currently, sawmill owners often have the sole power to decide land use; they tend to harvest trees too often, to neglect by-products that they cannot market, or to charge resin tappers high fees to enter the forests, forcing the tappers more deeply into poverty.[41]

Rights and Responsibilities of Lumber Companies

Central American lumber companies do not pay taxes on illegal operations, though they may pay bribes to corrupt officials. When they are granted legal concessions, sawmills pay very little for the forests over which the state has given them monopoly power. A modern land tax would define rights more clearly and could easily support a system under which the tax rate is lower when the forest is managed in a sustainable way, and much higher when it is exploited thoughtlessly.

Throughout Central America, local and national governments are deeply mired in deficits, unable to provide necessary services or to implement environmentally friendly policies if they cost more than present policies. The game has no clear rules; boundaries are ill-defined, as are the rights of land program beneficiaries. The traditional rights of squatters undermine the stable legal guarantees needed to encourage investment in reforestation and other renewable forest products. Thus Central America needs to expand the definition and legal protection of the rights of all landholders, large and small.

Definition of Small Farmer Rights in Land Programs

All beneficiaries of government land redistribution programs should have a legal right to buy the land assigned to them and become independent. They might be required to prove some effort and competence; the U.S. Homestead Program of a century ago required settlers to qualify for title by living on the parcel and cultivating at least 20 percent of the land assigned them within the first five years.[42]

Protecting Forests with Tax Credits

To protect the remaining old-growth forests, Central American governments should not only identify and demarcate them but also establish clear "carrot-and-stick" rules. Forests qualifying as old growth could be taxed more lightly than cutover land, by giving the owner a tax credit for keeping the forest intact and extracting products only on a sustained-yield basis. However, the annual tax credits would be provisional, subject to immediate and cumulative repayment if the forests were ever clear cut. Enforcement would probably require annual aerial photography, as well as a legal lien on the properties themselves and on any logs cut from them.[43]

Land Taxes

A modern land tax could contribute to the combination of political will and real resources needed to support cadastral surveys, definitions of rights to land, and the protection of forests.

Tax reform would involve a partnership. The national government would supply technical supervision and a legal framework to ensure universal, equitable application of the tax. Local staff would handle the actual assessment of individual farms and the collection of the tax proceeds. Above all, interested citizens would be invited to participate in the processes of setting relative taxable unit values and of deciding how the money raised by the tax should be spent.

This tax reform program is a package of policies that each country could finance on its own. Yet financial help is available through external agencies interested in supporting inventories and definitions of land and land rights. Along with creating a fair tax based on land, it is time to make it much easier for small farmers and laborers to buy or rent land through the market. Then, at last, it will be time to repeal laws and customs that encourage squatting on public and private lands.

CREATION OF A MODERN LAND TAX

The creation of a modern tax on land and buildings is well understood.[44] Basically, two parallel efforts are required: an inventory and a valuation. First, information from aerial photos and maps is combined with existing data from the land registry on the legal ownership of land and on improvements such as buildings, roads, fences, drainage systems, and other structures that increase the land's value. These data are supplemented with information from owners and from field visits. The end product is a geographic information system and property registry—the basis for establishing and defending all rights to land.

Second, the economic value of the land is estimated. New land taxes or major reforms no longer attempt to determine the market value of each property; that costs too much, and the result will be challenged in the courts. Instead, a modern land-tax reform is based on a system of estimated average or normal unit values for typical types of land and improvements.

To start, a country's ministry of agriculture staff prepares a typology of soil types, as well as typical improvements in each province or zone. A map is prepared, showing approximate boundaries of the main soil types. This can be done quickly and inexpensively, based on photo interpretation, previous soil studies, and spot field checks.

Citizen Participation in Setting Unit Values

Local participation in establishing relative land values may be critical to the political acceptability of a land tax. In each region real-estate brokers, commercial farmers, attorneys, bankers, and anyone else with an opinion should be invited to review a tax service proposal on land unit values and suggest modifications. It is essential to the success of the tax system that all influential citizens feel that their voices were heard in the process of deciding values assigned to various classes of soils.

Also, the community is in the best position to define the effect on land values of access or lack of access to a paved road. Technical land-tax staff should facilitate the meetings, and, based on local information, develop unit values per hectare and adjustments for the quality and distance of roads to the nearest market. These proposals, along with any written dissents by the citizenry, are subjected to a similar process at the national level, involving national organizations, until some consensus is reached on relative unit values among provinces.

The highly successful Chilean land-tax reassessment of 1965 pioneered the methods just described. In that case the President of the Republic made the final decision on disputed unit values, making some small adjustments suggested by dissenters. In another country the decisionmaker might be the supreme court or the legislature. The important point is that at all levels there be citizen participation in defining unit values.

Preparation of the Actual Tax Roll

Finally, the two efforts—the cadastral survey and the tables of unit values—are merged by computer to create the tax roll. A statement is issued to each identified landowner specifying the location and size of the property, the area of each soil type, and the quality and distance of access to a market. Buildings and other taxable improvements are described by size, type of construction, and quality (average, above average, or below average). For urban property, location values depend on the street or neighborhood.

After discrepancies reported by owners are resolved, the actual tax bills are prepared. Areas of land and buildings are multiplied by unit values to produce tax values, and by the tax rate to produce the amount of tax due.

Eliminating Traditional Appeals

Readers accustomed to individual property valuations in the United States or other industrial countries can appreciate the justice and efficiency of the unit value system. Unlike older systems that try to estimate values for each property, the unit system is simple and fair among neighbors. Above all, costs are reduced because the courts are not clogged with costly appeals.

In the unit value system the appeals are heard in the setting of unit values, and not on the values assigned individual properties. Unit values apply equally to everyone in like circumstances. Once the tax bills are sent out, owners can only appeal administrative errors as to area, soil type, or the like—all readily verified and stable from year to year.

Finally, provisions must be made for continual updating of the cadastral survey. Land transfers must be recorded, and unit values must be adjusted yearly for inflation and for new bridges, roads, or other changes in the economic value of land.

In short, an environmentally friendly development strategy requires financing. A modern land tax not only can provide the resources with which to address many local problems, but can also be an instrument to provide powerful incentives and accurate information about land rights. This tax would be levied on the market value of the land and adjusted to provide clear incentives to protect existing old-growth forests and reforestation projects.

The actual tax rate may be decided by law or may be left to local governments to set according to their budgets. However, acceptability of a land tax depends greatly on the feeling that the relative values assigned each farm (or urban property) are fair. This is accomplished by the unit value method—thus increasing the political viability of a land program to protect both people and the environment.

REVENUE POTENTIAL OF A MODERN LAND TAX

So few developing countries have created a modern land tax that it is difficult to project potential revenues. In Chile's very successful reform of 1963–65, the revenue was roughly tripled—an increase amounting to about 2 percent of GDP.

Few countries have any comprehensive estimates of the national capital stock, but many have estimates of the contribution of the agricultural and urban housing sectors to their GDP. One can attempt to approximate the amount of exempted property, the amount of property eligible for tax reductions, and the ratio of market value that will actually be achieved by the assessment process. The proposed tax rate can then be applied to this calculation.

For example, if national planners believe that the value added by agriculture accounts for about 40 percent of GDP, and that net income in agriculture is about one-half of the value added for land, one-quarter for labor, and one-quarter for machinery and inventories not subject to a land tax, then one can make a crude estimate of potential revenue. On the assumptions stated, the revenue potential might be between 2.5 and 3.0 percent of GDP from agricultural land; urban real estate would probably yield a similar amount.[45] Of course, the share of rural and urban property in total national wealth varies greatly among countries, and so the potential revenue from a land-tax system will also differ.

In practice, revenue potential would also be estimated by extrapolating from existing land taxes, inadequate though they are. And once a serious cadastral survey is under way, it quickly becomes possible to make refined estimates generated by the survey itself. It is also necessary to adjust revenue estimates to allow for any trade-offs; that is, if export taxes are to be repealed when a land tax is created, total revenues will rise less. And if the land-tax revenues are earmarked largely for local governments, central governments will be able to reduce annual grants—so the land-tax revenue will not be all gain for local governments. It will, however, give them greater autonomy and decisionmaking power.

USES OF THE NEW REVENUE

Land-tax revenues are usually assigned to local governments, which use the monies to finance roads, bridges, and community services of obvious need and benefit to the community. This is the practice in Chile, the United States, and in other countries with a modern tax. It would also be possible, however, to earmark part of the tax for certain other uses. For instance, one-half of the proceeds might be paid into a land bank to provide the landless and small farmers with mortgage loans to purchase land.

When revenues are used to meet local needs, the taxes enjoy a greater degree of political support. The land bank could be required to lend at least 80 percent of the land-tax revenues in the municipality from which they came. This would be popular with the landless, who need credit to buy land, and with the sellers, who want more of the purchase price in cash than the poor can pay. The remaining revenues, as well as funds obtained from international agencies and bilateral donors, would be available to increase the loanable funds for the poorest areas of the country.

Finally, to enhance the environmentally friendly aspect of the land tax, revenues should never be used to build roads into protected areas, although improving access to other areas should be a priority. As "matching" or "counterpart" funds, land-tax proceeds could also leverage significant external resources to finance conservation plans for environmentally threatened lands.[46]

CONCLUSION

Land-tax reform is needed throughout Central America. Technological advances make it possible to identify rural properties efficiently and to arrive at approximate unit values in an equitable manner as part of a cadastral survey. Reform is feasible because external donor agencies are willing to help finance the necessary land inventory survey, and because part of the resultant tax proceeds can and should be allocated to pay for maintaining and updating the land records and valuations.

The economic advantages of land taxation are well known. The tax is relatively onerous for owners who do not cultivate their farmland. For those who invest and manage their land relatively well, the tax is much gentler than existing taxes on sales, production, and export, which would be replaced in whole or in part.

Politically, land taxation provides revenues for local services and infrastructure investment. It may also lead taxpayers to demand of their officials a degree of accountability that is missing when municipalities are funded by grants from the central government. In addition, the consensus building needed to define unit values of land and various kinds of construction encourage participation in local democracy.

Land taxation contributes greatly to protecting the environment by requiring an inventory of natural resources, defining rights, and identifying occupants and owners. Land taxes also provide revenues to help meet local expenses. Costs will vary widely from place to place; however, in fragile land areas, they may well include forest guards and small ecotourism facilities to give the poor a stake in preserving the natural resources that tourists come to experience. Finally, when the land tax is high enough to be noticeable to owners, exemptions from it for environmentally sound practices become valuable incentives.

Land taxes are no panacea, but they can be a significant policy tool to help solve the problems of poverty, underdevelopment, and environmental destruction.

Notes

[1] For a description of the relationship between poverty and environment, see H. Jeffrey Leonard, *Environment and The Poor: Development Strategies for a Common Agenda*, U.S.-Third World Policy Perspectives No. 11 (New Brunswick, NJ: Transaction Publishers in cooperation with the Overseas Development Council, 1989).

[2] Some U.S. states apply lower tax rates or lower assessment-to-market value ratios to farmland than to commercial or industrial property. Even after these reductions, the average U.S. farm owner paid $5.22 per acre in property taxes in 1990. The rate in Wisconsin, which taxes all real estate alike, averaged $17.16/acre in 1990; that was 2.14 percent of full market value. See U.S. Dept. of Agriculture, *Farm Real Estate Developments* (Washington, DC: USDA, June 1991), pp. 27-32.

[3] World Bank, *World Development Report, 1988* (New York: Oxford University Press, 1988).

[4] Some examples of such major luxury items bought by the rich but rarely taxed are private school tuition fees, fees paid to private clinics and doctors, travel abroad, goods purchased while abroad and not taxed upon return, the cost of building mansions, and clothing made by dressmakers and tailors rather than bought in stores.

[5] The *World Development Report, 1988* treats taxation and the need for tax reform in developing countries in considerable depth, op. cit.

[6] Land taxes normally include the value of buildings and other improvements, although a good theoretical case can be made for the temporary exemption of productive improvements as an incentive.

[7] Food and Agricultural Organization (FAO), *Examen de las Políticas y Estrategias para el Desarrollo Rural* (San José, Costa Rica: FAO, April 1985), p. 21.

[8] John D. Strasma, "Agricultural Taxation in Costa Rica," paper presented at the International Seminar on Real Property and Land as Tax Base for Development, Taiwan, November 14-17, 1988. Reprint available from the Land Tenure Center, University of Wisconsin, Madison, WI 53706.

[9] John D. Strasma, Peter Gore, Jeffrey Nash, and Refugio I. Rochin, *Evaluation of El Salvador's Land Reforms* (San Salvador: USAID, 1983). Reprint available from the Land Tenure Center, University of Wisconsin, Madison, WI 53706. Most owners of large farms appear to have declared values for land tax purposes considerably below the actual market values in 1976 and 1977. Fewer than 10 percent appear to have anticipated land reform or sought larger bank loans with their farms as collateral, the usual reasons that landowners would declare more than true market value for land tax purposes.

[10] The highest rate is only 2.5 quetzales per hectare, well under $1.00. By way of comparison, an average Wisconsin farmer would pay land taxes of about $60 per hectare ($24/acre) per year, though the market value of his land is well under that of the best Guatemalan farm land.

[11] John D. Strasma, James R. Alm, Eric N. Shearer, and Alfred Waldstein, *The Impact of Agricultural Land Revenue Systems on Agricultural Land Usage in Developing Countries* (Burlington, VT: Associates in Rural Development, 1987).

[12] John D. Strasma, "Tributación Agrícola en Honduras," paper presented at the International Seminar on Land Taxation and Land Markets, Tegucigalpa, Honduras, August 1990. Reprint available in English or Spanish from the Land Tenure Center, University of Wisconsin, Madison, WI 53706.

[13] Bureau of the Land Survey, "Exposición Cadastral a los Miembros del Consejo Superior de Planificación Económica," (Tegucigalpa, Honduras: Bureau of the Land Survey, February 13, 1988).

[14] By way of comparison, local property tax rates in Wisconsin average about 2.0 percent a year on market values.

[15] Law 6184, November 29, 1977, quoted in *Investor's Guide to Costa Rica* (San José, Costa Rica: Costa Rican-American Chamber of Commerce, November 1989), p. 150.

[16] John D. Strasma and Robert Waugh, *Agrarian Reform, Land Purchase and Productivity* (San José, Costa Rica: USAID, 1984). Construction of the road was financed with a grant from USAID. The Ministry of Public Works was supposed to maintain it but did not, considering this road a low priority in times of budget cuts. The municipality refused to maintain the road, because by law the beneficiaries of the land distribution program were exempt from the land tax. Many beneficiaries paid their share willingly, but a few "free loaded," refusing to pay. The efficient and logical answer is to have land program beneficiaries pay taxes on their parcels just like any other owners.

[17] A progressive tax on each person's holdings is worth study in Nicaragua because of the conflictive land situation. Normally, it is much wiser to tax each parcel by itself at a fixed rate. Then each municipality taxes land in its own jurisdiction; this is much simpler to assess, bill, and collect.

[18] See Jonathan Skinner, "If Agricultural Taxation Is So Efficient, Why Is It So Rarely Used?" paper presented at the Conference on Rural Organization and Credit Markets, Annapolis, MD, June 1989. Skinner gives a fifth reason. He sees taxes on income and exports as a form of partnership or risk sharing between government and producers. We have yet to find farmers in land-tax countries who would prefer to pay export or income taxes instead of land taxes of equal average amount per year, for the risk-sharing or insurance element that is theoretically present in output-based taxes. Anyhow, governments routinely forgive land tax due in drought-stricken or other disaster areas, so in practice there is partial insurance even under a land tax.

[19] Ministry of Justice and The Kingdom of the Netherlands, Bureau for International Assistance, project and first quarterly report, San José, Costa Rica, 1991.

[20] Even Belize has a program, based in part on the failed effort by The Coca Cola Company to buy up about 10 percent of the farmland for citrus plantations.

[21] Each country's reform has been studied carefully by various scholars. The best recent surveys are in William C. Thiesenhusen (ed.), *Searching for Agrarian Reform in Latin America* (Boston: Unwin Hyman, 1988).

[22] David Kaimovitz, "The Role of Decentralization in the Recent Nicaraguan Agrarian Reform" and Nola Reinhardt, "Contrast and Congruence in the Agrarian Reforms of El Salvador and Nicaragua," in Thiesenhusen, ibid.

[23] Antonio Morales Ehrlich, who became the head of the Salvadoran land reform agency (ISTA) after the murder of José Rodolfo Viera, was a strong and effective proponent of this view despite an overwhelming desire of the beneficiaries to farm in individual parcels or small cooperatives. In the Chilean land reform of 1966-1970, in contrast, the Christian Democrats let the beneficiaries themselves decide among individual parcels, collectives, or hybrids, after three years of experience working together.

[24] John D. Strasma, "What Does it Mean to be a Beneficiary? Rights and Responsibilities of Members of Land Reform Cooperatives in El Salvador," Staff Paper No. 203 (Madison, WI: University of Wisconsin, 1986).

[25] John D. Strasma, *The Debt Situation of Land Reform Beneficiaries in El Salvador, 1990* (Madison, WI: University of Wisconsin, 1990).

[26] Alexander Coles, "Land Markets and Titling Programs in Honduras," unpublished doctoral dissertation, University of Wisconsin, Madison, WI, 1990.

[27] Ironically, bans on sales *cause* reconcentration. They force the poor to borrow from village merchants instead of selling their parcels. If unable to repay, they turn their land over to the merchants, just what lawmakers tried to prevent by forbidding land transfers without permission of the reform agency.

[28] Coles, op. cit.

[29] Hans Binswanger and Miranda Elgin describe this problem eloquently in "Reflections on Land Reform and Farm Size," in Carl K. Eicher and John M. Staatz, *Agricultural Development in the Third World*, 2nd ed. (Baltimore: The Johns Hopkins University Press, 1990), pp. 343-54.

[30] For specific examples of successful credit programs, see John D. Strasma, "Making Land Banks Viable," Staff Paper No. 242 (Madison, WI: Department of Agricultural Economics, 1990). A key element is recognition that not every rural worker is cut out to be a farm owner/operator and that unsuccessful farmers can and should sell their interests to another *campesino*, rather than waiting passively for a bailout or foreclosure.

[31] For detailed accounts of these problems, see the January 1991 issue of *Tapir Tracks*, the quarterly newsletter of the Monteverde Conservation League, Costa Rica.

[32] Ernest Lutz and Herman Daly, *Incentives, Regulations and Sustainable Land Use in Costa Rica* (Washington, DC: World Bank, July 1990), p. 7.

[33] Ibid.

[34] For examples, see almost any issue of the *Tico Times*, an English-language weekly published in San José.

[35] An owner who does hire guards may also face criminal charges if the guards use violence to repel squatters; there are problems of this sort currently in the Pavones area in southern Costa Rica, see *Tico Times* (April and May 1991).

[36] Dale Adams and Claudio Gonzalez-Vega have led efforts to analyze the problems of agricultural credit programs in developing countries. For example, see Claudio Gonzalez-Vega, "On the Viability of Agricultural Development Banks: The Case of the Banco Nacional de Costa Rica" (Columbus, OH: Department of Agricultural Economics, Ohio State University, May 1990) ESO No. 1735.

[37] Costa Rican cattle ranchers recently won enactment of a law forcing banks to renew overdue debts, at interest well below expected inflation. This left the banks close to insolvency, and the legislature did not replenish their capital. Naturally, no banker there has the slightest interest in making new loans to farmers, large or small.

[38] Brazil recently changed policy and now encourages land rentals. Priority is given to credit for tenants who sign graduated leases for at least five years. In one popular model, no rent is payable the first year while the tenant clears the brush and plants the first crop, but thereafter the tenant pays a cash rent indexed for inflation.

[39] Strasma, Gore, Nash, and Rochin, op. cit.

[40] Agrarian tribunals have been highly successful in several countries and are being studied intensely by specialists in agrarian law in Central America. Typically, they use two non-lawyer members who know a great deal about farming in the region, plus one lawyer who presides and sees to it that the statutes are carried out.

[41] Denise Stanley, "Demystifying the Tragedy of the Commons," in *Grassroots Development: The Journal of The Inter-American Foundation*, Vol. 15, No. 3, 1991, pp. 26-35.

[42] The Homestead Act of 1862 gave farmers clear title to up to 160 acres of public lands free, after they lived on it and cultivated at least part of it for five years. Settlers who changed their minds sold their rights to others, who stuck it out and obtained titles.

[43] Similar measures are used in some U.S. states, such as Wisconsin, to discourage the subdivision of farms near cities. The land is taxed at its use value in farming, rather than its market value for housing. If converted, the accumulated tax difference is due and payable immediately, with interest.

[44] For instance, the International Association of Assessing Officers and the Lincoln Institute of Land Policy held a major world conference and training program on land taxation in Cambridge, Massachusetts, in September 1991. A detailed chapter on the creation of a modern land tax appears in Strasma, Alm, Shearer, and Waldstein, op. cit.

[45] That is, gross domestic product (GDP) $\times$ 0.40 $\times$ 0.5 = 0.20 $\times$ GDP. Capitalize this at the interest-rate estimate appropriate for the sector; if this were 10 percent, the capital value of the land would be estimated as 0.20 $\times$ 1/0.10, or 2.00 $\times$ GDP. If the assessment process expected to achieve 90 percent of market value, on average, then the tax base would be about 1.80 $\times$ GDP. If about 10 percent of the property would be exempt (religious, government, the poor, etc.) and another 10 percent would be exempt under incentive provisions, the base falls to 1.80 $\times$ 0.8, or 1.44 $\times$ GDP. Finally, if the proposed tax rate were to be 2 percent a year, the revenue estimate would be 1.44 GDP $\times$ 0.02, or just under 3 percent of annual GDP.

[46] See, for instance, World Resources Institute, *Natural Endowments: Financing Resource Conservation for Development*, project report commissioned by the United Nations Development Programme (Washington, DC: World Resources Institute, 1989).

Part IV
Appendix

Beatrice Bezmalinovic
Cynthia Knowles

FIGURE 1. POPULATION GROWTH IN CENTRAL AMERICA[a]

At the present rate, the population of Central America will double in 28 years. Because of the extension of agricultural practices that erode and deplete the land–in particular, cattle ranching–there is much less arable land available today than there was 30 years ago. Yet, the same land surface that supported about 12 million people in 1960 may have to support over 60 million people in 2025. Raising the standard of living for the rural poor, while protecting a tiny, overused resource base, is Central America's key environmental challenge.

	Belize	Costa Rica	El Salvador	Guatemala	Honduras	Nicaragua	Panama	Central America	United States
Population Estimate 1991 (millions)	0.2	3.1	5.4	9.5	5.3	3.9	2.5	29.9	252.8
Population 1960 (millions)	0.1	1.2	2.6	4	1.9	1.5	1.1	12.4	180.7
Population Projected to 2025 (millions)	0.5	5.6	9.4	21.7	11.5	8.2	3.9	60.7	333.7
Population Density (per square mile)	26	159	656	225	122	77	83	151	68
Annual Natural Increase[b] (percent)	3.3	2.4	2.8	3	3.1	3.4	2.1	2.5	0.8
Birth Rate (per 1,000 population)	38	28	35	38	39	42	26	31	17
Death Rate (per 1,000 population)	6	4	8	8	8	8	5	6	9
Married Women Using Modern Contraceptive Methods (percent)	--	58	45	19	31	23	54	42	69
Population "Doubling Time" at Current Rate of Increase (years)	21	28	25	23	23	21	34	28	88

[a]Unless otherwise noted data is from late 1980s.
[b]Population growth rate excluding migration.

Sources: Population Reference Bureau, Inc., *1991 World Population Data Sheet* (Washington, DC: Population Reference Bureau, 1991); and World Resources Institute, *World Resources 1990-1991* (New York: Oxford University Press, 1990), Table 16.1, p. 254.

FIGURE 2. URBANIZATION IN CENTRAL AMERICA

Forty-six percent of the population of Central America lives in urban areas, far less than in the rest of Latin America (76 percent). Nevertheless, the urban population is growing rapidly—compounding at rates between 2.9 and 5.6 percent a year for the past 30 years. If cities absorb the region's rapidly growing population, massive increases in already severe urban poverty are highly likely.

	Largest City and Its Population	Urban Population 1991 (millions)	Urban Population 1960 (percent of total)	Urban Population 1990 (percent of total)	Average Annual Urban Population Change, 1960-1990 (percent)
Costa Rica	San José (275,000)	1.6	37	54	4.3
El Salvador	San Salvador (336,000)	2.4	38	44	2.9
Guatemala	Guatemala City (754,000)	3.9	33	42	3.7
Honduras	Tegucigalpa (598,000)	2.2	23	44	5.6
Nicaragua	Managua (608,000)	2.3	40	60	4.7
Panama	Panama City (424,000)	1.3	41	55	3.5

Note: San José, Tegucigalpa, Managua, and Panama City are estimates.

Sources: World Resources Institute, *World Resources 1990-1991* (New York: Oxford University Press, 1990), Tables 16.1 and 17.2, p. 254; major city figures from J. W. Wilkie, E.C. Ochoa, and D.E. Lorey (eds.), *Statistical Abstract on Latin America*, Vol. 28 (Los Angeles: Latin American Center Publications, University of California, 1990), p. 127.

FIGURE 3. BASIC ECONOMIC INDICATORS: GROWTH, DEBT, AND TRADE, 1991

The countries of Central America maintain heavy debt burdens relative to their GDP and export earnings. Despite spotty resurgence of growth in the 1990s, countries such as Nicaragua, Honduras, and Costa Rica have debts greater than or nearly equal to their GDP.

	Costa Rica	El Salvador	Guatemala	Honduras	Nicaragua	Panama
GDP ($ millions)	4,870	6,022	8,642	2,967	2,594	5,062
GDP Per Capita ($)	1,933	961	750	403	879	1,960
Consumer Price Inflation (annual average percent)	28.7	14.5	36.9	34	n.a.	1.4
Value of Exports ($ millions)	1,580	620	1,250	925	300	4,100
Value of Imports ($ millions)	1,820	1,275	1,650	995	650	4,700
External Debt ($ millions)	4,050	2,200	2,700	3,150	9,205	6,700

Notes: Data for 1991 are estimates; data for Nicaragua are estimates for 1989-1990, based on available data.

Sources: Economist Intelligence Unit (EIU), *Guatemala, El Salvador, Honduras: Country Report*, No. 1 (London: Business International Ltd., 1992), pp. 3, 5, 7; EIU, *Nicaragua, Costa Rica, Panama: Country Report*, No. 1, (London: Business International Ltd., 1992), pp. 3, 5, 7; and World Bank, *World Development Report 1991* (New York: Oxford University Press, 1991), p. 245.

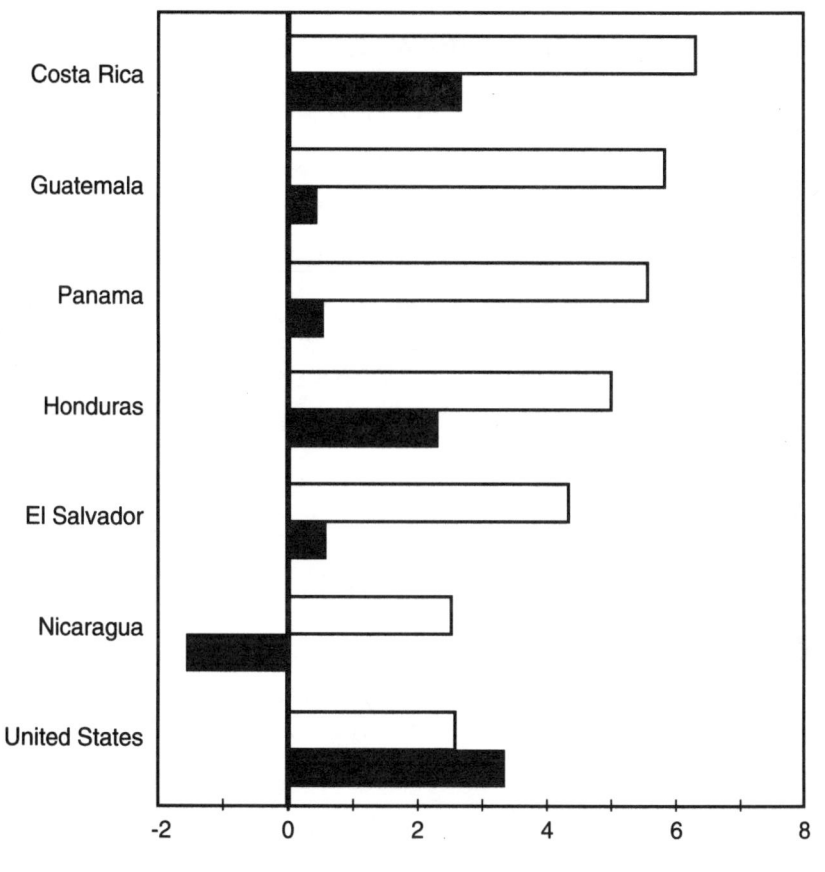

FIGURE 4. GROWTH IN GDP SLOWS: THE "LOST DECADE" IN CENTRAL AMERICA
(average annual growth, percent)

After strong growth in GDP from 1965 through 1980, the 1980s were generally an economic disaster for Central America. The United States, by contrast, grew faster in the 1980s than the 1970s. While recovery is beginning in the 1990s, it is uneven among countries and within social groups.

☐ 1965-1980   ■ 1980-1988

Costa Rica

Guatemala

Panama

Honduras

El Salvador

Nicaragua

United States

-2   0   2   4   6   8

Note: For Guatemala and El Salvador, GDP and its components are at purchaser values.

Source: World Bank, *World Development Report 1990* (New York: Oxford University Press, 1990), Table 2, p. 180

FIGURE 5. U.S. AID TO CENTRAL AMERICA BY EXPENDITURE
1978-1990 ($ millions)

U.S. military and economic assistance to Central America has decreased since its peak in 1985. Increases in overall assistance during the 1980s were largely accounted for by growth in Economic Support Funds, which now account for about half of overall assistance.

Year	Economic Support Funds	Military Assistance	Food Aid	Development Assistance	Total
1978	0	4	9	75	88
1979	8	4	20	96	128
1980	10	10	34	144	198
1981	102	45	74	113	334
1982	177	121	75	133	506
1983	373	138	96	171	778
1984	290	304	105	132	831
1985	767	245	116	326	1,454
1986	458	200	111	272	1,041
1987	684	184	85	310	1,263
1988	458	133	97	236	924
1989	474	137	99	219	929
1990	425	172	97	238	932
1991	513	102	149	164	928
1992	380	112	123	189	804
1993	345	53	108	183	689

Source: Congressional Research Service (CRS), *Central America: Major Trends in U.S. Foreign Assistance Fiscal 1978 to Fiscal 1990* (Washington, DC: CRS, 1990), p. 61, and various updates.

FIGURE 6. U.S. AID TO CENTRAL AMERICA BY COUNTRY, 1978-1991 ($ millions)

The buildup of U.S. aid to the region began in 1979 and peaked in 1985. El Salvador (with 18 percent of the region's population) still accounts for about half of all U.S. aid.

Year	El Salvador	Costa Rica	Guatemala	Honduras	Nicaragua	Panama	Belize
1978	11	8	11	19	14	23	1
1979	10	17	24	30	21	22	1
1980	65	16	14	58	39	3	1
1981	156	17	20	56	62	12	1
1982	280	57	16	112	8	18	1
1983	327	217	30	154	—	13	18
1984	413	182	19	171	—	25	6
1985	571	220	99	297	1	80	25
1986	437	154	115	191	—	34	12
1987	556	180	182	255	—	13	11
1988	402	106	147	199	—	2	16
1989	396	118	158	187	3	1	11
1990	390	89	165	215	1	1	13
1991	292	54	90	151	262	58	n.a.
1992	294	43	85	132	205	58	n.a.

Notes: Data may not add due to rounding; – indicates less than $1 million; n.a. indicates not available.

Source: Congressional Research Service, *Central America: Major Trends in U.S. Foreign Assistance Fiscal 1978 to Fiscal 1990* (Washington, DC: CRS, 1990), pp. 59-64, and various updates.

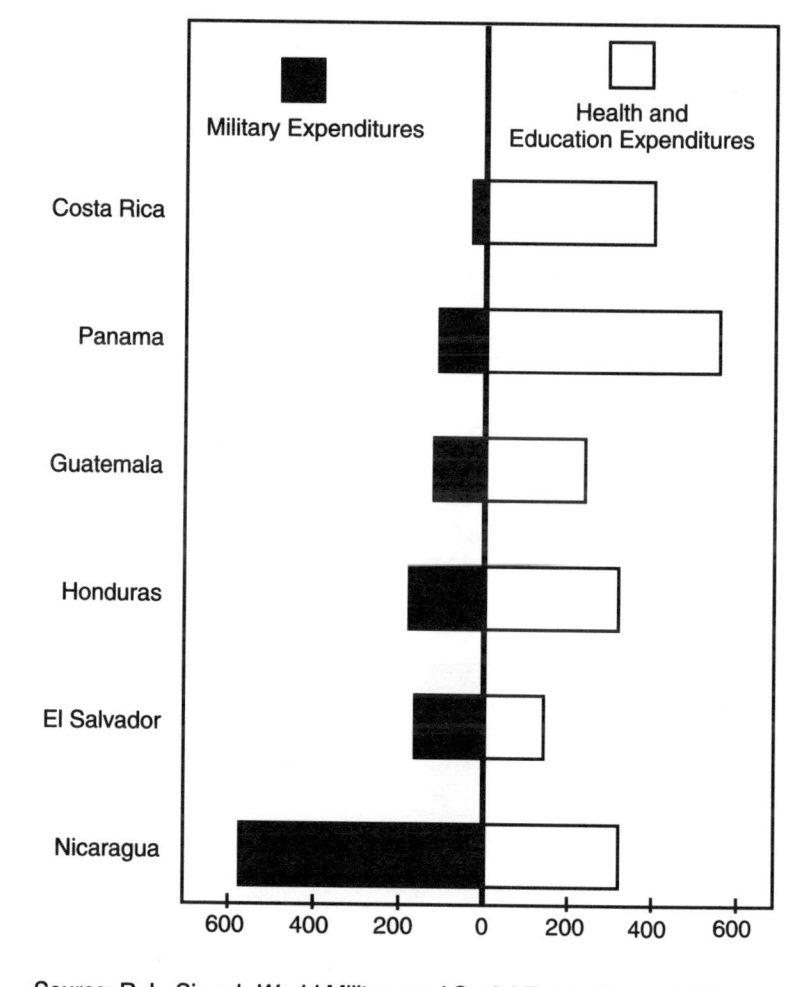

FIGURE 7. MILITARY EXPENDITURES TO HEALTH AND EDUCATION EXPENDITURES, 1987 ($ millions)

In the late 1980s, military expenditure was about 6 percent of health and education expenditure in Costa Rica, but 126 percent of health and education expenditure in El Salvador, and 180 percent in Nicaragua. With the end of the fighting in Nicaragua and El Salvador, Central America now has a historic opportunity to reverse its spending priorities.

Military Expenditures

Health and Education Expenditures

Costa Rica

Panama

Guatemala

Honduras

El Salvador

Nicaragua

600 400 200 0 200 400 600

Source: R. L. Sivard, *World Military and Social Expenditures 1991* (Washington, DC: World Priorities, 1991), Table II, p. 51.

FIGURE 8. INFLATION IN GUATEMALA: WHY THE POOR ARE POORER THAN EVER (quetzales)

In Guatemala, the cost of just about everything that poor people consume has skyrocketed–but wages have not increased with prices. In the countryside, a rural worker earns approximately 10 quetzales ($2) per day, about the same as 10 years ago.

Item	Cost December 1989 (quetzales)	Cost October 1991 (quetzales)
Tortillas (1 pound)	0.56	1.01
Eggs (1 dozen)	2.37	4.30
Black Beans (1 pound)	0.90	1.43
Coca Cola (1 soda)	0.54	1.09
Sugar (1 pound)	0.39	0.95
Tomatoes (1 pound)	0.57	1.31
Powdered Milk (1 pound)	5.21	10.78
Public Bus Fare	0.20	0.40

Note: Prices in Guatemala City only. Exchange rates were 5.24 quetzales per $1 in December 1989 and 5.10 quetzales per $1 in October 1991.

Sources: Instituto Nacional de Estadística, *Indice de Precios al Consumidor,* Boletín No. 50 (Guatemala: Instituto Nacional de Estadística, November 1991); and Instituto Nacional de Estadística, *Compendio Estadística sobre Variables Económico Sociales Año* 1990 (Guatemala City: Instituto Nacional de Estadistica, 1990).

FIGURE 9. DISTRIBUTION OF INCOME (percent)

The distribution of income was skewed in every country in Central America in 1980, and available country studies suggest that the situation generally stayed the same or worsened during the disastrous 1980s. If economic growth resumes in the 1990s, it is likely to continue to benefit the wealthier segments of the population disproportionately, and income disparities are likely to widen.

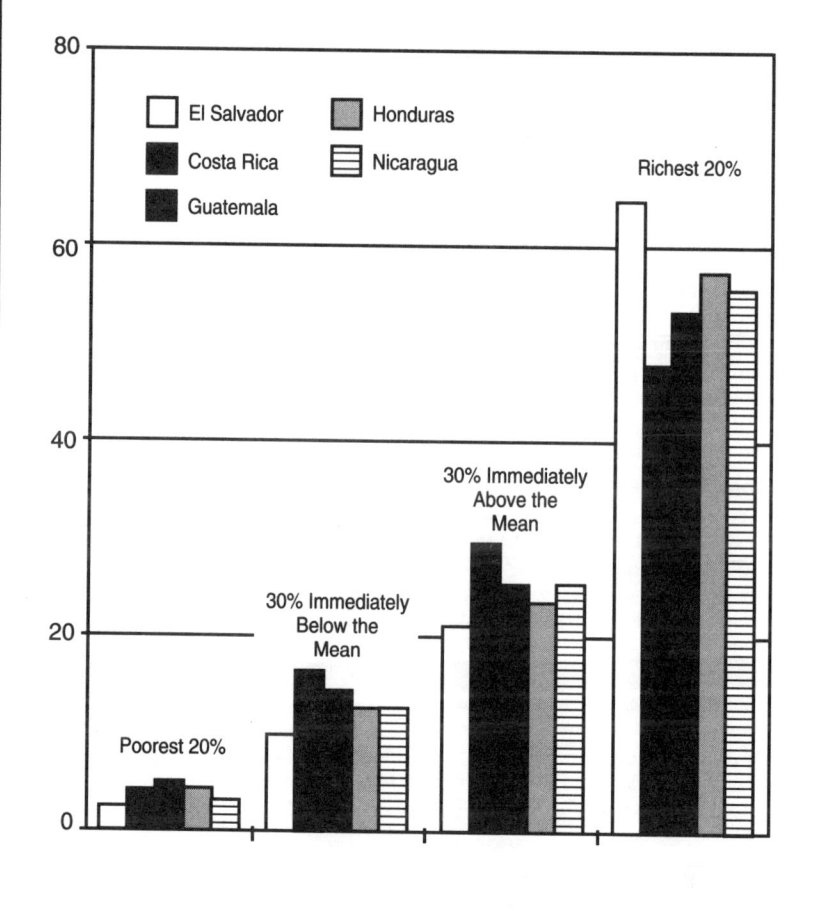

Source: Economic Commission for Latin America and the Caribbean, "Central America: Bases for a Reactivation and Development Policy," *CEPAL Review*, No. 28 (April 1986), Table 4, p. 9.

FIGURE 10. POVERTY IN CENTRAL AMERICA

In rural Central America, between 34 and 84 percent of the population is poor or extremely poor (see chart A). In urban areas, some 14 to 58 percent live in poverty (see chart B). However, data on poverty in Central America is uneven at best. The most commonly used definitions of poverty are based on income per capita. The World Bank defines persons who are "poor" as those with per capita incomes of less than $370 per year and "extremely poor" persons as those with per capita incomes of less than $275 per year.[1]

It is extremely difficult to measure individual or family incomes, much less the distribution of these incomes within countries. Poor families typically have a large number of very small, nonmonetary sources of income (e.g., in-kind income from agricultural labor, unpaid work contributed by children or the elderly). Census techniques seldom aggregate and measure the multiple, minuscule incomes of the poor; and if they do, country-to-country comparisons are at best rough approximations. Further distortions are introduced when local incomes are converted into dollar quantities that can be compared or aggregated.

Site-specific studies of poverty are usually more meaningful than national, regional, or global estimates. For more narrowly focused studies, many indicators other than per capita income are commonly used—for example, the proportion of income recipients earning less than a constant minimum wage, the proportion of families consuming a certain number of calories, or the proportion of families whose income can purchase a certain standard of living or minimal basket of goods.

The Central American and Panamanian Institute for Nutrition (INCAP)[2] distinguishes between "poor" and "extremely poor" with a definition that is based on a family's capacity to purchase a minimal standard of nutrition. INCAP's poverty estimates for countries and the region as a whole are based on extrapolation from smaller samples. These estimates are slightly higher than World Bank country figures.[3]

---

[1]For a discussion of some basic definitions of poverty and alternative indicators, see World Bank, "What Do We Know About the Poor?" *World Development Report 1990* (New York: Oxford University Press, 1990), pp. 24-38.

[2]INCAP, Análisis de la Situación Alimentaria Nutricional en Centroamérica y Panama (Guatemala City: INCAP, June 1989), Vol. 1.

[3]United Nations Development Programme, "Population Below Poverty Line, 1977-1986," *Human Development Report* 1990 (New York: Oxford University Press, 1990), Table 3, pp. 132-33.

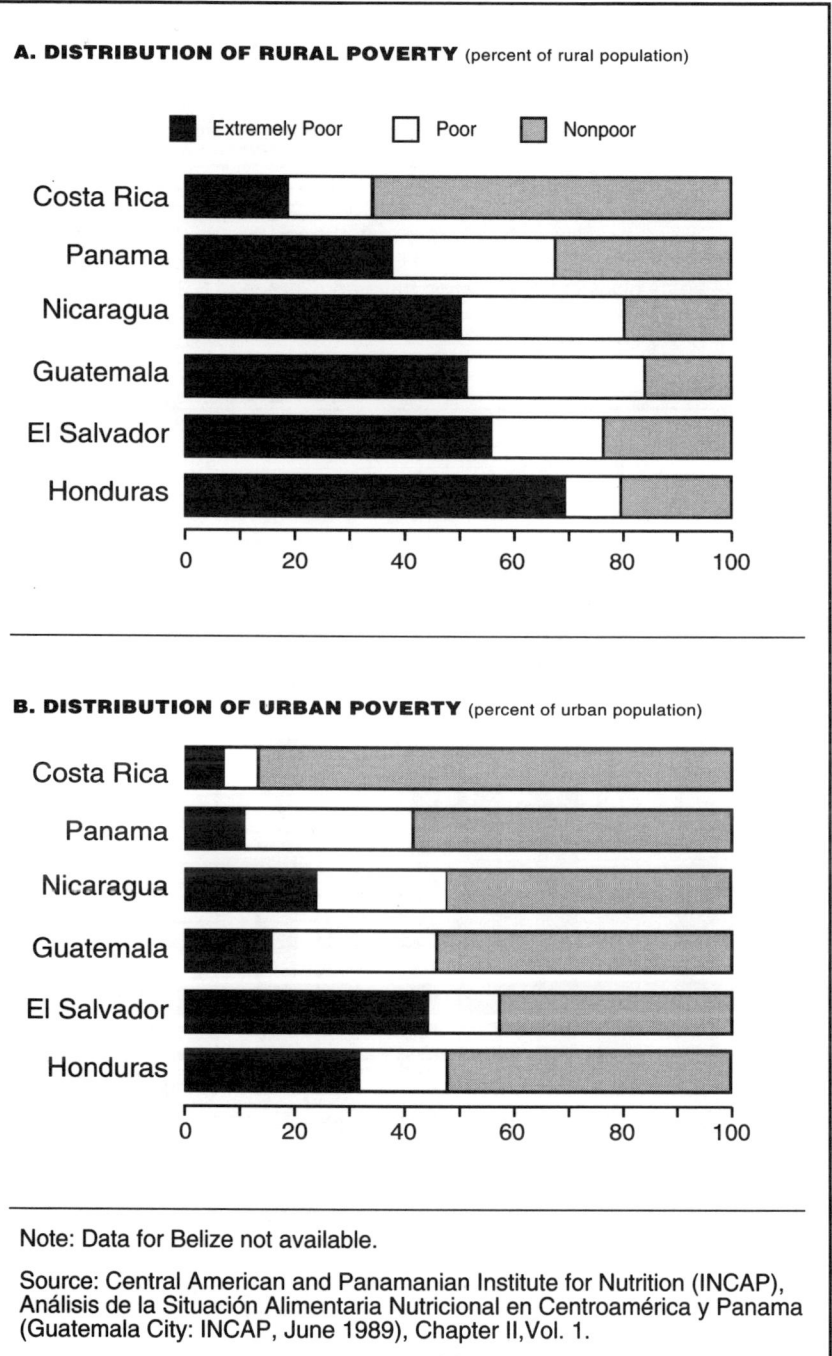

A. DISTRIBUTION OF RURAL POVERTY (percent of rural population)

■ Extremely Poor   □ Poor   ▨ Nonpoor

Costa Rica
Panama
Nicaragua
Guatemala
El Salvador
Honduras

0   20   40   60   80   100

B. DISTRIBUTION OF URBAN POVERTY (percent of urban population)

Costa Rica
Panama
Nicaragua
Guatemala
El Salvador
Honduras

0   20   40   60   80   100

Note: Data for Belize not available.

Source: Central American and Panamanian Institute for Nutrition (INCAP),
Análisis de la Situación Alimentaria Nutricional en Centroamérica y Panama
(Guatemala City: INCAP, June 1989), Chapter II,Vol. 1.

FIGURE 11. ILLITERACY IN CENTRAL AMERICA, 1960-1989 (percent)

All countries in Central America have made substantial strides against illiteracy during the past 30 years, but there are significant differences among countries. Nicaragua has made the most progress, Costa Rica has nearly achieved universal literacy, while Guatemala and Honduras have far to go. Illiteracy is linked to environmental stress through the effects of education on population growth. In El Salvador, for example, women 35 to 44 years old with no education have an average of 6.2 children, while women in this age group with more than 10 years of education have an average of 2.2 children.

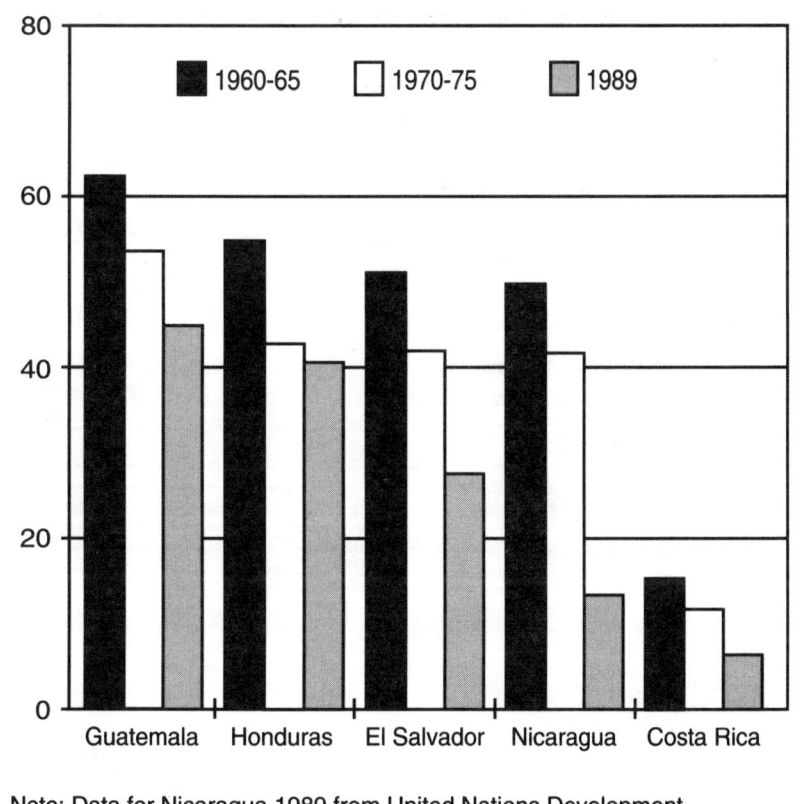

Note: Data for Nicaragua 1989 from United Nations Development Programme, *Human Development Report* (New York: Oxford University Press, 1990).

Sources: World Bank, *Social Indicators of Development 1989* (Baltimore, MD: Johns Hopkins University Press, 1989), pp. 71, 93,125,135, 227, 239; and *Family Health Survey, El Salvador 1988* (San Salvador: Asociación Demográfica Salvadoreña and Center for Disease Control, 1989), Table 3.2.

FIGURE 12. RURAL ACCESS TO POTABLE WATER, 1980 and 1990
(percent of population)

Access to safe drinking water generally improved in Central America during the 1980s. Still, six out of ten rural Central Americans do not have reasonable access to potable water.[a]

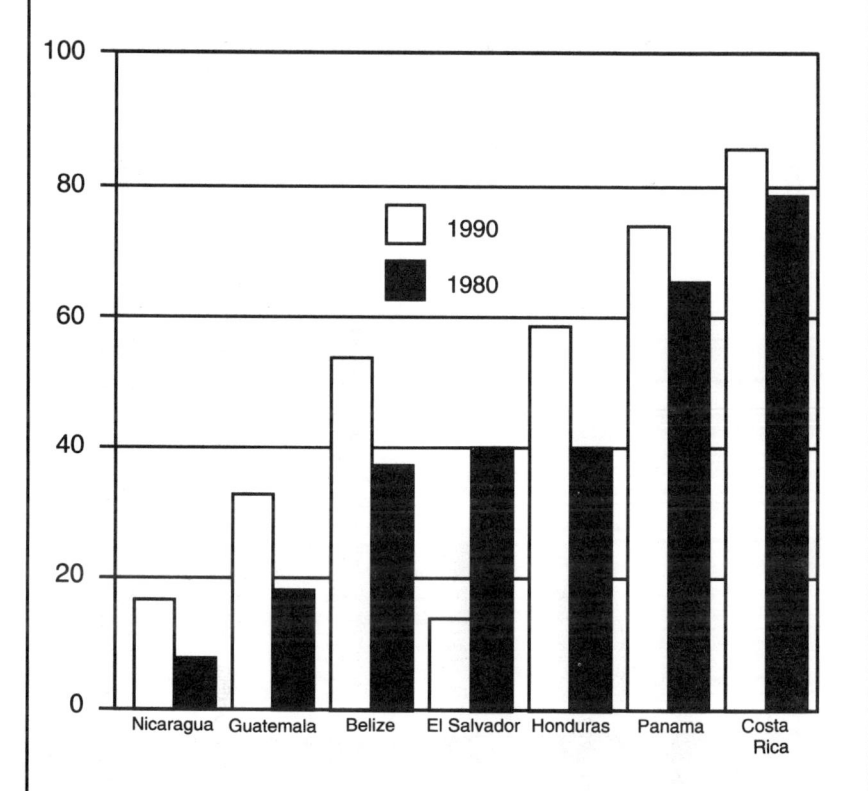

[a] Potable water is defined as treated surface water or untreated but uncontaminated water such as that from springs, sanitary wells, and protected boreholes.

Source: CDM and Associates, *Planning for Water and Sanitation Programs in Central America,* Field Report No. 334 (Washington, DC: USAID, 1991), Table 1, p. 17.

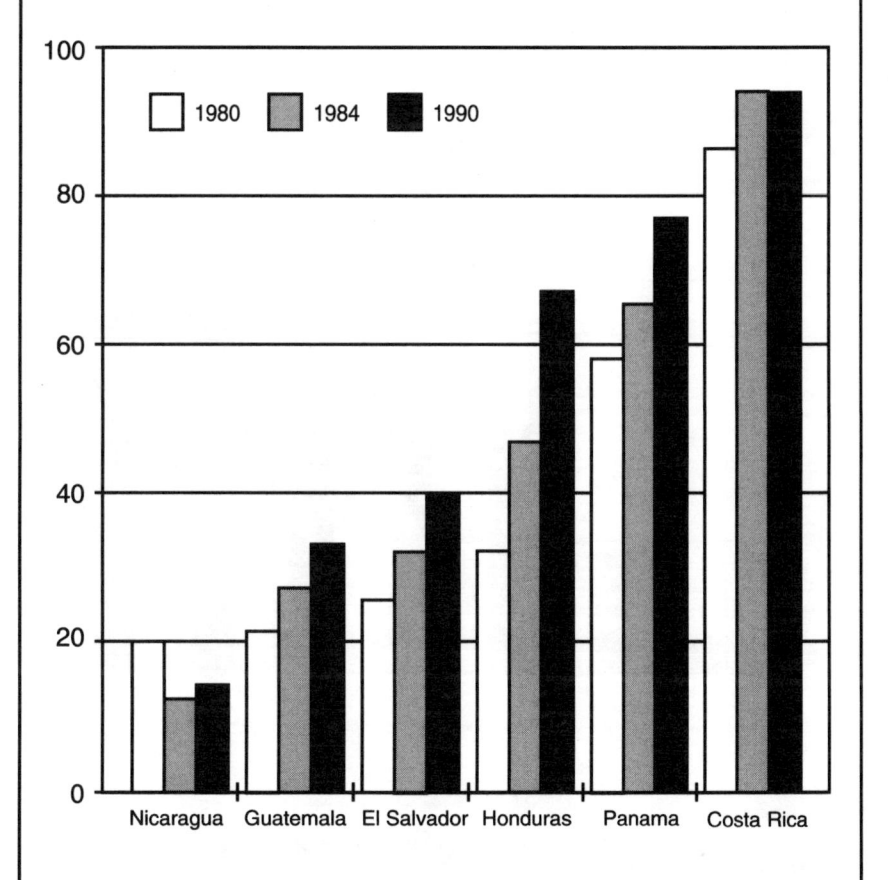

FIGURE 13. RURAL ACCESS TO SANITATION, 1980-1990
(percent of population)

Development agencies, nongovernmental organizations, and governments placed great effort in improving sanitation in rural areas during the 1980s. Overall, coverage in Central America went up from one-third to nearly one-half the rural population.

Legend: 1980, 1984, 1990

100
80
60
40
20
0

Nicaragua   Guatemala   El Salvador   Honduras   Panama   Costa Rica

Source: CDM and Associates, *Planning for Water and Sanitation Programs in Central America,* Field Report No. 334 (Washington, DC: USAID, 1991), Table 2, p. 18.

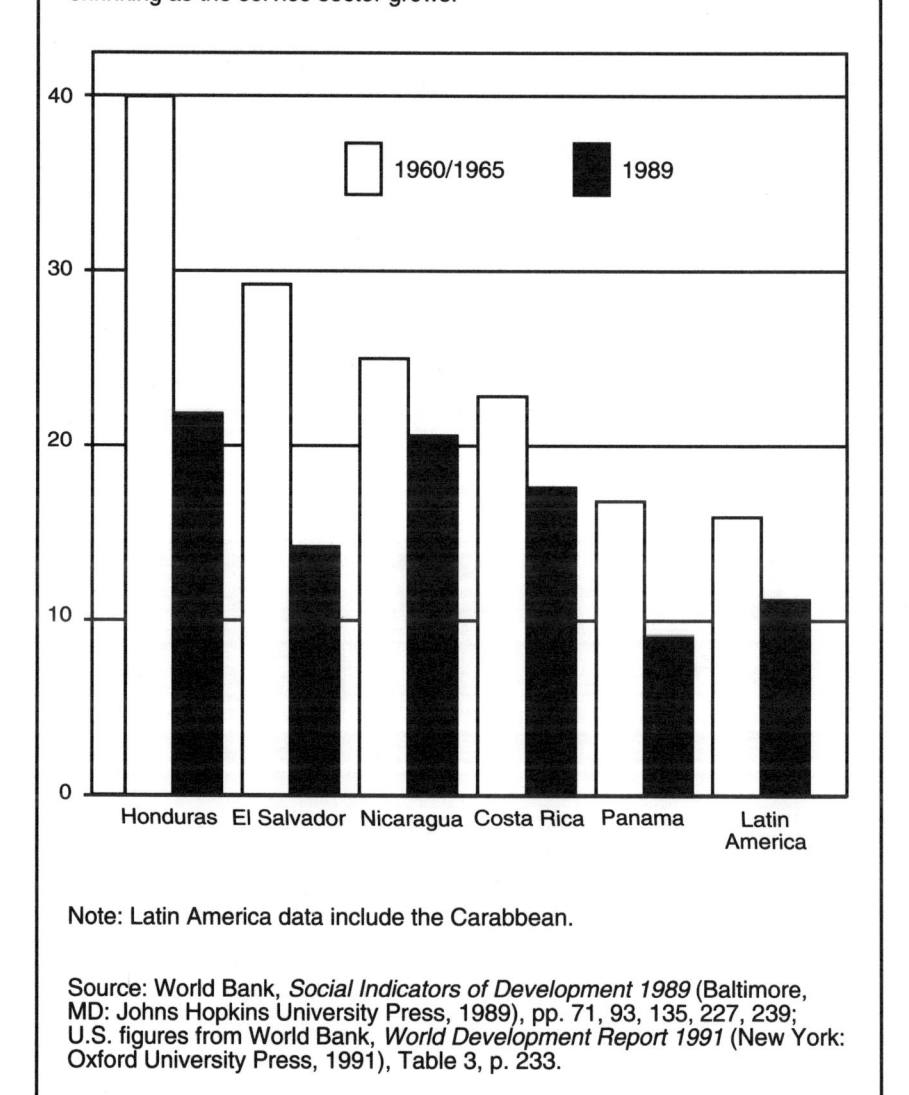

FIGURE 14. AGRICULTURE'S CONTRIBUTION TO GDP, 1960/65 AND 1989 (percent of GNP)

Agriculture accounts for only about 20-25 pecent of total GDP in most countries of the region, although more than 50 percent of Central America's population is rural. Moreover, agriculture's importance to the economy is shrinking as the service sector grows.

| | 1960/1965 | 1989 |

| Honduras | El Salvador | Nicaragua | Costa Rica | Panama | Latin America |

Note: Latin America data include the Carabbean.

Source: World Bank, *Social Indicators of Development 1989* (Baltimore, MD: Johns Hopkins University Press, 1989), pp. 71, 93, 135, 227, 239; U.S. figures from World Bank, *World Development Report 1991* (New York: Oxford University Press, 1991), Table 3, p. 233.

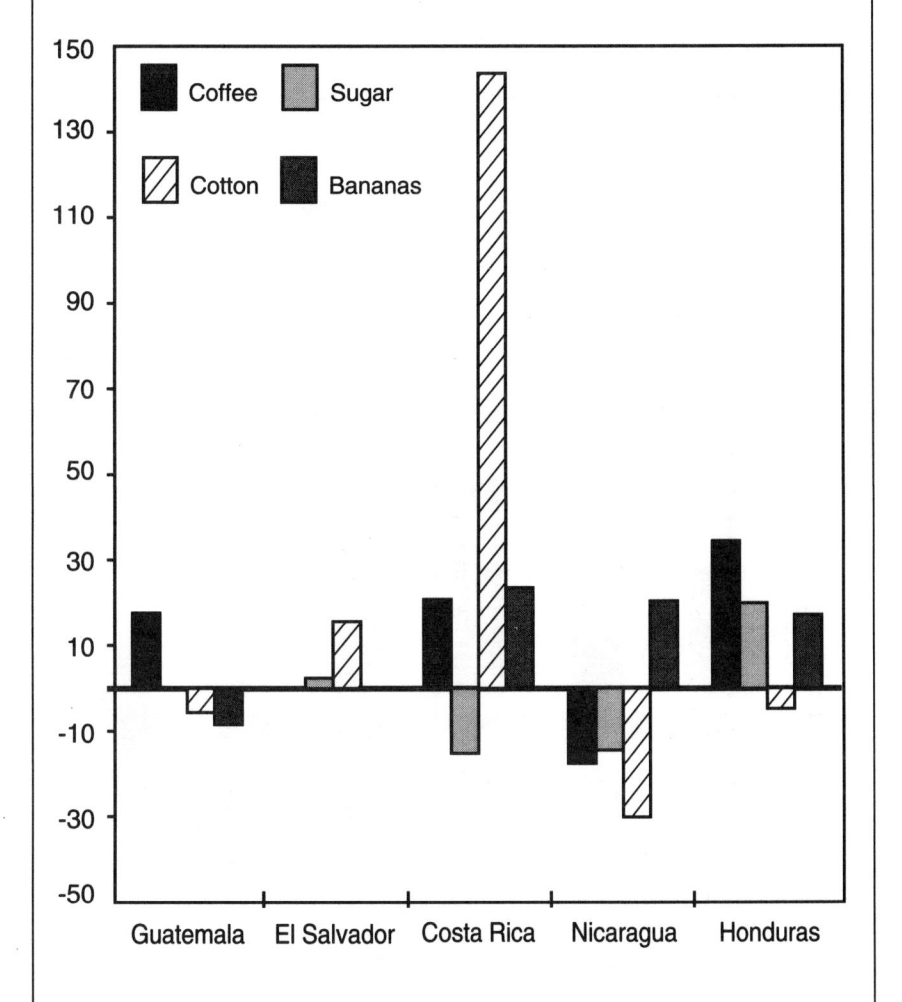

FIGURE 15. CHANGE IN YIELDS OF TRADITIONAL AGRICULTURAL EXPORT CROPS, 1981-1987 (percent change per hectare)

Yields for most traditional agricultural exports were stagnant in the 1980s, especially in Nicaragua.

Note: Coffee and banana data for El Salvador and sugar data for Guatemala are not available.

Source: SIECA, *Series Estadísticas Seleccionadas de Centroamérica,* No. 22 (Guatemala City: SIECA, April 1989), Tables 31-38.

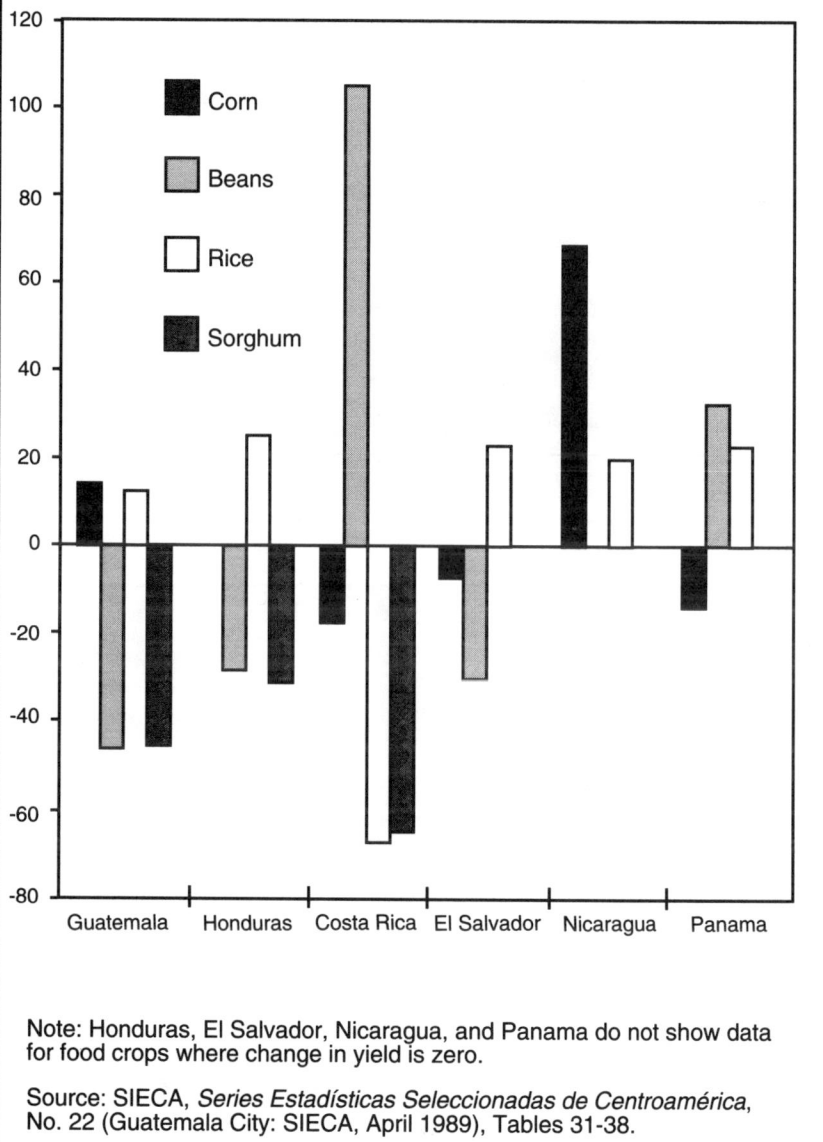

FIGURE 16. CHANGES IN YIELDS OF BASIC FOOD CROPS, 1981-1987
(percent change in yield per hectare)

With the exception of corn in Nicaragua and beans in Costa Rica, yields of most basic food crops declined in Central America during the 1980s.

Corn

Beans

Rice

Sorghum

Guatemala   Honduras   Costa Rica   El Salvador   Nicaragua   Panama

Note: Honduras, El Salvador, Nicaragua, and Panama do not show data for food crops where change in yield is zero.

Source: SIECA, *Series Estadísticas Seleccionadas de Centroamérica*, No. 22 (Guatemala City: SIECA, April 1989), Tables 31-38.

FIGURE 17. COMPARISON OF PESTICIDE USE[a] (grams per hectare)

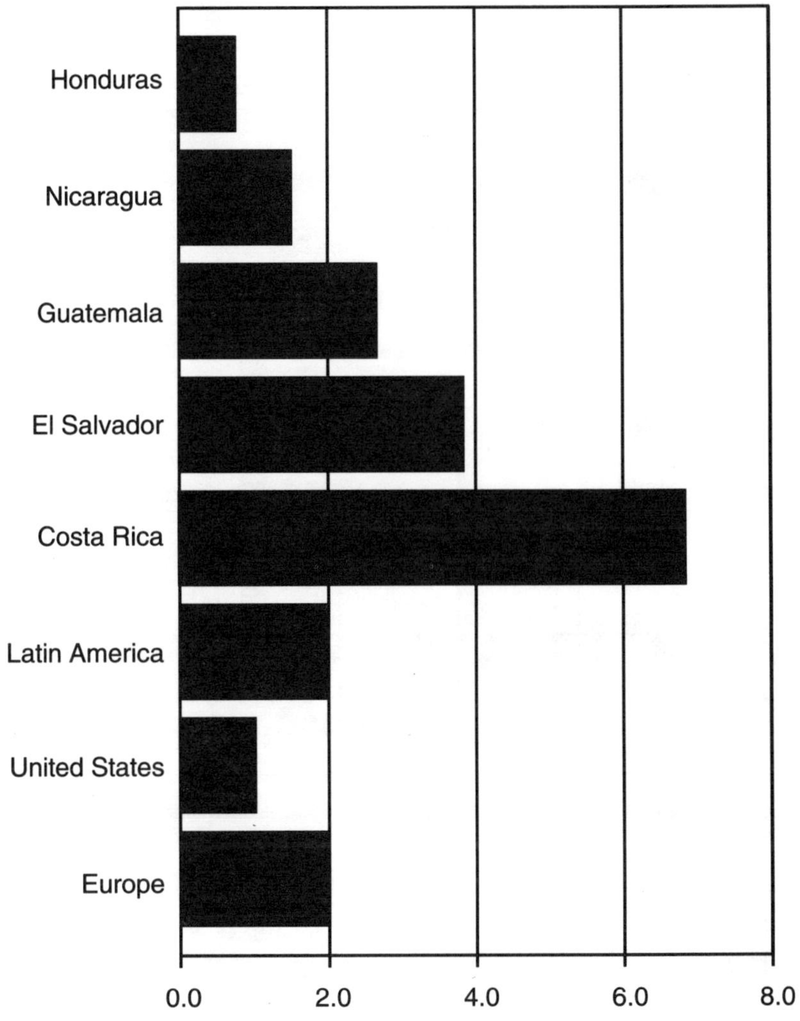

[Bar chart showing pesticide use in grams per hectare for:]

- Honduras
- Nicaragua
- Guatemala
- El Salvador
- Costa Rica
- Latin America
- United States
- Europe

[X-axis: 0.0, 2.0, 4.0, 6.0, 8.0]

[a]Data from early 1980s.

Source: World Resources Institute, *World Resources 1990-1991* (New York: Oxford University Press, 1990) Table 18.2; General Accounting Office, *Food Safety and Quality* (Washington, DC: GAO, 1989), Appendix 1.

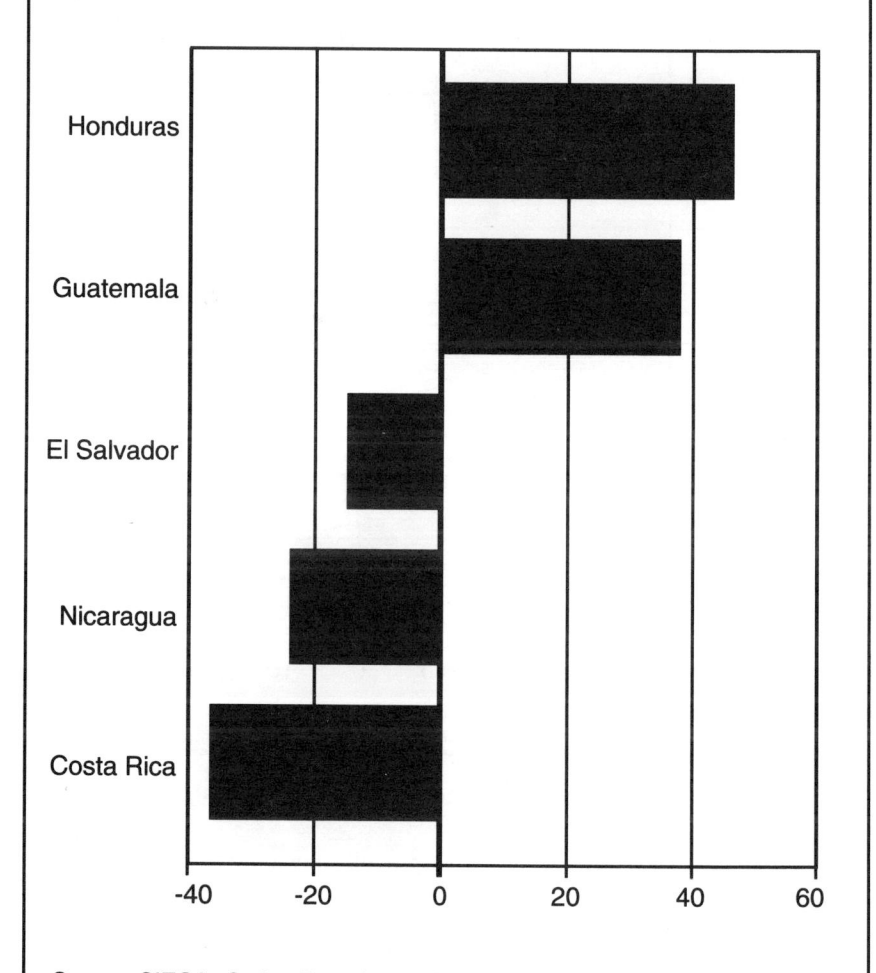

FIGURE 18. CHANGES IN SIZE OF NATIONAL CATTLE HERDS,
1971-1988 (percent change in number of cattle)

In Honduras and Guatemala, cattle herds have expanded over the past 20 years in part because of continuing availability of cheap forest land for pastures. In Costa Rica and El Salvador--where available forest lands are now nearly exhausted--cattle herds are diminishing. Cattle ranching in Nicaragua slowed with the war but is resuming with post-war colonization, settlement, and repatriation programs. Low international beef prices are further depressing herd size.

Source: SIECA, *Series Estadísticas Seleccionadas de Centroamérica*, No.22 (Guatemala City, SIECA, April 1989), Tables 31–38, 61.

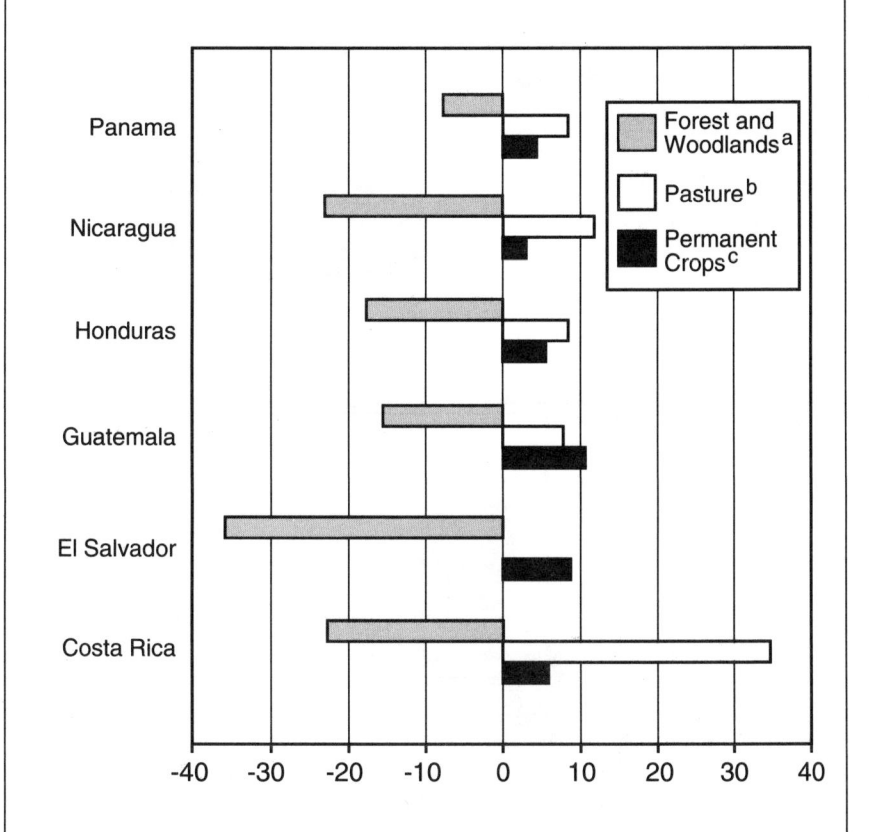

FIGURE 19. TRENDS IN LAND USE 1975-1977 TO 1985-1987 (percent)

Central America's forests have been converted to pasture and permanent crops at an extraodinary rate. In just a decade, about 20 percent of remaining forests disappeared. In El Salvador, forests are almost completely gone.

Panama
Nicaragua
Honduras
Guatemala
El Salvador
Costa Rica

Forest and Woodlands[a]
Pasture[b]
Permanent Crops[c]

-40 -30 -20 -10 0 10 20 30 40

Note: Percent change in pasture land in El Salvador equals zero.

[a] Forest and woodlands includes uncultivated land, grassland not used for pasture, built-on areas, wetlands, and roads.

[b] Permanent pasture is land used five or more years for forage, including natural and cultivated crops.

[c] Permanent cropland includes land under temporary and permanent crops, temporary meadows, market and kitchen gardens, and temporary fallow.

Source: World Resources Institute, *World Resources 1990–1991* (New York: Oxford University Press, 1990), Table 17.1, p. 267.

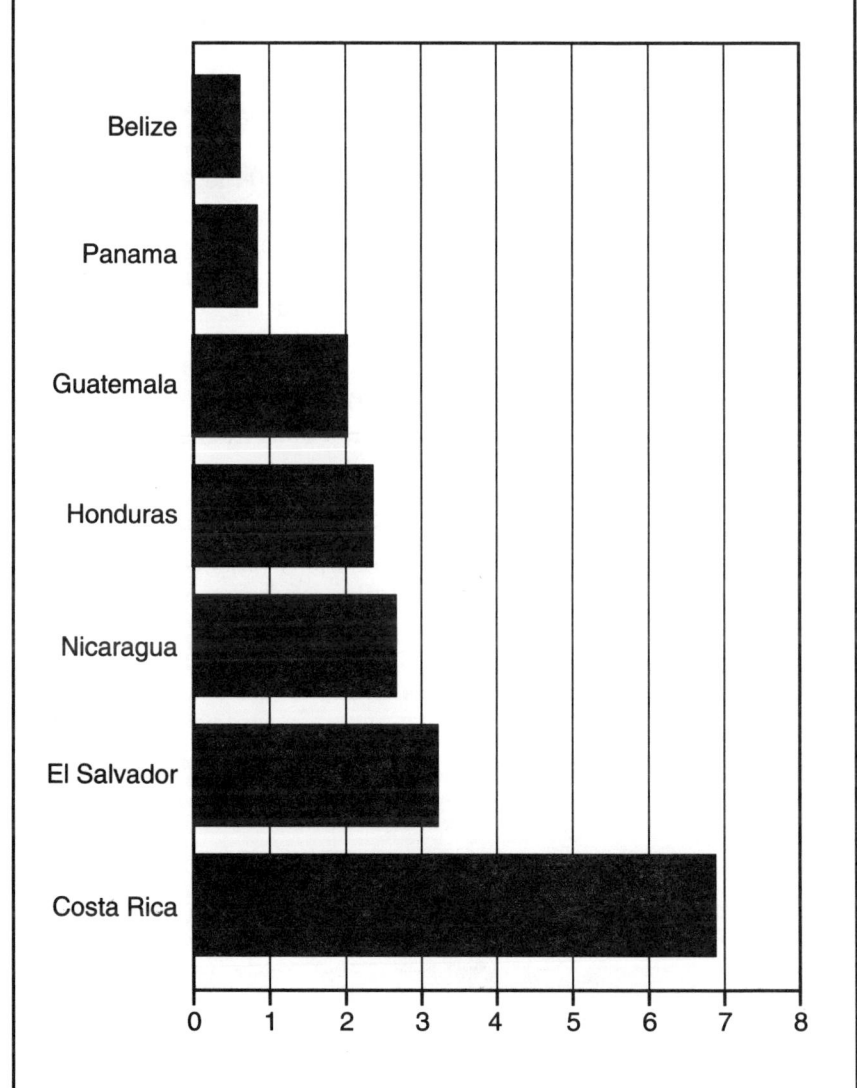

FIGURE 20. AVERAGE ANNUAL DEFORESTATION IN CENTRAL AMERICA IN THE 1980s (percent of total forest area)

Costa Rica still had the region's highest rate of deforestation during the 1980s, despite its innovative programs in the creation of protected areas.

Source: World Resources Institute, *World Resources 1990-1991* (New York: Oxford University Press, 1990), Table 3.1, p. 42.

About the Overseas Development Council

The Overseas Development Council's programs focus on U.S. relations with developing countries in five broad policy areas: U.S. foreign policy and developing countries in a post-Cold War era; international finance and easing the debt crisis; international trade beyond the Uruguay Round; development strategies and development cooperation; and environment and development.

Within these major policy themes, ODC seeks to increase American understanding of the economic and social problems confronting the developing countries and to promote awareness of the importance of these countries to the United States in an increasingly interdependent international system. In pursuit of these goals, ODC functions as:

■ A center for policy analysis. Bridging the worlds of ideas and actions, ODC translates the best academic research and analysis on selected issues of policy importance into information and recommendations for policymakers in the public and private sectors.

■ A forum for the exchange of ideas. ODC's conferences, seminars, workshops, and briefings brings together legislators, business executives, scholars, and representatives of international financial institutions and nongovernmental groups.

■ A resource for public education. Through its publications, meetings, testimony, lectures, and formal and informal networking, ODC makes timely, objective, nonpartisan information available to an audience that includes but reaches far beyond the Washington policymaking community.

Stephen J. Friedman is the Chairman of the Overseas Development Council, and John W. Sewell is the Council's President.

O | D | C

Overseas Development Council
1875 Connecticut Ave., NW
Washington, DC 20009
Tel. (202) 234-8701

195

Overseas Development Council
Program Advisory Committee

About the Authors

Project Director

SHELDON ANNIS is an associate professor of geography and environmental studies at Boston University. Previously, he was senior research associate at the Overseas Development Council. Before that, he was senior research officer at the Inter-American Foundation, where he also edited the journal, *Grassroots Development*. His recent publications include *God and Production in a Guatemalan Town* and *Direct to the Poor: Grassroots Development in Latin America*. Dr. Annis lived in Guatemala for many years and has worked in rural Central America for international development agencies, foundations, and environmental and nongovernmental organizations.

Contributing Authors

OSCAR ARIAS, former President of the Republic of Costa Rica, earned the 1987 Nobel Peace Prize for his efforts to encourage peace in Central America, culminating in the signing of the Central American Peace Plan in August 1987. Most recently, he established the Arias Foundation for Peace and Human Progress. Dr. Arias served as the head of the National Liberation Party for five years before being elected President. He also was a congressman, the Minister of Planning and Economic Policy, and a political science professor at the University of Costa Rica.

JAMES D. NATIONS, an ecological anthropologist, has spent the past 15 years working for the conservation of tropical ecosystems in Latin America. Currently, he is vice president for Latin American Programs with Conservation International in Washington, DC. His publications include *Tropical Rainforests* and a dozen book chapters on park planning, natural resource use, and environmental protection. While in Latin America, he lived for three years with the Lacandon Maya, a rainforest tribe in Chiapas, Mexico; worked as a technical advisor to Guatemala's National Council for Protected Areas; and worked in Ecuadorian Amazonia.

STEPHEN B. COX is the founder and director of Acceso, a nonprofit organization that offers communication services, information, and training in strategic planning and institutional development to Central American organizations. He is also director of the Office of Planning and Development of the Central American Institute for Business Administration (INCAE) in San José, Costa Rica. From 1985 to 1991 he worked for The

Ford Foundation as the representative for Mexico and Central America, and as a program officer in Lima, Peru. Before that, he joined the Inter-American Foundation to support development programs in Peru and Bolivia and helped manage Agua del Pueblo, a Guatemalan organization dedicated to rural development.

ALVARO UMAÑA, an environmental leader who pioneered the implementation of debt-for-nature swaps in Costa Rica, is a faculty member of the Central American Institute for Business Administration (INCAE) in San José, Costa Rica. He served as Costa Rica's Minister of Natural Resources, Energy, and Mines from 1986 to 1990, where he formed debt-for-nature swaps that sold $95 million of Costa Rican commercial debt to support projects enhancing the country's tropical rain forest reserves. He has also served as an international fellow at the World Resources Institute; energy planner for the Latin American Energy Organization; vice president of the International Union for Conservation of Natural Resources; and president of the Arias Foundation for Peace and Human Progress.

KATRINA BRANDON is a senior fellow at the World Wildlife Fund and a consultant on biodiversity policy, most recently for The Rockefeller Foundation and the Policy and Research Division of the World Bank's Environment Department. Since 1987 Dr. Brandon has worked at the World Wildlife Fund on policies and projects designed to link conservation with development. She coordinated a program in four Latin American countries that promoted sustainable development by incorporating environmental concerns into economic decisionmaking. She is co-author of a World Bank study entitled "People and Parks: Linking Protected Area Management with Local Communities" and co-editor of the April 1992 volume of World Development on "Linking Environment and Development."

STUART K. TUCKER was a fellow at the Overseas Development Council until December 1991 and is now a freelance writer, editor, and statistician in Michigan. A public policy analyst and economist, he works primarily on international trade policy and Latin American development issues. He has written numerous articles on international economic policy, co-edited *Growth, Exports, and Jobs in a Changing World Economy: Agenda 1988* (Transaction Publishers in cooperation with ODC, 1988), and co-authored *Trade Policies Toward Developing Countries.* Prior to joining ODC in 1984, he was a research consultant for the Inter-American Development Bank, the Urban Institute, and the Roosevelt Center for American Policy Studies.

JOHN D. STRASMA, professor of agricultural economics at the University of Wisconsin–Madison, teaches courses in public finance and environmental economics. He is currently involved with the Lands Commission of the African National Congress planning for the creation of a tax on rural land in post-apartheid South Africa. He also helped plan land-tax reforms in Bolivia, Chile, Dominican Republic, Honduras, and Peru. Dr. Strasma has worked on land market research and land bank projects in Costa Rica, Dominican Republic, El Salvador, Guatemala, and Honduras. The World Bank recently published his study on the feasibility of land tax reform in Zimbabwe.

RAFAEL CELIS is the director of the Sustainable Agricultural Production and Development Program at the Center for Tropical Research and Training (CATIE) in Turrialba, Costa Rica. From 1985 to 1989 he was a research fellow at the International Food Policy Research Institute (IFPRI) in Washington, DC. IFPRI recently published his monograph *The Role of Agriculture in the Development of Costa Rica.* He also is a board member of the Center for the Promotion of Sciences and Socioeconomic Development, in San José, Costa Rica.

BEATRICE BEZMALINOVIC is a graduate student in the John F. Kennedy School of Harvard University.

CYNTHIA KNOWLES is a graduate student in the Energy and Environmental Studies program of Boston University.

THE PREMISE AND THE PROMISE: Free Trade in the Americas

Sylvia Saborio and contributors

The vision of a hemispheric system of free trade charts a bold new course for U.S.-Latin American relations that promises to transform the economic and political landscape of the hemisphere well into the twenty-first century. In this volume, analysts from the United States, Latin America, and Canada explore the dynamics of the process under way in the Western Hemisphere today, what features free trade areas ought to have, how the process of regional integration ought to proceed, and how the regional architecture ought to relate to the international trading system.

CONTENTS:

Sylvia Saborio:	Overview: The Long and Winding Road from Anchorage to Patagonia
Peter Morici:	Free Trade in the Americas: A U.S. Perspective
José Manuel-Salazar Xirinachs with Eduardo Lizano:	Free Trade in the Americas: A Latin American Perspective
Richard G. Lipsey	Getting There: The Path to a Western Hemisphere Free Trade Area and Its Structure
Refik Erzan and Alexander Yeats:	U.S.-Latin American Free Trade Areas: Some Empirical Evidence
Craig VanGrasstek and Gustavo Vega:	The North American Free Trade Agreement: A Regional Model?
Andrea Butelmann and Alicia Frohmann:	U.S.-Chile Free Trade
Sylvia Saborio:	U.S.-Central America Free Trade
DeLisle Worrell:	U.S.-Caricom Free Trade
Alberto Pascó-Font and Sylvia Saborio:	U.S.-Andean Pact Free Trade
Roberto Bouzas:	U.S.-Mercosur Free Trade

O | D | C

U.S.-Third World Policy Perspectives, No. 18 July 1992, 304 pp.

ISBN: 1-56000-060-0 (cloth) $29.95

ISBN: 1-56000-619-6 (paper) $15.95

AFTER THE WARS:

Reconstruction in Afghanistan, Indochina, Central America, Southern Africa, and the Horn of Africa

Anthony Lake and contributors

After a decade or more of fighting and destruction in various regions of the world, new policies in Washington and Moscow as well as the fatigue on the ground are producing openings, at least, for peace. Negotiations are at different stages regarding Afghanistan, Indochina, Central America, Southern Africa, and the Horn of Africa—but all share new possibilities for peace.

This volume analyzes the prospects for post-war reconstruction and development in these regions, tackling the difficult quandaries they face individually and collectively: Among realistic potential alternatives, what kind of new political structures can best manage post-war reconstruction/development? Which economic policies would be most effective in maintaining peace and political coalitions? Should the focus be on the reconstruction of pre-war economic life or on creating new patterns of development? What are the prospects for democracy and human rights?

The authors thus consider the relationship of economic planning and likely political realities: For example, might diplomats seeking to stitch together a fragile coalition to end the fighting also be creating a government that cannot make the hard economic choices necessary for sustained peace? Might economists calling for post-war economic programs that are theoretically sound but politically unsustainable threaten a tenuous peace?

CONTENTS:

Anthony Lake:	Overview: After the Wars—What *Kind* of Peace?
Selig S. Harrison:	Afghanistan
Nayan Chanda:	Indochina
Benjamin L. Crosby:	Central America
Mark C. Chona and Jeffrey I. Herbst:	Southern Africa
Carol J. Lancaster:	The Horn of Africa

Anthony Lake is Five College Professor of International Relations at Mount Holyoke College. He was Director of Policy Planning from 1977 to 1981 at the U.S. Department of State, and before that a member of the National Security Council staff. He has also been director of the International Voluntary Services and of various projects at the Carnegie Endowment for International Peace and The Ford Foundation. Between 1963 and 1965, he served on the U.S. embassy staff in Hue and Saigon, Vietnam. His most recent book is *Samoza Falling*.

O | D | C

U.S.-Third World Policy Perspectives, No. 16 1990, 224 pp.

ISBN: 0-88738-880-9 (paper) $15.95

ISBN: 0-88738-392-0 (cloth) $24.95

FRAGILE COALITIONS:

The Politics of Economic Adjustment

Joan M. Nelson and contributors

The global economic crisis of the 1980s forced most developing nations into a simultaneous quest for short-run economic stabilization and longer-run structural reforms. Effective adjustment is at least as much a political as an economic challenge. But political dimensions of adjustment have been much less carefully analyzed than have the economic issues.

Governments in developing countries must balance pressures from external agencies seeking more rapid adjustment in return for financial support, and the demands of domestic political groups often opposing such reforms. How do internal pressures shape external bargaining? and conversely, how does external influence shape domestic political maneuvering? Growing emphasis on "adjustment with a human face" poses additional questions: Do increased equity and political acceptability go hand-in-hand? or do more pro-poor measures add to the political difficulties of adjustment? The capacity of the state itself to implement measures varies widely among nations. How can external agencies take such differences more fully into account? The hopeful trend toward democratic openings in many countries raises further, crucial issues: What special political risks and opportunities confront governments struggling simultaneously with adjustment and democratization? The contributors to this volume explore these issues and their policy implications for the United States and for the international organizations that seek to promote adjustment efforts.

CONTENTS:

Joan M. Nelson:	The Politics of Long-Haul Economic Adjustment
John Waterbury:	The Political Management of Economic Adjustment and Reform
Stephen Haggard and Robert R. Kaufman:	Economic Adjustment in New Democracies
Laurence Whitehead:	Democratization and Disinflation: A Comparative Approach
Joan M. Nelson:	The Politics of Pro-Poor Adjustment
Thomas M. Callaghy:	Toward State Capability and Embedded Liberalism in the Third World: Lessons for Adjustment
Miles Kahler:	International Financial Institutions and the Politics of Adjustment

Joan M. Nelson is a senior associate at the ODC. She has been a consultant for the World Bank, USAID, and the IMF, as well as a staff member of USAID. She has taught at the Massachusetts Institute of Technology, the Johns Hopkins University School of Advanced International Studies, and Princeton University's Woodrow Wilson School.

O | D | C

U.S.-Third World Policy Perspectives, No. 12 1989, 186 pp.

ISBN: 0-88738-283-5 (cloth) $24.95

ISBN: 0-88738-787-X (paper) $15.95

ENVIRONMENT AND THE POOR: Development Strategies For A Common Agenda

H. Jeffrey Leonard and contributors

Few aspects of development are as complex and urgent as the need to reconcile antipoverty and pro-environmental goals. Do both of these important goals—poverty alleviation and environmental sustainability—come in the same package? Or are there necessary trade-offs and must painful choices be made?

A basic premise of this volume is that environmental degradation and intractable poverty are often especially pronounced in particular ecological and social settings across the developing world. These twin crises of development and the environment can and must be addressed jointly. But they require differentiated strategies for the kinds of physical environments in which poor people live. This study explores these concerns in relation to irrigated areas, arid zones, moist tropical forests, hillside areas, urban centers, and unique ecological settings.

The overview chapter highlights recent efforts to advance land and natural resource management, and some of the real and perceived conflicts between alleviating poverty and protecting the environment in the design and implementation of developing policy. The chapters that follow offer economic investment and natural resource management options for reducing poverty and maintaining ecological balance for six different areas of the developing world.

CONTENTS:

H. Jeffrey Leonard:	Overview
Montague Yudelman:	Sustainable and Equitable Development in Irrigated Environments
J. Dirck Stryker:	Technology, Human Pressure, and Ecology in the Arid and Semi-Arid Tropics
John O. Browder:	Developmental Alternatives for Tropical Rain Forests
A. John De Boer:	Sustainable Approaches to Hillside Agricultural Development
Tim Campbell:	Urban Development in the Third World: Environmental Dilemmas and the Urban Poor
Alison Jolly:	The Madagascar Challange: Human Needs and Fragile Ecosystems

O | D | C

U.S.-Third World Policy Perspectives, No. 11 1989, 256 pp.

ISBN: 0-88738-282-7 (cloth) $24.95

ISBN: 0-88738-786-1 (paper) $15.95

ECONOMIC REFORM IN THREE GIANTS:

U.S. Foreign Policy and the USSR, China, and India

Richard E. Feinberg, John Echeverri-Gent, Friedemann Müller, and contributors

Three of the largest and strategically most important nations in the world—the Soviet Union, China, and India—are currently in the throes of historic change. The reforms of the giants are transforming global economic and geopolitical relations. The United States must reexamine central tenets of its foreign policy if it is to seize the opportunities presented by these changes.

This pathbreaking study analyzes economic reform in the giants and its implications for U.S. foreign policy. Each of the giants is opening up its economy to foreign trade and investment. What consequences will this new outward orientation have for international trade, and how should U.S. policy respond to these developments? Each giant is attempting to catch up to global technological frontiers by absorbing foreign technologies; in what areas might cooperation enhance American interests, and in what areas must the U.S. protect its competitive and strategic assets? What role can key international economic institutions like the GATT, the IMF, and the World Bank play to help integrate the giants into the international economy?

Economic reform in the giants has important consequences for their political systems. What measures can and should the United States take to encourage political liberalization? How will the reforms affect the foreign policies of the giants, and what impact will this have on U.S. geopolitical interests? The contributors suggest how U.S. foreign policy should anticipate these new circumstances in ways that enhance international cooperation and security.

CONTENTS:

Richard E. Feinberg, John Echeverri-Gent, and Friedemann Müller:	Overview: Economic Reform in the Giants and U.S. Policy
Friedemann Müller:	Economic Reform in the USSR
Rensselaer W. Lee III:	Economic Reform in China
John Echeverri-Gent:	Economic Regorm in India
John Echeverri-Gent, Friedemann Müller, and Rensselaer W. Lee III:	The Politics of Economic Reform in the Giants
Richard P. Suttmeier:	Technology Transfer to the Giants: Opportunities and Challenges
Elena Borisova Arefieva:	The Geopolitical Consequences of Reform

O | D | C

U.S.-Third World Policy Perspectives, No. 14 1990, 256 pp.

ISBN: 0-88738-316-5 (cloth) $24.95

ISBN: 0-88738-820-5 (paper) $15.95

PULLING TOGETHER:

The International Monetary Fund in a Multipolar World

Catherine Gwin, Richard E. Feinberg, and contributors

Side-stepped by the developed countries, entangled in unsuccessful programs in many Latin American and African nations, whipsawed by heavy but inconsistent pressure from commercial banks and creditor countries, and without effective leadership from its major shareholders, the IMF is losing its bearings. It needs a sharp course correction and a strong mandate from its member countries to adjust its policies on each of five critical issues: global macroeconomic management, Third World debt, the resuscitation of development in the poorest countries, the integration of socialist nations into the global economy, and relations with its sister institution, the World Bank. In addition, the IMF needs to bolster its own bureaucratic, intellectual, and financial capacities.

In an economically interdependent but politically centrifugal world, a strong central institution is needed to help countries arrive at collective responses to complex global economic problems. But only if its member states are willing to delegate more authority to the IMF can it help pull together a multipolar world.

CONTENTS:

Richard E. Feinberg and Catherine Gwin:	Overview: Reforming the Fund
Jacques J. Polak:	Strengthening the Role of the IMF in the International Monetary System
Peter B. Kenen:	The Use of IMF Credit
Jeffrey D. Sachs:	Strengthening IMF Programs in Highly Indebted Countries
Guillermo Ortiz:	The IMF and the Debt Strategy
Louis M. Goreux:	The Fund and the Low-Income Countries

O | D | C

U.S.-Third World Policy Perspectives, No. 13 1989, 188 pp.

ISBN: 0-88738-313-0 (cloth) $24.95

ISBN: 0-88738-819-1 (paper) $15.95

POLICY ESSAYS

ODC's new publication series explores critical issues on the U.S.-Third World agenda in 80-120 succinct pages, offering concrete recommendations for action from the perspective of experts, practitioners, and innovative thinkers in the field.

Pressing for Peace: Can Aid Induce Reform?
Nicole Ball
Policy Essay No. 6, September 1992
ISBN: 1-56517-006-7 $9.95

North-South Environmental Strategies, Costs, and Bargains
Patti L. Petesch with Foreword by Maurice F. Strong
Policy Essay No. 5, May 1992
ISBN: 1-56517-005-9 $9.95

Encouraging Democracy:
What Role for Conditioned Aid?
Joan M. Nelson with Stephanie J. Eglinton
Policy Essay No. 4, April 1992
ISBN: 1-56517-004-0 $9.95

Debt Reductions and North-South Resource
Transfers to the Year 2000
Richard E. Feinberg, Eduardo Fernández-Arias, and Frank Sader
Policy Essay No. 3, 1991
ISBN: 1-56517-002-4 $8.00

Debt Conversion in Latin America: Panacea or Pandemic?
Mary L. Williamson
Policy Essay No. 2, 1991
ISBN: 1-56517-001-6 $8.00

Modular Multilateralism:
North-South Economic Relations in the 1990s
Richard E. Feinberg and Delia M. Boylan
Policy Essay No. 1, 1991
ISBN: 1-56517-000-8 $8.00

CHALLENGES AND PRIORITIES IN THE 1990S:

An Alternative U.S. International Affairs Budget FY1993

John W. Sewell, Peter M. Storm, and contributors

The massive political, social, and economic changes in the world over the last two years present an unprecedented opportunity to rethink an reorganize U.S. government budget priorities in the field of international affairs. The second in ODC's series of alternative international affairs budgets is offered to encourage debate over the policies needed to address key global challenges central to U.S. interests in the 1990s.

ISBN: 1-56517-008-3 $9.95

Special offer: Order *Challenges and Priorities in the 1990s* and receive at no additional cost the FY1992 alternative international affairs budget, *United States Budget for a New World Order.*

Reactions to *United States Budget for a New World Order:*

". . . I do commend you on the thought process and your spirit of innovation. It is precisely that which we need at this point in time."
—Frank Carlucci, former Secretary of Defense

"Many of your 'alternative budget' proposals would be worth pursuing."
—Lee H. Hamilton, U.S. House of Representatives

"Your ideas are certainly worthy of consideration by the Congress and the President as a starting point for debate."
—Charles S. Robb, U.S. Senate

Overseas Development Council

SPECIAL PUBLICATIONS SUBSCRIPTION OFFER

U.S.-Third World Policy Perspectives

Policy Essays • Policy Focus

As a subscriber to the ODC's three publications series, you will have access to an invaluable source of independent analyses of U.S.-Third World issues—economic, political, and social—at a savings of 30 percent off the regular price.

■ Brief and easy-to-read, each **Policy Focus** briefing paper provides background information and anaylsis on a current topic on the policy agenda. In 1992, 6-8 papers will cover aspects of U.S. trade, aid, finance, and security policy toward the developing countries.

■ **Policy Essays** explore critical issues on the U.S.-Third World agenda in 60-80 succinct pages, offering concrete recommendations for action. In 1992, a special "conditionality series" will explore the potential utility and the limits of attaching conditions to aid, trade, and technology transfers to encourage sustained changes in certain policies and behavior of other governments. A separate essay explores the North-South environmental strategies, costs, and bargains to be raised at the U.N. Conference on Environment and Development.

■ **U.S.-Third World Policy Perspectives,** ODC's policy book series, brings a wide range of expertise to bear on current issues facing American policymakers. Each volume presents creative new policy options or insights into the implications of existing policy.

SUBSCRIPTION OPTIONS

Special Publications Subscription Offer*	$65.00
(All U.S.-Third World Policy Perspectives (1), Policy Essays (5-6), and Policy Focus briefing papers (8-10) issued in 1992.)	
1992 Policy Focus Subscription Offer*	$20.00
(Foreign)	$19.00
Individual Titles	
U.S.-Third World Policy Perspectives	$15.95
Policy Essay	$9.95

* Subscribers will receive all 1992 publications issued to date upon receipt of payment; other publications will be sent upon release. Book-rate postage is included in price.

All orders require prepayment. For individual titles, add $1.00 per item for shipping and handling. Please send check or money order to:

0 | D | C

Publication Orders
Overseas Development Council
1875 Connecticut Avenue, NW
Suite 1012
Washington, DC 20009